Everyday Law on the Street

THE CHICAGO SERIES IN LAW AND SOCIETY

Edited by John M. Conley and Lynn Mather

Everyday Law on the Street

City Governance in an Age of Diversity

MARIANA VALVERDE

THE UNIVERSITY OF CHICAGO PRESS   CHICAGO AND LONDON

MARIANA VALVERDE is professor in and director of the Centre for Criminology and Socio-legal Studies at the University of Toronto. She is the author of several books, including *Law's Dream of a Common Knowledge*.

The University of Chicago Press, Chicago 60637
The University of Chicago Press, Ltd., London
© 2012 by The University of Chicago
All rights reserved. Published 2012.
Printed in the United States of America

21 20 19 18 17 16 15 14 13 12   1 2 3 4 5

ISBN-13: 978-0-226-92189-1 (cloth)
ISBN-13: 978-0-226-92190-7 (paper)
ISBN-13: 978-0-226-92191-4 (e-book)
ISBN-10: 0-226-92189-1 (cloth)
ISBN-10: 0-226-92190-5 (paper)
ISBN-10: 0-226-92191-3 (e-book)

All photographs are by Greg Duke.

Library of Congress Cataloging-in-Publication Data

Valverde, Mariana, 1955–
    Everyday law on the street : city governance in an age of diversity / Mariana Valverde.
        pages ; cm. — (The Chicago series in law and society)
    Includes bibliographical references and index.
    ISBN-13: 978-0-226-92189-1 (cloth : alkaline paper)
    ISBN-10: 0-226-92189-1 (cloth : alkaline paper)
    ISBN-13: 978-0-226-92190-7 (paperback : alkaline paper)
    ISBN-10: 0-226-92190-5 (paperback : alkaline paper)
    [etc.]
    1. Municipal government. 2. Municipal corporations. 3. City planning and
redevelopment law.   I. Title. II. Series: Chicago series in law and society.
    K3431.V35 2012
    320.8'5—dc23

                                                                    2012007985

♾ This paper meets the requirements of ANSI/NISO Z39.48–1992 (Permanence of Paper).

Contents

Photo gallery follows page 140.

Acknowledgments

I came to urban studies relatively late in life and could not have made such a significant turn in my scholarly journey without a great deal of support and help. Evelyn Ruppert and Engin Isin's generosity toward a rank amateur was essential in the early days. Later on, I became indebted to Nick Blomley, Davina Cooper, Dave Cowan, and Peer Zumbanssen, as well as colleagues at the University of Toronto's Cities Centre, especially Larry Bourne, Philippa Campsie, Paul Hess, Michael Shapcott, Richard Stren, and Richard White. But taking up urban studies has not made me abandon other interests: Xiaobei Chen, Kelly Hannah-Moffat, Franca Iacovetta, Audrey Macklin, Paula Maurutto, Renisa Mawani, Pat O'Malley, Kunal Parker, Annelise Riles, Nikolas Rose, and Chris Tomlins have been and I hope will remain important interlocutors as well as valued friends.

My colleagues at the Centre for Criminology and Sociolegal Studies have over the years built a wonderful work environment, and, in relation to this book, showed a touching faith that something worthwhile would emerge from a messy and protracted research project. Tony Doob and Ron Levi deserve particular thanks for not shutting their office doors whenever I barged in with half-baked ideas. Jessica Cheblowski, Rita Donelan, and Lori Wells's administrative competence and good humor made it possible for me to serve as director while writing this book.

Several current and former doctoral students played important roles in the project—some as research assistants in the field (Dena Demos, Mike Mopas, Karrie Sandford, and Rashmee Singh) and some by sharing information and ideas (Brenna Keatinge, Karrie Sandford, and especially Lisa Freeman). Brenna Keatinge and Jordana Wright did some crucial documentary research in the late stages and shared their own enthusiasm for researching urban issues. Research assistants' excellent notes are cited only occasionally, but they were tremendously important in shaping questions and themes.

Initial funding for a related project on municipal law (carried out with Ron Levi) was given by the late lamented Law Commission of Canada. The bulk of the funding, however, was provided by the Social Sciences and Humanities Research Council. A standard research grant was used to do most of the empirical research for the project, from 2003 to 2007. Another grant (2007–11) with a much broader historical and geographical scope allowed me to place the empirical findings in a larger context, and to produce related historical and/or theoretical publications. The continued willingness of the government of Canada to provide a funding stream that avoids micromanaging the research process, the budget, and the "deliverables" is close to miraculous, given current trends; I hope that civic leaders who read this book and find it useful will support the continuation of funding for "basic" social science research when the time comes.

The empirical research on municipal practices of inspection and dispute resolution was facilitated by two senior city managers who gave my assistants and me full access to the everyday work of officials. Their openness is exemplary and gives the lie to popular images of "the bureaucracy." I am sorry that research ethics rules make it impossible for me to thank them by name, or to acknowledge those inspectors who generously agreed to have their work scrutinized. Similar restrictions apply to acknowledging most of the numerous current and former city politicians and staff who agreed to be interviewed, and who often gave me insightful analyses, not just information. But many others answered questions and gave me information, and I want to especially thank the late Bill Bosworth, Hongmei Cai, Joy Connelly, Paul Dowling, Diane Dyson, Tim Groves, Marianne Maroney, Katie Rabinowitz, former mayor John Sewell, Michael Shapcott, Paul Young, Councillor Paula Fletcher and her staff, Councillor Adam Vaughan and his staff, the Homecoming group and the East Toronto Community Coalition. Last but not least, I want to thank my partner Maggi Redmonds, whose own long experience in community and city agencies—and the wisdom gained through reflecting on the experiences—is not directly cited, but has greatly influenced the book. She and our son Nick Valverde also gave editing advice upon request. Finally, Nick, our daughter Ming Redmonds, and their teenage friends, who as a group embody the most hopeful aspects of Toronto's urban diversity, served as a constant source of inspiration. As I worked on the book I kept in mind that it is their generation that will pay the price if we middle-aged folks fail to address the governance problems on which this book, I hope, sheds some new light.

CHAPTER I

Introduction

W hy is the word "urban" so often followed by the word "problems"? The countryside, after all, is hardly a haven of stability: the swallowing up of family farms by corporations and the prospect of catastrophic climate change are only some of the tremendous challenges faced by rural populations around the world. But people of all classes tend to think of the country and the small town as "good" places to live. By contrast, ever since the discovery of new forms of misery in the industrializing cities of mid-nineteenth-century Europe, the urban has been regarded as a symbolic space as well as a physical place that is by nature full of all manner of dangers and risks.

An important reason for the traditional association of "urban" with "problems" is that cities have always contained more social diversity than the surrounding countryside. Cities in the Roman empire welcomed merchants and settlers from diverse ethnic, language, and religious groups: today, cities remain the primary magnet for permanent migrants as well as short-term travelers. That "the cities of the 21st century will increasingly be characterized by the challenges of multiculturalism,"[1] as one British scholar puts it, is now an almost trite remark. But multiculturalism and diversity have acquired different meanings. While in the 1950s and 1960s, cultural and racial diversity were regarded as inherently problematic, there has been a shift in numerous city regions around the world toward regarding diversity as a good thing, even as a resource.

Whether accompanied by fears or by hopes, however, diversity does pose new challenges for governance, since the existing governance structures were developed during far less diverse times. To compound cities' difficulties, these challenges are taking place in a global context in which central governments have downloaded many responsibilities to local governments and local community agencies, without a concomitant increase in fiscal capacity and politico-legal resources. From the extreme pressures faced by American municipalities in states that are nearly bankrupt, to the sudden loss of central government funding experienced by British local communities in the postfinancial crash period, to the complete abdication by the Canadian federal government of such issues as housing and public transportation, city officials, politicians, and civic leaders have been abandoned by senior levels of government just when greater resources are needed. And these resources are not only monetary. Cities are also in great need of what in industry would be called "R & D"—that is, the people and the mechanisms needed to learn from collective experience, creatively devise innovative solutions, and ensure that legal powers are flexible enough to allow cities to tackle new problems. If this book helps both citizens and leaders to think creatively about the governance challenges of today, it will have served its purpose.

While this study began as an open-ended look at the mundane details of how cities regulate space, settle disputes, and interpret ordinances and regulations, without any single theme being chosen beforehand, it became clear that the issue of diversity, while rarely explicitly addressed, was always hovering in the background. People rarely stopped to think about just what "diversity" means, however. Nearly everyone whose work was studied expressed a sincere commitment to the idea of diversity if the topic came up (though neither my research assistants nor I asked, since the focus of the study was how things are done, not what people say about what they're doing). "Diversity is our strength" is Toronto's motto; and unlike in many parts of Europe, in Toronto one is hard-pressed to find anybody who explicitly opposes diversity as such. But in practice, certain dimensions of diversity were more valued than others, in different ways depending on the context. This is hardly surprising, since activists as well as scholars have long noted that there's a tendency for institutions and individuals to imagine they're promoting equality or diversity in general when in fact they're only addressing a single factor (gender, say, or race). It was thus not unexpected to find that certain vectors of diversity—socioeconomic status, most glaringly, but also housing tenure—were often trampled in the collective rush to express pride in Toronto's cultural/racial diversity.

The shortcomings of what one could call "diversity in practice," diversity on the ground, could be studied by the use of aggregate data, as has been done in important reports replete with discouraging graphs showing that like many other "global" cities, Toronto is becoming more unequal and poverty is increasingly racialized.[2] These studies have certainly informed my analysis, since to correctly interpret microlevel interactions, it is important to have a good grasp of the underlying structural trends.[3] However, this book is concerned mainly with processes that are not visible to those who work with aggregate data—the everyday interactions that make up the ever-shifting dynamics of urban governance on the ground.

Detailed studies of the dynamics of local governance are extremely scarce; but there are some precedents. Notably, many years ago Michael Lipsky carried out a study entitled *Street-Level Bureaucracy: Dilemmas of the Individual in Public Services*. Like the present book, Lipsky's influential study focused on the microdetails of the governance process, rather than on the big-picture outcomes.[4] However, his study included officials from a variety of levels of government, and so he was unable to shed light on the specificity of governance at the local level. In addition, it was limited to bureaucrat-client interactions, whereas I include civil-society groups, city councillors, planners, and a variety of other actors in my purview. Thus, my study paints a broader picture than Lipsky's; but more important, it shows that city governance, urban governance, has its own dynamics. Cities are not simply smaller versions of states: there is such a thing as "seeing like a city," as distinct from "seeing like a state," as this book demonstrates.[5]

If multiculturalism and diversity are the key governance challenges for today's cities, Toronto is an appropriate site for the empirical study of street-level urban governance, since it has distinguished itself for warmly embracing the idea (and to some extent the practice) of diversity. It is significant that in the late 1990s, many people came to believe that UNESCO had officially declared that Toronto was "the world's most diverse city." This claim proved to be an urban legend,[6] not surprisingly given that there are many different measures of diversity, and no consensus about which variables are most important. The "most diverse" claim was thus eventually revised: the "Equity, Diversity and Human Rights" web page within the city of Toronto's website stated (in 2010) that it's "one of the most diverse" cities. The Tourism Toronto website, however, still claims Toronto as "the world's most ethnically diverse city." And in the course of my research I encountered many savvy civic actors who believed that some UN agency had in fact given Toronto the "most diverse" award. Clearly, Torontonians passionately want to believe that they/we live in "the most diverse city in the world," and a nerdy social scientist pointing out that there is no agreed-upon measure of diversity in general cannot dent that pride.

In the United States there are cities that pride themselves on diversity as well, but, with the partial exception of multicultural New York City (which is significantly whiter than Toronto), American cities of diversity are Hispanic cities. Miami is 65 percent Latino, while in Los Angeles, the Hispanic/Latino population is now 48 percent of the LA total, and it's projected to soon rise to 60 percent. In Toronto, the 2006 census showed that the city, once almost completely white, is now almost majority non-white: 47 percent of Torontonians said they were "visible minorities," in the city, while 42 percent of the larger census metropolitan area fell in that category. But there is no equivalent to Miami's or LA's Latino blocs. South Asians make up 12 percent of the Toronto total, closely followed by people of Chinese descent (11.4 percent), blacks (8.4 percent), and Filipinos (4.1 percent). In addition, there are dozens of ethnic and language groups with significant representation—for instance, Somalis, whose Toronto community is the largest in the world outside of Somalia. These demographic facts make Toronto a wonderful urban studies laboratory.

A factor that makes this study particularly relevant elsewhere is that it does not focus on the official bureaus specifically devoted to promoting diversity. Instead, it studies a wide array of low-level governance processes and analyzes them in an open-ended manner. Studying how the local ethic of diversity works in everyday governance processes that do not come with "diversity" labels already attached gives us great insight into basic questions of urban governance.

So what exactly was studied for this book? Clearly, no one person could study the whole field of urban governance, even in one city; such an enterprise would require a team of experts.[7] I was limited both by the time and the research funding available and by my own background. Other scholars have worked with large data sets to shed light on a variety of crucial policy issues. But while reading such studies has been crucial in sketching for me the social and economic context, and thus indirectly shaping this book, I decided to draw on my sociolegal studies background and contribute to urban studies through a detailed qualitative study of "everyday law" in the law-and-society tradition.[8]

This multiyear project had several parts. First I worked with a legally trained colleague, Ron Levi, to study the formal law, including the mind-numbing details of the 2003 Ontario Municipal Act and the 2006 City of Toronto Act.[9] As we shall see throughout the book, even after the supposed empowering of Canadian cities in recent legislation and court decisions, cities have very limited powers to shape their own destiny. But while cities in the United States generally have more legal autonomy than cities in Canada, the basic legal architecture is the same across North America. Just as important, municipal inspectors go about their work in a similar manner, as far as one can judge from the scarce empirical studies available.[10] Therefore, despite the differences in formal law across borders, the dynamics of urban governance documented here are by no means limited to either Toronto or Canada.

After concluding the formal law research, I devised a four-part empirical study. Planning decisions at the lowest level were studied by a systematic observation of Toronto's four "Committees of Adjustment" (the local equivalent of boards of zoning appeals). Simultaneously, I and another research assistant studied the work of the licensing tribunal, which handles disputes between the city and licensed businesses. Thirdly, with the generous support of two senior city officials (who unfortunately cannot be thanked by name due to research ethics rules), I was able to place two doctoral students in "ride-alongs" with the so-called generalist officers from Municipal Licensing and Standards who respond to citizen complaints about such matters as unsightly yards and noise. Finally, I participated in planning consultations going on in the city and in my own neighborhood, focusing not only on citizen-city interactions but also on the division of labor between politicians and bureaucrats, which turned out to be different than what textbooks suggest. The study began in mid-2003. Most of the research, and all of the research-assistant work, was concluded by 2007, but I continued to attend meetings and to follow various issues. The book is thus reasonably up-to-date through October 2010, when sending the first draft to the publisher coincided with a municipal election that unexpectedly brought to power a mayor and a council majority with Tea Party tendencies. Given that my research found that politics in the big *P* sense plays a relatively small role in the legal and enforcement matters I studied, however, the research presented here should remain timely for a while, just as it should prove relevant to cities with different political alignments.

Having explained the scope of the project, I will proceed in the rest of the introduction as follows. First I will delve a little more into the question of law's role in urban governance, in a section that takes the life and work of Toronto-based urban guru Jane Jacobs as an occasion to reflect on the distorted view of law that characterizes urban studies today. Next comes a section focusing on governance more than law. Here I show that the Jacobs ideal of a city of villages, which sounded so good when first put forward, in the sixties, has turned out to have serious defects when used as a model to govern large and very heterogeneous cities. Developing the city-village theme, this section will introduce the idea of "scales of governance" and will reflect on how the study's own chosen scale, which is somewhat ant-like,[11] limits what I have been able to discover.

The final section of this introductory chapter will ask some probing questions about the various meanings of the ubiquitous term "diversity." In keeping with findings of research elsewhere, such as John and Jean Comaroff's *Ethnicity, Inc.*,[12] I find that the capitalist quest for global competitiveness has been able to absorb and use a notion that had been originally democratic and antiestablishment; but I also document the persistence of the older, more inclusive and democratic meaning of "diversity," which in the city of Toronto, and I expect elsewhere as well, has not disappeared. This is followed by an overview of the chapters that follow.

Law versus the Street? The Legacy of Jane Jacobs

It would be silly to claim that legal mechanisms are the golden key to understanding how urban life is organized. The politicking that goes on in city councils; the machinations of real estate moguls; the engineering expertise that channels people and vehicles like so many ants along streets and highways; the cultural preferences that draw people with money to certain spots and away from others; the aesthetic ideas of architects and planners; the electronic transfers that keep global capital going—all of these processes shape urban life. Law is only one of the many dimensions of the fabric of our cities.

But without exaggerating law's importance, the everyday experience of living in cities, whether in the global South or in the global North, suggests that law does matter. Of course, many laws are not enforced, or are enforced very unevenly. And local law is often powerless to prevent environmental calamities or to control such things as capital flows. But anyone who is familiar with the host of everyday interactions that involve urban law—from the rigors of parking fines to the red tape needed to open a small business—will agree that the little-understood agglomerations of laws, ordinances, bylaws, rules, policies, inspection practices, and regulatory fines that cities have, and which do not seem to be known, in their totality, by anyone, do in fact shape the experience of urban life to a great extent. The most striking feature of law at the local level is its heterogeneity and lack of clear organizing rationales.

In addition, local law is different from most other spheres or scales of law in that in many cases we have to ask for permission to do all manner of mainly private things—renovating one's own house, for instance, or letting one's own front yard revert to nature. Studying urban law, one cannot but be struck by the fact that the lofty constitutional principles of individual freedom that guide national-scale law have very little bite at the local level. Cities will tell us we can't sleep in parks even though that's a breach of individual rights. And it's not just homeless citizens who experience "the city" as a kind of feudal lord: just try arguing your way out of a parking ticket by claiming that citizens have already paid for the streets and so the streets belong to them.

Despite the obvious importance of local legal and regulatory mechanisms in daily life, and despite the fact that local law is not understood by those who only study state law, when one casts an eye over the vast literature that describes how city life works, in the present and in the past, it is surprising to find that law has been systematically neglected. An important anthology notes in its introduction that most urban research "takes the legal phenomenon for granted." While some high-profile ordinances (say, banning panhandlers) have drawn much attention from both activists and scholars, the mundane operation of lower-profile laws that don't look political remains invisible as one reads the latest in urban sociology or urban geography.[13]

The failure to analyze, and even to see, the legal dimensions of routine urban life is a product of systematic biases among writers on things urban. Many amateurs of things urban take an aesthetic perspective, focusing on the latest waterfront design improvements while neglecting the drab reality of run-of-the-mill streets.[14] Urban geographers and qualitative sociologists, on their part, study sociocultural processes, sometimes through quantitative analyses of aggregate data, and, less frequently, by means of anthropological studies of the everyday interactions of citizens—but these studies tend to focus exclusively on marginal groups. Law here appears in a distorted manner; it appears only as it bears down coercively on the impoverished or the racialized, and, in addition, it is studied usually only in relation to particular campaigns or crises, not over a period of several years. The much larger areas of law that work without fanfare and without police—paving roads, maintaining parks, dictating the size of yards, inspecting homes and public buildings, regulating city traffic, and issuing marriage licenses, taxi plates, and building permits—remain wholly invisible in these studies.[15]

While what one could call "culturalism" is arguably the key reason for the neglect of law in urban studies writing, many urban sociologists do pay attention to economic and demographic change as well as culture; but they too pay scant attention to legal and regulatory mechanisms. Focusing on aggregate data and time series, American urban sociology renders law largely invisible—it is not a variable. On their part, critical urban writers in all disciplines who are influenced by the Marxist tradition tend to share Marxism's narrow view of law as a mere "superstructure" that does not need to be closely analyzed because it is a reflection of and explained by class interests.[16] For a variety of reasons, then, the main scholarly literatures on the urban either ignore law's power or show it only as an exceptional force or a set of antiquated rules.[17]

Jane Jacobs's tremendously influential study of street life in the Greenwich Village of the 1950s, the most important urban studies work of the twentieth century, shares this general neglect of the power of law. *The Death and Life of Great American Cities* (the 1961 book that made her famous, several years before she and her family left New York for Toronto) pays little attention to law. But the main problem is not the absence of law but rather its distorted portrayal. In keeping with the ethos of the sixties, insofar as law is discussed, legal mechanisms appear as bureaucratic obstacles to the flourishing of spontaneous civic interaction. In one place Jacobs does look at law more constructively, famously advocating "zoning for diversity"[18]—a planning idea that has now become commonplace in regeneration projects but which was then quite revolutionary. But that is an exceptional and undeveloped passage.

Jacobs's work paid little attention to the fact that legal mechanisms matter not only when they are moralistic or archaic and thus highly noticeable but even—perhaps especially—when they quietly facilitate the complex array of interactions that urban life involves (though often the interactions facilitated are not the ones that were originally targeted). Admittedly, the specific laws found in municipal law books are to a large extent outdated and/or dysfunctional. However, if one's engagement with law is limited to ridiculing silly rules, as is ritually done by lovers of edgy urban life (often invoking Jacobs), one misses a great deal. That Jacobs's account idealized spontaneous interactions, largely ignoring the fact that large cities cannot be run like preindustrial villages, or even like federations of villages, is an insight which slowly came to prominence as I witnessed countless unproductive well-meaning efforts by self-appointed village elders to "get people together" or "consult the community."

Jacobs's idealization of civic spontaneity was part and parcel of the same sixties ethos that gave us self-help groups, women's consciousness-raising, and cooperatives, which is probably why it remained uncriticized. Jacobs and her family moved to Toronto in 1968, mainly in protest against the Vietnam War, as she and her husband were very concerned about their boys being eventually drafted. In hindsight we can see that the same ethos that gave us the peace movement and the myriad cooperative experiments of that generation also undergirded her well-known praise for the spon-taneous ballet of sidewalk life—a phrase that in retrospect seems more than a little naive. The ideals that she shared with her contemporaries gave her a very sharp eye for any abuse of state power; but they also led her to idealize street life. For example, if African-Americans and racialized im-migrants had formed a significant proportion of the population of Jacobs's beloved Greenwich Village then, as they do now, her rosy-colored account of how neighbors look after each other might have had to be substantially modified (as Mitchell Duneier pointed out in his own study of sidewalk life in the Greenwich Village of the late 1990s).[19]

Settling in the Annex neighborhood—a then-bohemian, now-bourgeois area near the university, with largish older homes lining leafy streets—Ja-cobs instantly became the patron saint of Toronto urban design and ur-ban politics. She soon decided to put the skills she had learned fighting New York's development czar Robert Moses and his proposed Manhattan freeways locally in fighting against the proposed "Spadina Expressway." Eventually abandoned in favor of a new subway line, this LA-style free-way would have run about a block from Jacobs's own house. The "Stop Spadina" movement became the training ground of a whole generation of "small is beautiful" civic leaders, who like Jacobs deplored suburban bore-dom and loved independent shops, pedestrianism, and tree-lined streets of older homes with tiny yards.[20] University professors, artists, and later, young professionals began to move into streets that were previously the domain of either immigrants or the old Anglo poor.[21] And "mixed use" slowly became the new, antisuburban rallying cry.[22]

While becoming a local icon—she was routinely featured, always glow-ingly, in the local press, usually wearing her trademark grandmotherly shawl and the archaic ear trumpet that she preferred to a hearing aid—Jacobs also became tremendously influential around the world. And as with all great successes, genius alone cannot explain her fame. A factor that explains why her ideas fell on fertile ground is that like many other progressive people of the 1960s, Jacobs had become very critical of the hierarchical, expert-dominated, centralized governance that was popular in the 1950s. The spontaneous, village-like, friendly, informal social life that Jacobs observed—and described, though often romantically—was a key part of the sixties Zeitgeist. This ideal deserves respect: the 1960s visionaries who gave us organic farming and alternative schools did serve the very useful function of dethroning the postwar experts who thought big and industrial. But like all other visionary myths, the city-as-village vision had many blind spots. The experts who gave us freeways, after all, also gave us old-age pensions, unemployment insurance, and, in many countries, fairly equal educational and health care opportunities for all, for the first time in history.

Village elders, whether in cities or in actual villages, can be wise and fair and sensible, and can "cut through red tape" in useful ways. But if they are not so wise, or if they only listen to the loudest voices, it is difficult to contradict them or seek redress. By the same token, informal interactions among neighbors can be positive—or they can degenerate into prejudice-driven attacks on outsiders. As we shall see in this book, the faith in local grassroots activism that Jacobs shared with sixties' activists throughout North America was and remains rather blind to the fact that it is dangerous to assume that those who show up (or phone their councillor) are those whose voices should matter the most.

The "dysfunctional dance of local governance" and the unreasonable constraints put on affordable-housing developments by neighborhood groups are complex processes for which Jane Jacobs and her reformer friends are certainly not wholly responsible. Nevertheless, Jacobs's friends and successors have not done much to reflect on the bitter lessons of the sixties' grassroots organizing ideals. Even in a polyglot city whose motto is "Diversity is our strength," city councillors, city staff, and neighborhood groups rarely notice that tenants and young people almost never show up at so-called community consultation meetings. The city as a group of ideal villages (a trope repeatedly invoked not only in Toronto but also around the world by promoters of microplanning) sounds homelike and friendly and antibureaucratic. But a city like Toronto, or San Francisco, or Seattle, is simply not a grouping of happy, autonomous, spontaneously organized villages. Democracy at the scale of the city, particularly in today's increasingly economically divided cities, requires careful attention to the mechanisms used to solicit input and allow for citizen participation. Jane Jacobs's front-stoop vision of spontaneous neighborhood action, somewhat naive even in her own time and place, has become completely inadequate, and it may be positively harmful as a model of governance in cosmopolitan cities riven by very sharp economic, social, and racial differences.

As someone who has lived in Toronto for thirty years, I am proud that diversity is a notable fact in my daily life. To give but a tiny example, when my daughter's school sent out an automated phone announcement just as I was writing this chapter, the message stated that a parent survey was available on the school's website in twenty languages. I'm even prouder of the fact that the marked racial, religious, and linguistic diversity of local public schools does not scare white Anglo parents: only 5 percent of Toronto parents send their children to private schools, a notable achievement in a context of growing economic inequality. But the fact that Toronto public schools include rich white children as well as poor immigrants will not by itself generate the civic leadership we need to face today's challenges.

When Jacobs was penning her ode to the "ballet" of spontaneous sidewalk interactions, she could not have known that what would succeed the postwar welfare state would be not a flowering of community-based alternatives, but rather a very marked resurgence of social inequality, a social inequality reflected in increased geographic concentration of both poverty and wealth. Like London and New York, Toronto (which replaced Montreal as the financial capital of Canada over the 1960s–1980s period) has witnessed rapid gentrification and new forms of downtown-based upper-class consumption—and like those cities, Toronto has simultaneously experienced the emergence of new forms of poverty (including homelessness, which had been virtually eliminated in the 1960s and 1970s but skyrocketed in the 1990s).

And if economic and demographic changes since the sixties have made the spontaneous village-life ideal anachronistic, the neglect of law that also characterized Jacobs's work similarly creates challenges. Jacobs had a very keen eye for the microlevel interactions that make up much of urban life (a way of seeing she shared with her friend, the neglected amateur sociologist William H. Whyte),[23] but her understanding of the complex network of legal and administrative mechanisms that constitute municipal governance in complex cities was less than thorough.

Jacobs's lack of attention to law and governance issues was quite forgivable in 1961. At that time, law teaching and legal scholarship were removed from social struggles, and "governance" was not a word in common use. Over the past forty years, however, legal scholars have become more aware of the social roots and consequences of laws and regulations, and are now using tools from the social sciences to understand law in its context. On their part, anthropologists have studied how ordinary people, including in First World cities, imagine law in their own everyday life. Sociologists and political scientists have in turn studied how law itself has changed as a result of social movements; and scholars in and out of law schools have produced thousands of studies of the workings of legal mechanisms, legal institutions, and legal personnel.[24] This vast body of work has greatly informed this book. But within urban studies too, especially urban geography, there is growing interest in studying legal mechanisms. Given this budding interest, this book contributes to urban studies as well as sociolegal studies.

Local and Global, Public and Private: Zooming In and Out in Studying Local Law

This book aims to shed light on the often unexpected ways in which law in the broad sense of the word—that is, including sublegal regulations and inspection and enforcement practices—shapes everyday urban life. But only some legal mechanisms and processes were available for inspection. Since I was given access to municipal inspectors' daily rounds, I could see exactly how they enforce—and often choose not to enforce—municipal ordinances. Attending numerous planning-related meetings, some at city hall and some at the neighborhood level, gave me insights into how local planning law serves as a funnel for conflicts about everything from pollution to who should be allowed to live where, conflicts that cannot be vented in any other arena or venue but that planning law cannot usefully address. Interviewing officials and observing both officials and city councillors at a variety of meetings was also informative—but needless to say, I did not have access to their phone calls and their backroom deals.

   The scale of my own work was thus both local (I did not study other cities, or higher levels of government, except by reading secondary sources) and limited to what was visible in public venues and documents or revealed through interviews and job-shadowing research. Before presenting the research, it is thus necessary to contextualize it by reflecting on the fact that there are other lines of legal force that greatly affect urban experience. I will briefly mention two.

First, there are developments in international law that negatively impact cities' ability to use law to address diversity issues. Trade and other agreements signed by nations—about which cities have had no say—are imposing new limits on the ability of local governments to make their own choices as to economic and social development. Such treaties as the North American Free Trade Agreement (NAFTA) impose constraints on local procurement and local planning policies under the guise of making trade easier and fairer. Gerald Frug and David Barron, noted American legal writers on urban issues, warn that many nation-states, including Canada, regard cities as children who must comply with the rules set by senior levels of government, even if those rules take away established local rights to influence economic development, protect the environment, and set labor standards.[25]

The Canadian Union of Public Employees, on its part, has commissioned legal research showing that while there are few international trade arbitration cases regarding municipalities, the ones that exist are of great concern, especially the *Metalclad v. Mexico* decision, which declared that a local choice to deny a hazardous waste company a permit—because an ecological preserve was in the works—amounted to expropriation.[26] Frug and Barron point out that the *Metalclad* decision and others along the same lines represent a decrease of local land-use powers—which few people would have thought would be affected by trade agreements. Municipal policies that encourage inclusiveness and diversity or promote environmental protection are thus vulnerable, given that cities have little or no political power at the international level. They also lack the research and legal capacity to make their needs heard even at the domestic national level.

The second legal line of force that needs to be mentioned here is also global in scale, but it involves corporate and contract law rather than international law. Increasingly, city governments interested in carrying out major improvements do not employ their own funds and their own personnel exclusively; instead, they use a variety of contractual techniques to set up "public-private partnerships." Much has been written about the privatization of public services from health care to correctional services, at all levels of government. But what is rarely mentioned is that a key feature of these now-ubiquitous contracts between city governments and private (often transnational) firms is that the accountability processes that apply to the public sector often don't apply to such contracts. The public may be informed about some of the features of the contract, in city-produced press releases using the language of win-win. But many of the crucial financial details, especially those dealing with future financial risks, are kept secret, in keeping with contract-law practice.[27] This means that the legal underpinnings for the public-private arrangements now routinely used for all manner of urban purposes cannot be easily studied, unless a scholar gains privileged access to the backrooms. The "deals" of which city leaders are now so proud often come under criticism years later, as citizens discover that they are on the collective hook as the latest toll highway or tunnel fails to realize the economic and transportation miracles that were promised. But as these deals are being written and signed, the public notice and public involvement processes that are standard for government and public law purposes are often set aside.

The fact that many of the corporations involved in transforming urban life are now increasingly transnational is of particular concern from the point of view of governance and accountability. For instance, the forests of fifty-story condos that have mushroomed in Toronto's former railway lands are alleged to contain a large proportion of units that are not owner-occupied but are rather investment opportunities for global capital. This rumor, which cannot be confirmed due to the secrecy of private contract law, suggests that shiny postmodern glass towers that most onlookers imagine contain home-owning young professionals and empty-nester retirees may soon lose their cachet, as absentee corporate owners neglect repairs in favor of lower condo fees. A shift from gentrified urban paradise to vertical slum could perhaps be prevented if the ownership details of the condo units were publicly available to condo boards and to officials who might then devise new rules. But contract law is part of private law, not public law, and hence not open to inspection by researchers like myself. Future researchers will need to devise strategies appropriate to pry contract details from real estate agents, infrastructure developers, and real estate lawyers.

It is a sign of the times that both of the lines of legal force just outlined are simultaneously global and local, public and private. Theorists have remarked that governance today is often "multiscalar" rather than limited to one jurisdiction or one scale.[28] Urban governance is certainly a case in point, since a complete understanding of today's urban politics and law would require pursuing lines of inquiry that stray not only into constitutional law but also into fields such as corporate law, contract law, and private international law. It would be impossible in the present work to map out all of these complex and often hidden forces; but as the book unfolds I will attempt to identify some of the global-local, public-private trends and pressures that impact on local public law.

If today's urban governance is characterized to a great extent by the fluidity and rapidity of exchanges that blur the line between public and private, and between global and local, the issue that is featured in Toronto's official motto and that serves as a key theme of this book, diversity, is also characterized by a marked fluidity. Given that diversity, now a global trend or fashion as well as the local motto, is itself shaped by the legal environment, a brief reflection on the shifting meanings of "diversity" is in order.

The Shifting Meanings of "Diversity": From Rainbow Nation to Neoliberal Urbanism

The tremendous success of diversity talk in recent years may give the impression that there is a single condition, or a specific set of values, that has come to be embraced by a whole series of governments, neighborhoods, and corporations. This is not the case. Motherhood-and-apple-pie words (e.g., democracy, freedom) are successful precisely because they are semantically flexible and can be adopted by a wide variety of groups in a variety of contexts, as the great cultural theorist Raymond Williams pointed out long ago.[29] The fact that a word or phrase stays constant as its political effects and its symbolic associations change, often beyond recognition, serves to conceal the political and social conflicts and struggles that underlie shifts in what the "same" word does in different contexts. "Diversity," like "freedom" and "equality" before it, has come to mean a lot of different things to different people. A brief sketch of some key trends in how "diversity" is seen and managed, trends that are relevant to urban politics, is necessary.

First, one could draw a dividing line between political contexts in which there is a backlash against diversity (many parts of northern Europe, for instance, as well as the state of Arizona) and those contexts, such as Toronto, Sydney, London, New York, Chicago, and many smaller centers in the United States, in which "diversity" is generally regarded as a good thing, and indeed as an important part of what makes citizens proud of their particular city. This kind of for-or-against classification, however, would not be at all useful: it would sweep under the rug the myriad conflicts about what diversity is, what it does, and what it should do that are at the heart of this book.

Thus, with some trepidation about the risks of oversimplification, I suggest that one can shed light on a large number of situations, conversations, and texts that all regard "diversity" as a good thing by drawing lines that are more nuanced than a for-or-against classification. Very roughly, there's a diversity tradition that comes out of grassroots politics—what was not so long ago known as "rainbow nation." Here, diversity is part of a social-inclusion political agenda and is connected to such policies as affirmative action and more generous immigration rules. In my research, I often encountered this particular meaning (or loosely linked set of meanings, to be more precise) in everyday speech and in official city pronouncements. The city's office of "Equity, Diversity, and Human Rights," not surprisingly, is a leading promoter of this socially progressive take on "diversity": it has a "Plan of action" that explicitly focuses on "the elimination of racism and discrimination" and that proclaims that Toronto "has an inclusive vision of [a] society which is equitable and built on the strength of its diversity."

The "rainbow-nation" diversity project emerged throughout urban North America from the 1960s onward, encountering resistance and backlash and reemerging, often in unpredictable locations. While national-scale diversity-as-inclusion developments received large amounts of attention (e.g., during Barack Obama's 2008 presidential campaign), diversity politics was and remains to a large extent specifically urban. But what urban diversity meant and means varies a great deal from city to city, and even among different groups in the same neighborhood. For example, Ellen Berrey's detailed study of a Chicago neighborhood famous for diversity reveals that white liberals love to take pride in their locale's diversity, Toronto-style, but African-Americans prefer to talk about housing problems and rarely wave the "diversity" flag. Berrey concludes that while many whites living in what would be common in Toronto but unusual in Chicago—a racially and economically mixed but stable neighborhood—are genuine liberals who reject racial segregation, "their use of the term [diversity] also downplays racial and class power disparities."[30] As Berrey's study intimates, as the rainbow-nation grassroots activity gave rise to myriad local groups and microinstitutions (such as city bureaus and programs focused on diversity issues), a different diversity project was also developing, on quite separate tracks.

During the 1980s and 1990s, the word "diversity" began to be used, approvingly, in corporate contexts, to accomplish objectives that differ markedly from those of the "rainbow-nation" project. These organizational developments do not share a single politic; but a common feature is that diversity, especially workforce diversity, came to be regarded as an important feature of the new economy, and thus a resource for contemporary capitalism, especially the knowledge industries that many struggling rust-belt cities sought to attract in order to reinvent themselves. The story told by the promoters of corporate diversity usually begins by explaining that the capitalism of the first half of the twentieth century had needed large and homogeneous groups of workers employed on a long-term basis: the almost all-white and all-male workforces of many industrial sectors, for example, or the all-female and nearly all-white armies of secretaries employed by corporations and by governments. In those contexts, introducing new types of workers was seen as inherently problematic. In the new economy, however, labor markets are unstable and unpredictable, and employee groups are rarely as homogenous as in the past. This diversity, if properly managed, can be a resource, especially vis-à-vis global flows of capital, labor, and commodities.

The new business-management literature seeks to educate managers to regard demographic and lifestyle diversity among their employees and potential employees as a resource rather than as a threat. The ultimate goal, however, is not to overcome racism or sexism because they are unjust, but rather to enable firms—and cities—to keep up with global economic and demographic shifts and deal successfully with the challenges of global trade and global migration. Diversity-management training decries discrimination, and to that extent shares a common history with the "rainbow-nation" diversity project mentioned above. But the key objective of managerial diversity is to generate a more productive labor force and greater efficiencies and profits for corporations. A study of management training in the 1990s observes that "the rise in managerial rhetoric about diversity . . . occurs at a time when support for civil rights appears to be waning and rules banning affirmative action are gaining legitimacy."[31]

In today's discussions about cities competing in a global economy, diversity talk has pride of place, often alongside the word "tolerance," a term that also signals a distaste for discrimination but lacks the left-wing grassroots baggage of "diversity."[32] In keeping with this trend, "diversity" and "tolerance" are crucial terms in the extremely influential documents, speeches, and consultants' reports generated by urban guru Richard Florida and his creative class / creative cities team. Florida is North America's best-known writer on urban affairs today; and like Jane Jacobs, he moved to Toronto from the United States. But unlike Jacobs, Florida had no history of being arrested for activism and has not been known to denounce

US-led wars. He moved to Toronto because he chose in 2007 to become a professor of "business and creativity" at the University of Toronto, where the Martin Prosperity Institute, named after Roger Martin, dean of the business school, was created for him.[33] The contrast between Jacobs's and Florida's journeys to Toronto can be used to illustrate broader trends: there are good reasons why Jacobs was the urban guru of the 1960s and 1970s while Florida is the urban guru of the early twenty-first century.

Florida is best known for his thesis that cities and city-regions that do well in today's economic climate are those that attract and retain the "creative class"—the web designers, artists, scientists, and other knowledge-economy workers who, Florida tells us, do not punch the clock at fixed hours, and who enjoy edgy downtown consumption rather than suburban family-oriented seclusion. In his best-selling work *The Rise of the Creative Class*, diversity appears as a key factor in cities' success or lack of it. Tellingly, rather trivial indicators of "diversity" (such as body piercings) are put on the same level as race and ethnicity:

> My focus group and interview participants consistently listed diversity as among the most important factors in their choice of locations. People were drawn to places known for diversity of thought and open-mindedness. They actively seek out places of diversity and look for signs of it when evaluating communities. These signs include people of different ethnic groups and races, different ages, different sexual orientations and alternative appearances such as significant body piercings or tattoos.[34]

Florida also states that tech-savvy smart young people like to work for companies that have same-sex partner benefits, because "many highly creative people . . . grew up feeling like outsiders. They may have odd personal habits or extreme styles of dress. . . . When they are sizing up a new company and community, acceptance of diversity and gays in particular is a sign that reads 'nonstandard people welcome here.'"[35] Reading same-sex partner benefits as an indicator of geek-friendliness is, needless to say, rather different from critiquing homophobia because it is unjust.

Florida's city-saving recipes—such as "Technology, Tolerance, Talent"—have appealed not only to cities that do have a significant involvement in science, technology, and the arts but also to places where, as one Baltimore civic leader put it, we "should be so lucky to have the problem of gentrification."[36] One reason for the great popularity of Florida's ideas, even among leaders of rust-belt cities that are unlikely to do well on the "gay index" and similar Floridian measures of talent and tolerance, is that cities everywhere are now being pressured to constantly compete with one another in races that (as the brief discussion of global trade rules showed) are not of their own making. Florida's myriad city league tables form but a tiny part of a veritable avalanche of printed charts and graphs that purport to compare and rank urban centers (as googling "city rankings" shows). Cities, these days, do not have the option of *not* competing in the "technology, tolerance" and so forth leagues. Why not?

Cities like Baltimore have to make efforts to attract creative-class jobs in large part because central governments have largely abandoned the sixties' programs to promote equality on a national scale and help disadvantaged cities and neighborhoods to get closer to the national norm. The large-scale urban renewal programs that in the United States began in the 1930s, and that also existed in different forms in the United Kingdom and elsewhere, are distant memories now. Equally important, citizens of urban centers no longer expect to receive income support from state and federal governments, given the "end of welfare as we know it." In this new harsh climate, cities are increasingly left to their own devices to cope with the new forms of long-term unemployment and underemployment that lurk in the dark, rarely mentioned underside of Florida's relentlessly optimistic narrative.[37]

A sign of the times we live in is that while there are lots of quarrels about what indicators one should use when ranking cities, nobody is questioning the idea of competitive city rankings. The very exercise of collecting indicators presupposes that cities, like the atomistic individuals of classical economics, are by nature destined to compete with one another. The rainbow-coalition diversity project had assumed that cooperation and coalition-building are the normal conditions of political life. The new, Florida-style diversity, by contrast, is neoliberal insofar as it assumes that competition (between cities) is both good and natural. That individuals as well as corporations will seek to maximize their individual advantage regardless of their roots or their community bonds, moving to whichever city seems most attractive, is the first presupposition of the city-ranking game, and it is clearly rooted in neoliberal economic dogma. The second and, for our purposes, more important assumption is that cities too ought to behave like rational-choice individuals by boosting the indicators used to generate the city rankings that savvy knowledge workers will in turn look up in order to make a rational decision to move.[38] This latter chain of thought is normative as well as descriptive; it sings the glories of globally competitive cities, just as Jacobs's life and work sang the virtues of spontaneous cooperative street interactions.

The term "gentrification" has become a term of abuse with little substance (and so is very sparingly used in the pages that follow); but there is no doubt that the kind of diversity that Florida promotes goes hand in hand with—and to a large extent coincides with—the real estate and labor force changes that many observers subsume under the banner of gentrification. One reason for being careful about the label "gentrification," however, is that simply dismissing Florida-style diversity talk as the ideology of a particular sector of the bourgeoisie would not be very helpful. There are after all important differences between economic conservatives who are also social liberals, like Florida and the knowledge workers he admires (and most Toronto civic leaders), and, on the other hand, conservatives who are also openly racist and Islamophobic—even though all of them are neoliberals in economics. And in the interests of fairness it should be added that in much of Florida's consulting work for the Ontario government and other bodies, he has warned that the increased concentration of racialized groups in poor areas is bad (bad for economic development, mainly, but for ethical reasons as well).

It seems, therefore, that the old, rainbow-coalition meaning of "diversity" is not completely rejected by the newer, neoliberal diversity project. Some elements (a positive attitude toward gays, for instance, and to some extent a positive attitude toward racial diversity) have been incorporated into the neoliberal urbanist version of diversity. Other elements—the quest for economic equality and the pursuit of cooperative political and economic options, notably—have been rejected, however, since they are not compatible with today's capitalism.

In the chapters that follow we will have the opportunity to see at close range how everyday governance in one cosmopolitan city constructs local citizenship one day at a time, with diversity always hovering over the participants even when it is not directly addressed; and we will see how some vectors or dimensions of diversity are systematically neglected. But all of these systematic exclusions do not mean that diversity talk is merely a ruse or a ploy. Diversity is many things to many people, and nobody has the copyright on the word.

Chapter Organization

To provide an overview of the legal toolbox that is available to municipalities in North America to regulate urban space, but in an accessible manner rather than through a dry recounting of legal doctrine, the next chapter carries out a legal inventory of the laws (and other quasi-legal rules, such as technical standards) that operate at one particular street corner on the edge of the University of Toronto, where I work. The main point here is to show that even when no coercive force is apparent—for example, I have not seen the local panhandler being hassled by police—law quietly shapes both the built space and the social interactions that take place in it. And as it does so, certain cultural values are literally built into the urban fabric.

This leads to the discussion in chapter 3 of how cities create and enforce rules in regard to questions of taste, aesthetics, and cultural norms. This might seem a little trivial given the severe economic crises around us; but it illuminates a key factor making municipal law different from better-known, higher-level systems of law. City inspectors cannot arrest anyone and don't even use their ticketing or citation powers much; but they can and do impose aesthetic standards, micromanaging private as well as public space. And only cities can compel citizens to perform what are essentially public works, for example, maintaining neat front yards and shoveling snow from the public sidewalk. The regulation of taste by law is very largely a municipal affair, and this chapter offers one of the very few looks at how this is done on a daily basis. And since questions of taste are never culture-free, examining both everyday enforcement and some battles about local ordinances proves revealing, in regard to local law's cultural assumptions.

In the work of enforcing rules—or choosing not to enforce them—however, inspectors and bureaucrats are not sovereign. Chapter 4 goes on to show that local politicians play a very important part not only in shaping policy, which is their job, but also in interfering to a surprising extent in the day-to-day work of municipal officials, in ways that support or promote some kinds of diversity but work to systematically exclude certain cultural preferences. The often hostile interaction between local politicians and low-level city officials is here described as "the dysfunctional dance of local governance."

Zoning powers are among North American cities' key legal tools, and so chapter 5 studies how both the zoning rules and the way in which the rules are interpreted and enforced work. Since zoning affects every activity in the city, the focus is here narrowed (in the interests of highlighting diversity dynamics) to those zoning and planning disputes that concern housing designed to serve low-income and disabled citizens. The main lesson of this chapter is that consultation mechanisms designed in Jane

Jacobs's day to maximize public participation in urban planning are more often than not hijacked by "squeaky wheels," mainly older homeowners, who use these mechanisms in ways that create more inequality and exclusion, rather than more grassroots-based, inclusive diversity. However, there is a bit of "light at the end of the tunnel" in this chapter, since I recount in some detail the efforts made by city officials and housing activists to reform the rules of the consultation game to promote social inclusion.

Chapters 6 and 7 move from housing issues to another (even less studied) area of municipal law, namely business regulation. Chapter 6 examines the hapless situation of street-food vendors, shedding much light on the stark contrast between the city of Toronto's official celebration of diversity and its collective inability to "diversify" even something as uncontroversial as street-food choices. In turn, chapter 7 looks at the regulation of the taxi business, which in Toronto as in many other North American cities has become largely a new-immigrant business.

The final substantive chapter (8) explores the consequences of the fact that local planning law has become a funnel for all manner of global-scale anxieties about diversity by studying local planning disputes about mosques. Given the phobias affecting Muslim communities all over the Western world, examining how Canadian cities that would never think of emulating Switzerland's ban on minarets manage the anxieties of "host" communities is of more than local interest. This chapter also shows that local planning law has global dimensions, just as international developments have implications for and echoes in local governance as well.

Chapter 9 then provides a brief concluding reflection. "The death of planning" of the chapter's title does not refer only to urban planners' work: it refers more broadly to the slow death, over the past couple of decades, of the postwar welfare state ideal of a well-organized society largely planned by a benevolent—and paternalistic—central state. A local story about the rise and fall of an attempt to rationalize zoning rules is used here to illustrate the conclusion that emerges out of the book as a whole, which is that, in the context of today's polyglot and unequal cities, Jane Jacobs's campaign against centralized planning has become a victim of its own success. Today's planners neglect the scale of the whole city and work on small projects to renew this or that small patch. But large diverse cities cannot rest content with microprojects, especially since the private capital now routinely involved in regeneration projects has a large say in choosing whose neighborhood will get the investment. The top-down, expert-controlled, highway-oriented urban planning of the 1950s was a huge historical mistake; but that does not mean that cities should give up on the idea of planning. Geographic as well as racial and socioeconomic inequalities, within cities as well as within and between nations, are very much on the increase, and cities that seek to support all forms of diversity need to find a way to renew citywide planning.

CHAPTER 2

The Law of the Street Corner

As I was starting to research municipal law, around 2002, a colleague and I speculated that it would be interesting to do an inventory of all the laws that converged upon the particular street corner in front of our office, to demonstrate to our thus far unimpressed students and colleagues that local law is more ubiquitous and powerful than people think. In some ways this book is the eventual outcome of that conversation, since it became quickly apparent that no good general account of what local law does and how municipalities use their legal tools existed.

A great deal of information about many parts of this process does exist, most accessibly in the form of media and blog coverage of local politics and neighborhood issues, and also in official city reports. But such accounts and reports almost always focus on particular issues. A general, bird's-eye view of the role played by laws and ordinances in municipal governance did not seem to be available in the literature, and not only for Toronto. Even for the best-documented cities in the world, New York and London, there are plenty of studies of controversial developments, but more systematic reflections on local law and urban governance are surprisingly scarce.

The focus on specific campaigns or special projects tends to exaggerate differences between one city and another and one administration and the next. We know that some cities encourage tall high-rises, while others persist in limiting any residences other than the culturally laden North American house ideal, that is, "single-family detached." One municipality may suddenly welcome open-air sidewalk cafés and bike lanes, whereas across the road, in another municipality, city officials continue to channel people to malls surrounded by acres of parking. And some cities let panhandlers ply their trade relatively freely, while others have draconian sidewalk rules (such as San Francisco's 2010 ordinance banning all sitting and lying on sidewalks from 7:00 a.m. to 11:00 p.m.).

Clearly, such differences are important at the level of everyday urban life, and not only for those (like panhandlers) who are directly affected. Citizens often move to a town or move across town due to the differences in urban form that are frequently attributed to local culture but are usually the product, at least in part, of law. But if we focus on new ordinances and rules only, to either praise them or damn them, this will seriously obscure from view continuities in the underlying legal and regulatory architecture. Whether used to allow for extra-high condo buildings or to impose the home-owning nuclear family as the paradigm of urban living, whether used to promote public housing or to curtail it, the legal tools that North American cities use do not differ radically from city to city. Indeed, even details, such as the amount of fines, seem to be directly copied from other cities, since there is no good reason why a homeowner who fails to clear the snow from the abutting sidewalk should be fined $50 rather than some other amount. Focusing on particularly archaic or socially unjust ordinances, writers on urban issues tend to neglect the much larger number of rules that don't attract attention but do a lot of work—standards for drinking water, for example, as well as building codes, recycling systems, restaurant health inspection, and, probably the most underrated field of local law, traffic rules.

This chapter therefore provides an overview, however brief, of the legal foundations, the basic legal architecture, of urban governance—the common denominator underlying the rules that nobody complains about as well as those petty rules that are controversial. The linchpin of this mostly unknown legal edifice is the municipal corporation, a distinct and little-studied legal and political form.

The municipal corporation developed over a period of several centuries along a path diverging in many important ways from the better-known story of the modern state. The municipal corporation is distinct in its ways of governing, not only in the amount of territory covered. As I have argued in detail elsewhere, while cities sometimes use top-down, coercive, sovereign-style measures, cities have developed, over many centuries, certain typical ways of seeing and managing issues that are simultaneously less and more coercive than state law.[1] Cities cannot arrest anyone, or for that matter send us to war. But this does not mean cities respect the security of one's body and one's property more than national-level governments. Few legal scholars have reflected on the fact that only municipalities can force homeowners to fix up their yards, even if the risks to neighbors are purely aesthetic, and to repair the abutting public sidewalk out of their own pocket. Those living in cities that do fix sidewalks may be surprised to know that the state of Washington's municipal law research center informs Washingtonians that cities may require private owners to contribute up to 50 percent of the valuation of their property for improvements to an abutting sidewalk; and all around the United States one finds ordinances such as the one prevailing in the city of DeWitt, Michigan, which, as summarized in the city's website, demands the following:

> Property owners are responsible for maintaining and keeping in good repair any sidewalk that abuts or is adjacent to their property. This includes replacing sidewalk squares that have heaved or cracked. No sidewalk may be repaired without first securing a construction permit from the city.

That citizens are on the one hand compelled to fix up the city's property, at their own expense, and that on the other hand the same citizens have to ask for permission—and possibly pay money for a construction permit—to perform what is in fact an obligation is a legal fact that sheds much light on the feudal origins of the municipal corporation. If the federal government required people whose property happens to border a highway to fix the road, at their own expense, there would be a Tea Party–style revolution; but when it's local authorities that demand that owners spend money on both their own property and on public works, nobody complains. Understanding something about governance logics that are associated with the municipal corporation will help to explain this dualism.

Very briefly, states rule mainly by governing persons, through the liberal machinery of rights and/or through the coercive authority of sovereignty. By contrast, the municipal corporation, which began as an association of guild masters needing to provide certain services to property in common, has to this day remained primarily concerned with organizing space in such a way as to facilitate commerce and ensure public health, public safety, and public morals (as the initial clauses of municipal codes remind us).[2] States are legal-political entities that encompass and govern territories and populations.[3] They therefore need to secure borders and to ensure the loyalty of their people. A host of legal and cultural forms work to continually draw sharp boundaries between one state and another and to produce the citizen-state link on an everyday basis. These sociolegal forms include not only immigration inspections but also such "voluntary" acts as chant-

ing "USA, USA" at an Olympic event. By contrast, municipal corporations do not ask to see travelers' passports and do not have any equivalent
of treason statutes. (They don't even have anthems, a less trivial fact than
one might think.) Cities' legal powers are certainly weaker than those of
states, since local ordinances can be trumped by higher-level laws; but as
the rest of the book will amply show, asking whether one level of government has more or less power than another is a misleading question, since
it prevents us from seeing the *qualitative* differences between jurisdictions
and between scales of governance. Local authorities are for the most part
concerned with regulating space and activities and providing services to
property, and they bear on individuals and their acts, and on populations
and their loyalty, only indirectly. And in regulating space and looking after
"the public welfare," municipalities can sometimes wield legal tools that
have no equivalent in higher levels of government. For example, private
homes that are not in disrepair and have not been condemned can be forc-
ibly expropriated, not only for public works purposes (to build a highway,
for instance), but even when the city merely wants to provide a private
developer with suitable land.[4]

It is the continuities in the basic legal architecture of the municipal
corporation, over time and across space, and in particular the continuities
that make cities different from states, that I will try to highlight in this
chapter. The inventory of the legal tools that cities use carried out in this
chapter picks most of its examples from one particular street corner; but it
analyzes the "law of the street corner" in such a way as to emphasize those
features of the legal structure that endure over time, across space, and
across left-right political divides. An inventory of the local law that acts
upon one particular corner in Toronto carried out in this manner is thus
informative for concerned citizens and municipal officials around North
America, since it is the underlying legal forms, not the specific choices
made by regulatory officials, architects, and building owners, that are
highlighted here.[5]

Since understanding "law in action" (as opposed to law in the books)
requires knowledge of its social and historical context, it makes sense to
draw on my own experience of and involvement in urban life to help do
the legal inventory that will serve here as an overview of municipal law.
Now, for many years, my office was on the eighth floor of the University
of Toronto's Robarts Library, located just south of the corner of Bloor
Street and St. George Street. The corner immediately below my old office
window would not be a good one to understand local law, since all the land

is owned by the university. The more legally diverse and more public space of St. George and Bloor, which I traversed every day, thus appeared as a logical choice.

The Holy Trinity of Urban Space: Sidewalks, Roads, Buildings

The intersection in question, which among other things functions a gateway to the downtown campus of the University of Toronto, appears to the casual onlooker as always already divided into three main kinds of spaces: (1) the sidewalks, (2) the roadway, and (3) the buildings placed at each of the four corners. Street corners in other parts of town might have some strips of green between the sidewalk and the buildings, bits of dirt and grass that can give rise to quite complex legal debates; but otherwise this tripartite division of urban space is clearly the norm. To begin to analyze how urban space is put together by the city's legal tools, we have to open each of the three key elements of the intersection to peer into their legal insides, as it were. We could start with any of the three, but for the sake of paying homage to urban guru Jane Jacobs, who for decades lived a few blocks west of our intersection, we will start with the sidewalk.

Let us begin by asking: what is a sidewalk anyway? Or more precisely: what is the character of the legal entity that is not only regulated but to a large extent produced by the invisible legal apparatus hovering over (or lurking under, or both) my street corner?

Like most other things, sidewalks can be usefully described as complex assemblages of human and nonhuman elements.[6] The particular sidewalks that I can see when standing at the southeast corner are composed of the following: cement; technical specifications; provincial planning law; construction workers' sweat; a few rather stunted trees; signs embedded in the concrete (some put up by the city, some by the university); lamp posts; posts to lock up bikes; an ornamental structure that looks like a grand gate over St. George street but is only half of an arch, and thus not a gate; a ream of municipal bylaws; and, last but not least, the "customary" social practices that govern the spatial distribution and the circulation of people, bikes, and objects. We will take a closer look at how local law shapes and then organizes the bits and pieces of the sidewalk in a moment, but first we need to introduce the two remaining members of the holy trinity of urban space, namely roadways and buildings.

The second element of the street corner, the roadway, is also a heterogeneous and complicated assemblage made up of asphalt, painted lines, traffic lights, vehicles, pedestrians, cyclists, cars, trucks, loose bits of junk, provincial traffic laws, municipal parking rules, and other formal and informal rules governing interactions among vehicles and between vehicles and other entities. The list just given covers only the surface of the road, however. If one were to do a full inventory of the law of the street, one would have to include such legal entities as the professional licenses of the engineers who designed the vast underground passages that make electricity, the Internet, sewage, drinking water, and, last but not least, the subway, run along their proper channels without disturbing other things and activities. We would also need to include the lines that separate the electricity company's property from spaces and conduits that are the property of telecommunications companies or the city proper. These jurisdictional lines become partially visible to the observer's naked eye when workers wearing safety vests wield spray-paint cans of different colors and make mysterious colored markings on roads and sidewalks (orange for gas and blue for telephone, for example).[7] The governance of underground things and activities is mainly done not by laws but by technical standards, however. Standards have law-like force, since they dictate what will be made and where and how it will be placed; but they are not publicly visible, since such quasi-legislative authorities as the International Standards Organization (responsible for the "ISO-certified" signs on factories and construction signs) do not have the same public accountability requirements as government organizations. Standards only emerge from their quiet home within the municipal department of public works when something goes wrong—such as when a flood in someone's basement leads to charges of faulty sewer maintenance, and someone, such as an insurance adjuster, has to decide what counts as "faulty." But even if there is no public information about the politics of technical standards, we know that the vast underground system of cables and pipes that each modern city has built under itself did not have to develop as it did. It has its own legal history, as full of "might have beens" as other histories. A part of the story has been told by Jamie Benidickson in a fascinating study that shakes up the taken-for-granted belief that human waste ought to be channeled into waterways; but he only tells us how nature's streams became sewers, in fact and in law, and does not tell us how sewers coexist with other hidden networks.[8] But we cannot linger any longer on the fascinating topic of standards.[9]

Shifting our combined legal and physical gaze upward from the ground, and so away from both sidewalks and roads, we discover that the third element of the St. George and Bloor intersection—the buildings at each corner—turns out to be tremendously complicated too, legally. First, each building is a distinct legal entity that, like a Russian doll, contains many other legal subentities. For example, the private club at the northeast corner, which is so exclusive that it does not show its name on the door or the garden wall, undoubtedly has a liquor license, a building permit, and a municipal public health seal of approval to serve food (since going by the club on my way to the subway, I have had some glimpses, through the partly curtained windows, of waiters serving cocktail food). It must also have a specific zoning designation, although my perusal of the city's one-thousand-page zoning bylaw did not reveal a "gentlemen's club" category.

But assiduous attendance at zoning hearings has taught me that the grandiose redbrick late Victorian creation that I can see from the sidewalk is not the important legal entity. For planning and other local legal purposes (e.g., garbage pickup and snow removal), buildings are secondary entities whose legal personality derives from the plot of land on which they stand—the "municipal address," as planning documents always say. The essential legal entity, the municipal address, only becomes visible to citizens when it is contested, as when two neighbors fight about the legal status of a driveway or a fence. In that case, the authoritative source is the municipal survey (now available online, and so available to inspectors or city committees if they have a computer linked to the Internet).[10] Critical geographers and postcolonial scholars have produced numerous analyses of the power relations embedded in, and fostered by, the practice of surveying (though national-level surveys have received more attention than local ones). From this literature we know that the municipal survey has deep roots in the colonial appropriation of aboriginal land, a process that, in the case of Toronto (incorporated in 1834), took place at a time when neat squares drawn on maps were the high point of civilization. Our sample intersection is one of thousands that together make up "the grid," a particular way of dividing land that reflects certain cultural sensibilities (a preference for long straight lines intersecting others at ninety-degree angles, basically). And the ninety-degree rule applies not only to streets but to buildings as well. Thus, mosques that need to face Mecca, for example, end up being channeled into the legal category of exceptions to the norm; and exceptions require permission, often from the neighbors as well as the city. The resulting fights are usually presented by the media as clashes of culture or disputes about diversity, but these debates do not mention that the normal North American street grid system, with its associated rules about the orientation of buildings, is as much the product of a particular culture as the mosque.

It should be stressed that the municipal survey divides up the land of the city into plots without any reference to persons. Owners and tenants come and go, but the survey and its addresses stay. The holy-writ status of the straight lines drawn on paper becomes apparent not only in property disputes but also when there are no disputes, such as when people want to build a fence or get a building permit. A fact about urban life rarely highlighted in urban studies is that most of the time, citizens interact with city officials—and often also with each other—not as human beings, but rather as owners (or legal occupiers) of properties marked out in the survey. (Traffic and parking are also major arenas of citizen-city interaction, but those interactions generally require owning a vehicle, so they too are essentially mediated through property.)

In his analysis of "commodity fetishism" in volume 1 of *Capital*, Karl Marx famously described capitalist society as one in which most interactions among humans are side effects of relations among commodities. He showed that it is one's commodities (including one's skills and one's education) that go to the market and there find other commodities, most often money, to effect an exchange—with people being dragged along by their commodities like so many dogs pulled on leashes by their owners. This applies to much of urban social life: citizens interact with the city and with each other mainly via property relations. We often don't see the property foundation of urban interactions because relations with both neighbors and officialdom are rarely cold and calculating; rational-choice theory cannot properly describe such things as why so many people persist in staying in their microneighborhood when they could get a better house somewhere else cheaper, for example. But even though property, especially residential property, comes to be imbued with all manner of less than rational emotions, a large part of what cities do by way of legal regulation—and so a large part of how citizens interact with city hall—operates through property.

Even horizontal relations among citizens rely on and presuppose property. Neighbors form social bonds after their separately purchased commodities (rented apartments or owner-occupied houses) have initiated the contact. Citizens show up at public meetings not just to exercise their civic muscles but also out of a concern with property in the large sense—that is, not just individual economic property, but the collective and only partially tangible property that is made up of parks, streets, and the somewhat vague collection of publicly available goodies known in plan-ning law as "amenities."

For purposes of constitutional law we are persons. But for local, munic-ipal legal purposes we only exist insofar as we have a place to stand, with the status of each place being determined by the economics of real estate and rental markets as well as the law of property. The municipal corpo-ration's origins in fraternities of wealthy businessmen, and the fact that its historic central mission is providing services to property, with welfare functions being quite limited, help to put current draconian and arguably unconstitutional rules that target propertyless people, such as those who sleep on sidewalks, in their historical context. Those targeted are those who do not own or rent property, which means that they have a very tenu-ous connection with the local state. It is still relevant today to note that for many years the municipal franchise was extended only to property owners. While tenants came to be eventually included as well—and ten-ants now have standing for purposes such as being notified about develop-ment in their area—it is significant that in many localities, business people who own property in a city still get to vote, wherever they live, something that would not be tolerated for purposes of federal elections. Those who have no place to stand, literally, cannot be enumerated for local voting purposes, even if they do in fact inhabit a local space, such as a piece of unclaimed land. They do not have that all-important source of municipal identity, the address, and hence they are not entitled to local citizenship. (In Toronto, homeless people can get social assistance, but only if a local shelter for homeless people agrees that the shelter's address can be used for that purpose.) And in relation to politics beyond voting, in relation to the larger realm of citizenship, people who do not have an address can't take advantage of the ready-made, property-dependent identities that are the bread and butter of local politics: business owner, homeowner, legal occupier/renter, and, perhaps most powerfully, in our current situation, the identity of taxpayer (even though they of course pay taxes every time they buy items such as a pack of cigarettes).[11]

But let us now return from that linchpin of local citizenship, the muni-cipal address, to the buildings themselves. It should be noted that in ad-dition to local ordinances, there are federal regulations governing the physical characteristics of building materials, carpets, and curtains (drawn up mainly from the point of view of preventing fires). Those too could arguably be included in the legal inventory of the street corner. There are also state/provincial regulations enshrined in detailed building codes that determine such things as ceiling heights and the physical features of windows (a third-floor window, for example, has to be designed so that a small child could not fall out of it). The state or province also regulates elevators and inspects them, and sets out detailed standards for any non-family kitchens that might exist in any of the buildings. In addition, there are labor and employment standards, usually set out in state/provincial statutes.

The combination of rules about objects and building materials and rules about work and workplaces amounts to a veritable mountain of law. The height of each step of the staircase, the brightness of the lights that shine in the hallways, the number and location of fire escapes—indeed, it seems as if absolutely everything except the height of persons and the nature of their conversation is subject to legal regulation. But in fact, the height of persons, while obviously not mandated by law, is shaped by law as well, to the extent that elevators and stairs and desks are all designed according to standards and specifications that have the force of law and that assume a person who is not disabled and is of average height. And the nature of conversation in offices and other public spaces is regulated too, by such legal mechanisms as labor law, workplace codes of conduct, sexual harassment policies, antiracism policies, and Criminal Code of Canada provisions on hate speech. So maybe there are no spheres of "free" activity anywhere in the buildings that I can see at my street corner; law does seem to be everywhere.

Let us now turn to a more detailed (but by no means exhaustive) consideration of the legal and governance underpinnings of each of the three elements initially identified by visual inspection—the sidewalk, the roadway, and the buildings.

Sidewalks: Neoliberal Urbanism and the Decline of Standard-Issue Gray Concrete

Sidewalks in Toronto were for many decades made of rectangles of standard gray concrete. Other cities enjoy long stretches of sidewalk, often along major boulevards and historic districts, featuring patterned tiles, interlocking bricks, cobblestones, or even granite. Cities in the Netherlands, for example, feature numerous hand-built brick or stone sidewalks, and not only in historic districts. But Toronto seemed for many years impervious to these design trends. The public spaces of the city looked the same throughout: efficient but dull, functional but ugly, safe for pedestrians but cheaply made.

However, in recent years, in Toronto as in many other cities, many neighborhoods in search of "distinction,"[12] particularly those geared to promoting tourism or niche boutique-style shopping, have persuaded city officials and politicians to embellish the sidewalk with cobblestone-style bricks, colored tiles, and other aesthetic features. The same quest for district distinction has given us veritable forests of expensive-looking lampposts and planters for flowers and small trees.[13] What these design changes, often associated with partial privatization of public space, mean in the context of global neoliberalism, is a question that has occupied many critical urbanists studying gentrified touristy spaces.[14] But my focus here is on the relation between law and the entities I can observe with my own eyes on the sidewalk, and these entities do not at first sight seem to include neoliberalism, or even the economic entity that is "privatization."

However, the sidewalk entities that I can see—the tiles, bricks, lamps, etc.—are not purely physical. They are simultaneously physical, economic (a public-private partnership is generally used to fund the embellishments), discursive/aesthetic, and, more relevant in the present context, legal. Thus, the ornamental iron and concrete quasi gate that was built a few years ago on either side of the official entrance to the university is at one level a piece of ornamental iron; but it is also a visible embodiment of a larger political process, namely, municipal encouragement of competition among neighborhoods. Official encouragement of district "distinction" stands in sharp contrast to the postwar consensus about treating all sidewalks equally. The politico-legal infrastructure that supports micro-local beautification projects has the effect of increasing inequalities between neighborhoods—since the drab inner suburbs now look even drabber, as the inhabitants of Chicago, Manchester, Barcelona, and numerous other cities know from their own experiences in microscale improvements. The legal tools required to isolate a small area of the city and put it under private-public rule are not local inventions; they are global. They were pioneered in New York City, in the Times Square Business Improvement District, set up in 1992, and in inner-city London, in Thatcher-era legal forms that led to Canary Wharf and other public-private mini-sovereigns of small parts of London.[15] Now, cities everywhere feel obliged to create public-private partnerships to spruce up a shopping area or to attract tourists to the waterfront. So maybe I was wrong—maybe I can actually see neoliberalism with my own eyes, on the sidewalk.

As Nicholas Blomley has shown, sidewalks are regarded by urban planners and engineers as standard-issue public spaces wholly devoted to purposive commercially oriented movement—spaces in which the capitalist logic of constant circulation treats any stationary object or merely idle person as an impediment to "proper" pedestrian movement.[16] The craze for marking off select districts and distinguishing them from the larger, grayer city by physically remodeling the sidewalk to add ornamental lampposts and flowerpots has somewhat dislodged the utilitarian, engineer-driven circulation rationality of earlier decades. But it is crucial to note that these improvements, which are never distributed equally throughout the city, require a certain legal infrastructure. Generally, city officials designate an area as an "empowerment zone" (in Bill Clinton's United States) or, in today's Toronto, an "area in need of improvement."[17] And special, one-off city monies usually flow to supplement or "match" private funding, funding that is only available in certain select areas.

The competitive logic that sets one district against another in the quest for cultural distinction and tourist dollars is a complex phenomenon with roots in global and national economic and governance trends. But in Toronto as elsewhere, district distinction requires certain legal changes. And once an area has been legally marked off from the rest of the city as a special space that is not only provided with flowerpots that do not exist in poorer areas but also policed by private security and/or cleaned by special, nonmunicipal cleaners—often dressed in uniforms advertising the local business association—the capacious neoliberal legal infrastructure that is the public-private partnership ends up having its own effects on the everyday life of the sidewalk.

Municipal Sovereignty and the Permit System

Parks, sidewalks, and other spaces that are experienced as "public" are not actually common property. Even the famous Boston Common is not in fact common. Rather, these spaces are the private property of the municipal corporation. For that reason, any objects placed on or near the sidewalk—the blackboards prompting passersby to enter the restaurants near our particular intersection; the newspaper boxes on the northwest corner—require permits from the municipality. If the spaces were actually common, as grazing lands still are in some parts of the world, anyone could use the space as long as others' rights were not being harmed. But they are not common; they are owned by "the city," as popular parlance puts it in a phrase that underlines the distance between the municipal corporation as property owner and the municipal corporation as a democratic coming together of citizens.

In addition, all outdoor signs, even if placed wholly on one's privately owned building, also require permits, and are subject to size and lighting restrictions. This is no dead letter: despite the fact that the city only has about 140 "generalist" bylaw enforcement officers (in contrast to over five thousand police officers), municipal inspectors do in fact enforce the sidewalk-object permit system, making occasional rounds to ask small business owners whether their outdoor signs, however small, have permits.

Furthermore, any architectural feature that extends over the sidewalk may require a zoning bylaw amendment that must be approved by the appropriate committees, and sometimes also by city council as a whole. No such projection exists in this street corner; but a building projection that created a "gated-community" aesthetic for the university at a nearby location had to obtain city council permission "to permit illuminated signage on condition that the owner [the university] enter into an Encroachment Agreement with the City of Toronto with respect to the glazed cornice" (Variance from chapter 297, Signs, of the former City of Toronto Municipal Code, 1999). This kind of document, reminiscent of feudal arrangements allowing peasants to use the lord's land, is routinely produced in North American municipalities. Through these agreements private owners receive permission to put up lights and signs on their own, supposedly wholly owned, fee-simple property.

Sidewalk Trees

The entities placed in sidewalk planters or small holes covered by grates are more than biological beings: they are a hybrid of vegetable matter and regulatory material. Elaborate sets of rules govern the size of the sidewalk holes in which trees are planted and the features of the grate that covers the hole—and also the size and type of tree. These rules, Irus Braverman's research shows, are the result of compromises between the conflicting logics of the urban foresters and arborists—who want more trees and more space for their roots—and the engineers, who want smoother and more spacious sidewalks.[18] One might think that a tree is a good example of the perfectly benign entity; but it turns out that each tree and each little planting hole is the vector sum of professional rivalries and regulatory fights.

Street Food

The only street foods one can buy in the vicinity of St. George and Bloor are the hot dogs and sausages sold by a man who has long operated a cart on the northeast corner. The license to sell previously frozen hot dogs and sausages, from carts that have to be taken away each evening, is municipal and costs many thousands of dollars per year (how much depends on the location). The number of licenses is capped at 176, regardless of demand, and there is a moratorium in certain wards of the city—downtown wards, which are the only ones where there is a reliable market for such food—due to local councillors' belief that hot dogs are somehow low-class or unsightly. The vending license is site-specific, so that the vendor cannot move even a few feet along the sidewalk to avoid sun or rain. It is also food-specific (though it has recently become possible for hot dog vendors to humbly beg, and sometimes be granted, permission to sell other, also specified foods, which have to be cooked in commercial kitchens and only reheated at the cart). A few larger trucks exist that have licenses to sell either Chinese food or chips, but there are no more than a handful of such licenses.

Over the 2007–9 period much energy was spent by vendors, groups supporting "ethnic" and healthy foods, and one lone city councillor in reforming the compulsory hot dog rule. This campaign was in part inspired by the "food truck" movement in the United States, which has seen street food, formerly associated mainly with Mexicans, become a trendy phenomenon, with trucks sending customers real-time information about their location and their daily specials using Twitter. But for economic reasons as well as legal ones (Toronto has almost no underused privately owned land in the downtown core, unlike many US cities), food vending has up until now been limited to municipally owned spaces, mainly sidewalks. The importance of the claim made earlier that public spaces are not really public but are the private property of a municipal corporation is well illustrated by the contrast between US cities, where food trucks have emerged with relative ease because private land is readily available for short-term rentals, and other cities where prospective vendors have to battle against mountains of municipal red tape.

Finally, while no ice cream (truck-based) vendor has a permit for our particular street corner, an ice cream vendor licensed to work two blocks away, outside the Royal Ontario Museum, is regulated not only by the same arcane vending license system that regulates hot dog vendors but also by a food-specific section of the vending bylaw that prohibits playing the distinctive ice cream truck music after dusk. (He has been fined for this offence.)

Begging

For the past ten years, sidewalk activity in Toronto and elsewhere in Ontario has been regulated by the Safe Streets Act, passed by the neoconservative government of the late 1990s but not repealed by the Liberals elected in 2003. This law prohibits begging near the bank machine at the northeast corner as well as "aggressive panhandling" anywhere. It also prohibits more enterprising activities, including squeegeeing. Law enforcement in this area is nevertheless quite uneven. Two blocks west of our intersection, at Spadina and Bloor, one can readily observe any number of people—many of them aboriginal men—idling away their time in a small park featuring a sculpture made of large blocks of black granite made to look like domino pieces. Many of these men panhandle a good part of the day, which gives this street corner a very different feel from the antiseptic and gentrified atmosphere that St. George and Bloor acquired once the university finished its major renovation schemes.

The contrast between the two neighboring intersections is telling. In the "nicer" street corner I have chosen for my example here, there is a lone panhandler, who was plying his trade outside the St. George subway stop long before the neoconservative changes to national and provincial welfare policies resulted in new forms of visible indigence in Toronto. In 2008–9 he was still working that corner—but otherwise the corner of St. George and Bloor does not seem to feature much begging activity or enforcement action.[19] The university is very committed to ethnic diversity, but the street improvements and the quasi-gated community architectural changes give the message that the underclass is not welcome. Whether the university uses the local force or its own police to actively drive out beggars is unclear. One effort to evict homeless people from campus buildings apparently failed when the first disheveled middle-aged man apprehended turned out to be a senior math professor.

The rumor about the math professor could not be confirmed, but it was told to me as an explanation for why there is so little by way of security at the university, despite the proximity of several soup kitchens and a large Salvation Army shelter. The anecdote, true or not, probably illustrates that in keeping with the local Toronto effort to somehow combine compassion with social exclusion, harsh law-and-order tactics are unlikely to be used to drive out the small number of indigent or mentally ill people who use the university's buildings. But electronic access cards or "fobs" are becoming increasingly common. This will likely lead to the closing down of spaces currently used by some local inhabitants who do not have bathrooms or bedrooms of their own and thus need to use public spaces differently than those of us who have private homes and also have the money to use restaurants and other facilities.

Entertainment

In Toronto, musicians are allowed to use amplification to perform in public only rarely—in programmed events at some designated squares and parks. An official told me that a license to play music (acoustically) and collect donations can be given to anyone who asks. One rarely sees such entrepreneurs, however—even at the corner of Bloor and St. George, which sees rivers of pedestrians during peak class times. This suggests that if there is such a permit system, it is not very accessible. When the same official was asked whether the reason for the dearth of buskers is that police or city staff would move buskers along for fear that the sidewalk might become obstructed—a hypothesis derived from anecdotal evidence—she responded that musicians might indeed be made to move from sidewalks, but would be quite free to play in parks. This is not a very practical suggestion, however, since Toronto follows the Anglo-Protestant theory of parks as restful refuges from commercial life: only two parks of the dozens I have visited over the years have restaurants or even small cafés.

By contrast with the sidewalk, musicians can and do play for donations inside the subway—the only place one can in any case comfortably play instruments throughout the long winter months. Subway musicians need to pass an audition and obtain a license from the transit commission; but the number of such licenses appears to be very limited, since only a small minority of subway stations have regular buskers.

Using the Sidewalk to Rest

Lying down or sleeping on the sidewalk is not forbidden by any law of general application in Toronto, unlike in many other cities. However, camping is not allowed either on sidewalks or in city parks, and it is difficult to sleep or even take a short nap outdoors, other than in the short summer months, without some kind of protection. (Whether cardboard boxes or sleeping bags count as "camping" is a contentious enforcement question.) Even if there is no law forbidding people from lying down on sidewalks, however, merely sitting on the sidewalk can be regarded as obstructing pedestrian traffic.

Sitting or lying on the sidewalk is thus not without its legal problems, then, given the tendency of North American urban authorities to treat purposeful walking as the only valid reason for occupying municipal concrete. Nevertheless, given that Toronto lacks the kind of draconian antihomeless laws that now exist in San Francisco and Seattle, one should treat the phrase commonly used by local activists "the criminalization of homelessness" with a grain of salt. Sleeping in public spaces is highly restricted by parks' bylaws and by site-specific bylaws. Notably, city hall square has its own bylaw, which bans sleeping at any time, although in keeping with the Toronto ethos of compassionate social exclusion mentioned above, the bylaw is used to move people on, not to charge them. By comparison with the United States, it has to be said that Toronto is a "soft on homelessness" city, since neither the criminal law nor provincial laws prohibit loitering or begging—or even sleeping, for the most part.

But much of what looks like public space is either actually private or is policed by private security guards (e.g, the sidewalks adjacent to banks or corporate offices). This is why the Trespass to Property Act, which is not criminal or quasi-criminal but rather designed to protect private property, seems to be more important in the everyday life of the urban indigent poor than the criminal law, according to local informants. It is this act that authorizes private security guards as well as police to move people who are sleeping in privately owned spaces such as doorways, stairs, parking garages, and subway stations. In this context it is important that the subway, which could potentially offer refuge during harsh winter weather, is privately owned by the Toronto Transit Commission, a city body that is a landowner like any other. The logic of "moving along" that is implicit in the Trespass to Property Act is more frequently used to govern visibly indigent people than actual criminalization.

Skateboarding

Again in contrast to other cities, Toronto does not prohibit skateboarding in any legal code of general application. However, much ingenuity has been used, along St. George Street as well as in numerous other inviting spaces, to make skateboarding physically impossible. The decorative quasi benches that contain the flowerbeds on St. George Street have been fitted with pieces of metal that make it impossible for skateboarders and Rollerblade virtuosos to use those inviting spaces. We see here that, as in the case of panhandling and lying on the sidewalk, law is only one of the techniques used by local governments and bodies such as universities to discourage activities to the point of making them invisible. As the "crime prevention through environmental design" literature shows, moving objects around can have more powerful effects than passing new laws. And yet, if only symbolically, it is positive from the point of view of diversity that Toronto does not have antiskateboarding or antibegging local ordinances.

Snow Removal: Making Niceness Compulsory

In the winter, large posters on public transit shelters exhort Torontonians: "Be nice! Clear the ice!" The posters fail to mention that—as is the case in most American municipalities as well—it is actually compulsory for owners and occupiers to shovel snow and remove ice from sidewalks abutting their property within twenty-four hours of a snowfall. (Elderly or disabled people can apply to have a city crew do the job.) Students of the French ancien régime will recognize the clearing snow and ice rule as a corvée, a feudal practice by which absolute monarchs used to demand that subjects personally carry out public works. The current discourse about cities' fiscal woes makes it unlikely that citizens anywhere in North America will rise up and demand that public sidewalks be cleared by paid public employees; but it is worth pointing out that higher levels of government do not demand forced labor on roads or bridges. It is perhaps significant, however, that instead of posting the law and the fine prominently, the city chooses to buy advertising space to disseminate the (false) message that Canadian "niceness" is what causes citizens to engage in public works. Occasionally, city staff do "sweeps" and ticket homeowners who don't clear the ice. But this is rarely done (in keeping with what happens in other US municipalities). By and large, citizens accept the civic obligation imposed on them with only very occasional enforcement. The municipal corporation and its peculiar legal powers seem to be able to fly below the political radar, in this as in many other areas.

The Roadway

The inventory of regulatory forces converging on Toronto's sidewalks may have given an Orwellian impression of sidewalk life. However, sidewalks are veritable gardens of edenic freedom compared to roadways. As Alan

Hunt has documented, the regulation of traffic has arguably played a great role in enabling what US law calls "the police power of the state" to proliferate,[20] and Toronto is no exception.

Walking/Marching

It is illegal to walk on the paved roadway except at designated crosswalks, and then only when the light is green. These are very significant restrictions on political freedom. In Toronto, the only demonstrations that can be held without a series of prior permits are those tiny enough to fit into Toronto's narrow sidewalks, or on the designated protest space that is the front lawn of the provincial legislature (where protesters, surrounded by four lanes of fast traffic on either side, have little chance of being heard or seen).

If one wants to take to the streets in Toronto, one will need to first go to the police services' traffic department to obtain a "road closing permit." Then one needs to proceed to a different department to obtain a "parade permit." Police being generally on the side of vehicular traffic, they will do their best to limit the time of the march/demonstration, and will often suggest that marches proceed on streets that are not very busy—which of course defeats the purpose of demonstrating. In addition, organizers of large events can be told to obtain liability insurance (so that anyone injured tripping on the sidewalk sues the organizers, not the city). Years ago I was involved in organizing a large peace demonstration, and we spent many days frantically phoning around to find an organization that would loan its liability insurance. The demonstration was saved by the United Church of Canada, which graciously offered to be the official sponsor of the anti–cruise missile march. Once more, the commons is not the commons.

Driving

Traffic stops and overenforcement of rules about signal lights and so forth are known to be widely used by police as ways to show who's in charge. But while the racial profiling that is enabled by traffic rules and driver's license rules has been studied and discussed, few people have gone on to ask questions about the role of traffic laws more generally in the illiberal governance of people and activities. That one can only drive by the grace of having a license and that the license system means that identification can be demanded from drivers (but not from pedestrians) are taken to be facts of life in urban North America, with no thought given to the fact that the ubiquitousness of the driver's license gives police and other state officials a great deal of power that they cannot exercise over those who take buses or walk. And since vehicles too have their own license, which again is a conditional privilege, like all licenses, cars can be stopped and in many instances searched, whereas pedestrians cannot, at least not without cause. If vehicular traffic were governed by different legal means, instead of by means of licenses, the main means used by governments to scrutinize their citizens in North America (where national identity cards are unknown but drivers' licenses are normal) would disappear.

I have not personally seen police stopping cars or drivers at this particular intersection to ask for identification or look for drugs or guns. But the absence of enforcement—especially in a space-time unit in which university people and tourists predominate—does not mean that law's power is diminished. Indeed, law's power to govern citizens illiberally through vehicle licensing and driver's licensing is increased by the fact that not all drivers or all vehicles are equally likely to be stopped, and not all intersections are equally likely to be under surveillance by the drug squad. After all, if white middle-aged university professors like me were as likely to be stopped while driving as young black men, the coercive underpinnings of the laws that govern urban drivers and their vehicles would begin to be scrutinized. Uneven enforcement results in a situation where the power of law is just as great in nice middle-class areas as in poorer areas, but the impression is created that the force of law exists only in certain targeted spaces. This chapter proves, I hope, that there is as much law in an unremarkable and largely middle-class location as there is in the city's skid row.

Parking

From the point of view of law's effects on urban experience, it is very significant that municipalities are authorized to demand substantial amounts of money from citizens for the privilege of temporarily leaving their vehicles on streets that are already paid for by the very same citizens. It is also significant that while complaining about the high cost of parking is a regular indoor sport, in Toronto as elsewhere, no legal challenges to the city's authority to exact street-parking fees have been recorded. That the city should charge for people to park in city-owned lots that have always been privately owned is not legally remarkable; but streets are not the same as lots, one would think, in terms of public ownership.

Over the years, free street parking—previously available during evenings and on Sundays—has become almost extinct. Having paid for one's car, for the plate, for the license to drive it, and for the roadway (though taxes), citizens could feel that they own the street and should be able to park on it, at least for short periods that do not interfere with others' enjoyment of the street—but the sovereignty of the municipal corporation is sufficiently strong as to deter potential challenges to using street-parking fees as a key revenue source.

Municipal Regulation of Privately Owned Buildings

The two key instruments of municipal sovereignty over private property are planning rules (especially zoning) and the property standards bylaw. There are other important legal-technical-cultural mechanisms—sewage and water provision and the municipal property tax regimes are two important ones—but for the sake of simplicity we will confine ourselves to the two legal tools that generally do the most work in the shaping of the publicly visible spaces that comprise "the street."

Zoning and Zoning Appeals: The State of Exception as the Rule

On the question of zoning, which in Toronto is arranged through a legal structure that is very similar to and probably copied from the New York City 1916 zoning ordinance, suffice it to quote a city staff report:

> The City of Toronto currently has 43 different zoning by-laws inherited from the six pre-amalgamation municipalities. The by-laws contain over 1 million words, over 13,260 regulations, over 10,000 site-specific amendments, 1550 definitions and 276 different zones. (City of Toronto, Chief Planner's report, March 27, 2009)

Since technical knowledge is often a useful and remunerative source of professional capital, one could hypothesize that planners and urban designers who do know a good part of the regulatory system are keen to preserve their knowledge monopoly, and that this is the reason for the irrational complexity of the system. However, my empirical observation of planning hearings and disputes suggests otherwise. City planners admit that even they cannot possibly know all of the rules. And the planning department made a great effort over many years to replace the forty-three zoning bylaws mentioned in the quote above by a somewhat unified zoning bylaw—an effort that ultimately failed.

My research suggests that it is the local legal system's very structure, its regulatory architecture, that encourages a constant proliferation of site-specific exceptions and legal black holes. What US planners call "spot zoning"—that is, obtaining a site-specific exception to the rules that generally govern height, density, parking spaces, uses, and other features of street life—is in Toronto the only practical way of getting ahead with development proposals. Why? Precisely because the incredibly cumbersome and geographically limited character of the zoning rules make more general, policy-driven, rational, citywide change difficult if not impossible. Given this decentralized system and given the custom of granting all "minor" variances that are not opposed,[21] neither developers nor neighborhood associations have any interest in looking at the city as a whole.

A curious legal-social fact that has greatly shaped the everyday life of the street in Toronto as in other North American jurisdictions with powerful zoning appeals boards is that the exception can easily become more prevalent than the "norm." On many streets in downtown Toronto, "legal nonconforming uses" (that is, properties that have been legally authorized, through grandfathering or though having "variances" granted) are more numerous than properties that actually conform to the zoning bylaw. I asked a city planner to confirm or deny my impression that well over half of the buildings in the older sections of Toronto were nonconforming; she replied that there is no master map from which one could calculate the difference between what is and what the law says, but she thought I might well be correct.

Edward Bassett, the lawyer who devised the most influential early US zoning ordinance (for New York City, in the 1910s), realized that without a mechanism that would grant exceptions fairly easily, private owners would combine to ensure that courts (which in the United States were often very protective of private property) would eventually invalidate whole zoning ordinances and perhaps even abolish the municipal power to zone.[22] He thus set up a zoning appeals mechanism, a governance safety valve that would ensure that disgruntled property owners were diverted from seeking overall legislative change and channeled instead into asking for special rules for their own property. His hope was that over the long run the city would begin to look more like the plan; but in retrospect it is clear that he underestimated the political usefulness of the exemption-granting mechanisms. The zoning appeals system created a constant demand for political favors, which in turn fueled the fortunes of ward-heeling (Tammany Hall–style) politicians whose fortunes were furthered by granting exemptions—a vicious circle well documented in Robert Caro's Pulitzer-winning biography of New York City's development czar, Robert Moses, who loved freeways and public works projects but was also—and not by accident—the acknowledged master of the semisecret, often illegal, one-off deal.[23]

Property Standards

Toronto's bylaw enforcement officers can demand that private buildings be fixed up and maintained. If owners do not carry out repairs, the city can hire contractors, have the work done, and put the cost on the property tax bill. Generally, this is only done when neighbors make repeated complaints and when there are at least some safety hazards involved. Occasionally, however, purely aesthetic repairs are carried out and charged to the owner. In 2007, a particularly vocal city councillor repeatedly called city inspectors to have the lawns and gardens of rooming houses in his district cleaned up and tidied, with the cost being put on the rooming house owner's tax bill.

None of the four properties at each of our intersection's corners have unkempt gardens or rickety porches: they are all well-maintained institutional buildings catering to the University of Toronto students, professors, and staff; tourists visiting the city; and trendy locals who like to frequent the two "Bar Mercurio" locations. But just as the zoning bylaw exercises its power silently and continues to shape the city's spaces even when no zoning variances are being negotiated, so too the property standards bylaw, which like many other city bylaws combines aesthetic and functional rationalities in a single legal text, quietly shapes the appearance of the buildings and yards even in the absence of graffiti or long weeds.

Conclusion

A casual visitor to the corner of St. George and Bloor Streets would likely say that the corner appears as peaceful, orderly, and not without some aesthetic charm, even though the sidewalks show significant activity only on weekdays during the school year. Is this the result of the prevailing law?

Mitchell Duneier's sociolegal study of Greenwich Village sidewalks in the 1990s is illustrative here.[24] Early in the decade, the numerous sidewalk vendors and hawkers who gave the streets much of their life seemed to get along with each other and with their customers, as if demonstrating Jane Jacobs's theory of the spontaneous "ballet" of the street. But after Mayor Rudy Giuliani introduced harsh ordinances against vending, the peacefulness suddenly turned into disorder, even violence. The power of law was more visible in that second period, since previously cooperative vendors had to compete with one another for customers and for space. But the law's power did not increase—it was simply used differently, more visibly in the second period.

In general, urban space-time units that look peaceful—Jane Jacobs's 1950s Greenwich Village, for instance—are as much the product of law as spaces in which one can directly witness illegally built shacks being razed or vendors and panhandlers being removed by police. Law is more visible at certain times than at others, but it works and has effects even when it is not visible. Jacobs's Village, as Duneier reminds us, was in no small measure a product of nationwide laws and regulatory practices that kept blacks "in their place" and out of Manhattan. Similarly, the relative order and peace visible at the corner of St. George and Bloor on a sunny May afternoon in 2008 have been produced not only by global economic forces and nationwide cultural trends but also by the force of local law.

CHAPTER 3

The Legal Regulation of Taste

Annoying Noises, Unkempt Yards, and the
"Quality and Tranquility of Life"

The Legal Foundations of Local Aesthetic Regulation

In 2004 I was told by a municipal official that a local bylaw makes it illegal to grow vegetables on one's own front yard. After seeing my dismayed reaction, the official quickly added that the bylaw is not enforced in areas of the city with large concentrations of Italian-Canadians. Thinking about a Chinese family living around the corner from my house, who use every inch of their yard as well as of the fence to grow vegetables—in contrast to their mainly Anglo neighbors, whose front yards are free of any useful plants—I wondered if the antivegetable rule had been passed at a time when Anglo Torontonians were feeling threatened by immigration.[1] But in scrutinizing the text of the relevant section of the property standards bylaw I discovered that vegetables, Italian or Chinese or otherwise, aren't actually named.

Like most municipal laws, the front-yard bylaw does not take the familiar legal form of a set of prohibitions. Criminal codes, for example, are designed on the assumption that the state's role is to ban what causes harm to others, not to tell people what ideals to aspire to. The "harm principle" associated with the great nineteenth-century liberal thinker John Stuart Mill has been used to decriminalize a range of activities, from homosexual sex through suicide, not because governments necessarily approve of them, but because the criminal law's scope is increasingly thought to be limited to banning conduct that causes harm to others.

Municipal law is based on a different, pre-liberal and premodern theory of law. Municipal corporations in Renaissance Europe promulgated intricate rules governing everything from trash disposal, noise, who could wear what clothes (sumptuary laws), and who could make and sell goods where and when. The official legal "city" was composed of economically successful heads of households who gave themselves the power to govern the city much as they governed their own patriarchally organized workshops and households, looking to secure order, peace, and prosperity by imposing rules conducive to civilization and urbanity. Municipal jurisprudence, in the United States as well as in Canada, is still heavily imbued with this historical legacy of city-father paternalism.[2]

In keeping with this history, the jurisprudence on municipal powers—especially that developed by American courts of appeal—tends to regard city fathers as wise figures who can and should set standards for citizen behavior and impose common cultural codes. The preamble of a city of Ottawa noise bylaw (discussed below) is typical of thousands of similar texts in that it blandly states that the purpose of the law is not only to forbid harmful conduct but to establish nothing less than the "tranquility of life": "to provide for an environment free from unusual, unnecessary, or excessive noises which degrade the quality and tranquility of life."

In contrast to the world of constitutional rights and criminal codes, at the local scale it is accepted that coercive law can and ought to be used not only to protect what tort law has long called "the quiet enjoyment of one's property"—a preference for quiet and tranquility, as against urban excitement, is one of the key cultural foundations of municipal law—but also to enshrine in law a particular theory of what John Stuart Mill called human flourishing. If one reads current cases on issues such as billboards, messy front yards, and noise, it is clear that the cultural preferences of middle-aged, middle-class, married folks who own and lovingly tend a piece of urban property are constantly reinscribed (even in "diverse" Canada) in law both by the petty legislators who draw up ordinances and by the judges who interpret them. That young people who go out late at night, and tenants of any age who spend money on beer rather than on house renovations, are not entitled to have their cultural preferences imposed on the city as a whole is such a basic assumption of local law that it goes without saying.

This cultural tilt is more than a legal bias in favor of certain persons, though of course it is partly that. And it is more than a bias in favor of property owners, important as ownership is in both municipal "law in the books" and municipal law enforcement. Urban aesthetic regulation does not only empower certain groups of persons. It also ranks activities and spaces along a kind of moral "chain of being," as Constance Perin's brilliant anthropological study of the cultural biases of the single-family detached home zoning category shows.[3]

The key (modern) American case authorizing municipalities to write aesthetic criteria into law was the 1954 case of *Berman v. Parker*, regarding the power of the legislature to pass a draconian urban renewal statute by which large numbers of Washington, DC, property owners, including some whose properties were not "blighted," and thus not subject to condemnation, were to be expropriated. In a much quoted decision, Justice Douglas stated that local governments need state authorization both to engage in projects to clear slums and for the more ambitious projects that target "the conditions that cause slums,"[4] but that once the legislature and/ or the city council has decided to engage in such a wholesale redevelopment, their decision will generally trump constitutional provisions regarding individual autonomy and property rights.

> The misery of [run-down] housing may despoil a community as an open sewer may ruin a river. We do not sit to determine whether a particular housing project is or is not desirable. The concept of public welfare [which undergirds eminent-domain local powers] is broad and inclusive. The values it represents are spiritual as well as physical, aesthetic as well as monetary. It is within the power of the legislature to determine that the community shall be beautiful as well as healthy, spacious as well as clean, well balanced as well as well patrolled. If those who govern the District of Columbia decide that the Nation's Capital should be beautiful as well as sanitary, there is nothing in the Fifth Amendment that stands in the way. (*Berman v Parker*, 348 US 26 [1954], 33)

While there has been some effort on the part of appeal courts since the 1950s to make municipalities tailor their ordinances somewhat, and to offer, when challenged, some kind of justification for breaching all manner of rights, the basic paternalist logic through which municipalities continue enforcing myriad culturally laden policies and rules has not been disrupted.

Of particular interest to urban governance is the fact that even when municipalities make little or no effort to try to gesture toward the harm principle by emphasizing sanitary and economic rationales rather than the "spiritual" welfare of the 1954 *Berman* decision, appeal courts are often happy to simply assume that city councils have adequate reasons to proceed with expropriations and other uses of coercion. The judicial willingness to attribute or impute knowledge of complex social problems and their causes to city councils or state legislatures is especially visible in judicial opinions involving morally disreputable activities, despite the fact that unless councillors previously worked in the police "vice" squad, it is hard to discern how they might have gained the knowledge attributed to them by courts.

For example, in a 2000 case concerning draconian local rules about the location of strip clubs, which reached the Supreme Court because in US law stripping is considered speech and thus has legal protections that would not be extended to other commerce, the US Supreme Court said: "The council members, familiar with commercial downtown Erie, are the individuals who would likely have first-hand knowledge of what took place in and around nude dancing establishments there, and can make particularized, expert judgements about the harmful secondary effects" (*City of Erie v. Pap's AM*, 529 US 298 [2000]).

No evidence that the councillors actually walked the streets documenting harms flowing from strip clubs was offered. But even if such evidence had been produced, this would hardly amount to transforming local politicians into "experts" on social and moral harms. In fact, if sociological expert evidence had been introduced, it would have suggested that sexually oriented businesses actually generate *fewer* disturbances around them than other businesses open late at night, such as convenience stores and gas stations.[5] Appeal courts, however, do not require cities to evaluate scientifically the effects of rules limiting the location and the manner of operation of sexually oriented businesses. Instead, courts impute knowledge, either "firsthand" or "expert" or both, to local councillors.

There are of course differences in both statute law and common law between states in the United States and between the United States and Canada. (For example, Canada does not enshrine property rights in the Constitution; but on the other hand, Canadian courts are less deferential to municipal policy decisions than is the case in the United States.) However, the question here is not the technical legal one of exactly how much deference courts pay to city councils. The key point here is that despite jurisdictional differences (which mainly concern how compensation to expropriated owners is determined), the constitutional rights doctrines that have become central in both national and transnational law sometimes vanish at the local scale. A national desire to beautify would not do much to uphold federal statutes that breached individual rights, but the local pursuit of local beautification has the blessing of the judiciary, by and large.

In general, the logic of *Berman*, by which higher courts blithely authorize municipal authorities to impose all manner of intrusive regulations to govern the supposed harms flowing from morally controversial or merely unsightly activity, has not substantially changed over the past half a century, and is visible in Canadian as well as American law. An example will suffice to illustrate the moral-paternal quality of local law (before we go on to case studies of noises and unkempt yards). The Toronto bylaw governing front yards with which this chapter started is typical in that it sets out in great detail not what is forbidden (as is the case in criminal law), but rather what privately owned residential property ought to look like, or more accurately, must look like. Section 629.11 of the property standards bylaw states that front yards must be graded, must not be used for parking unless a special permit is obtained, and must have a "suitable ground cover to prevent recurrent ponding of water." In addition, front yards "shall be"

A. 3.   Landscaped, so as to prevent unstable soil conditions or erosion, with any combination of the following:
   a. trees, shrubs, grass or flowers
   b. decorative stonework, walkways or screening; and
   c. any other horticultural or landscape-architectural elements. . . .
   B.   Where grass forms part of the ground cover, it shall be maintained in a living condition and at a height of no more than 20 cm.
   C.   All lawns, shrubs and hedges shall be kept trimmed and not be overgrown.

The combination of these "shalls" and "musts" makes it clear that the inhabitants of Toronto are being told not only what their privately owned space must look like, but, implicitly, what it is *for*: one's private front yard has to be used to generate beauty, not to grow food. In practice, as the official mentioned at the beginning of the chapter told me, inspectors usually turn a blind eye to vegetables in areas of the city in which Torontonians of non-Anglo-Saxon origin grow tomatoes or eggplants. Turning a blind eye, however, is not the same as changing the law to make it less culturally biased and less nanny-state-like. Even when laws are not actually enforced, they are often used to warn and morally regulate private citizens. For example, a Toronto inspector responding to a neighbor's complaint about "garbage" in a backyard commented that the large number of tools and garden equipment strewn around might well be classified as "treasure" rather than "trash." He mentioned that his own parents are "European" and that they too tend to "hoard things": "it's a cultural issue," he concluded. But, typically, this remark did not stop him from gently encouraging the owner to tidy up the backyard. The cultural norms enshrined in law are at work even when no fines or sanctions are being imposed.

In recent years there have been a few challenges to the cultural norms imposed by the property standards law; but what is interesting in relation to changing demographics is that these have been articulated strictly as environmentally driven reforms, not as diversity measures. For example, a long-standing (seldom enforced) ban on hanging laundry out to dry on one's yard was revoked locally in 2007, and in the spring of 2008 the province of Ontario took this one step further by passing a law, under its environmental jurisdiction, prohibiting municipalities from banning clotheslines. The province went as far as to invalidate the private covenants (also known as deed restrictions) that had until that time ensured that new subdivisions would be free from the working-class and immigrant taint of clotheslines—though condominium anticlotheslines rules were explicitly exempted from the provincial law. (This is in keeping with moves elsewhere: for example, an Ohio bill similar to the Ontario law mentioned excluded condominiums and quoted one condominium board president who said that he moved to the "community" in question specifically because of "its strict regulations." "Those rules are why when I look out of my window I now see birds, trees, and flowers, not laundry," he said.[6])

Throughout North America, the discussions that led to a proliferation of state statutes invalidating local anti-laundry-lines ordinances were about the evil of wasting electricity—not about the class and cultural bias of those who regard laundry lines as unsightly and inappropriate. In other words, the cultural bias of the original rules was left untouched, with legal reform addressing only electricity conservation issues. Similarly, the Toronto compulsory front-lawn rule discussed later in this chapter was challenged by a middle-class, white, environmentally conscious artist, and supported by local environmentalists. It was not challenged or to my knowledge discussed by Italian-Canadian or Chinese-Canadian families wanting to grow vegetables on their front yard. That such rules should be considered as environmental rather than diversity issues illustrates the unpredictability of what does and does not become a diversity issue in public discourse.

A final preliminary note in regard to the legal regulation of matters of taste involves the already mentioned interaction between public law (e.g., municipal ordinances) and the private legal regimes set up by condominium boards and gated communities. Currently, numerous "gated communities" make even more exorbitant aesthetic demands on their members than municipalities. The color used to paint the house and even the size of one's pets can be (legally) subject to coercive regulation by the community board. Now, it is of course true that a gated community may have been designed specifically to establish and enforce certain norms (though one wonders about the rights of self-expression of the teenagers living in such communities). A city is clearly a much larger, more open and diverse space than a gated community or a condominium. And yet, questions could be raised about the extent to which gated communities or condominiums, especially larger ones, should be allowed to impose all manner of culturally specific rules on their members. In a city such as Toronto, in which tens of thousands of citizens now live in homes that are legally part of condominiums, one could ask whether a forty-story condo building that contains a very wide variety of people should be regarded, in law, as if it were a small homogeneous community. But the question of the legal regulation of aesthetics and culture by private law can only be mentioned briefly here; we must return to our public law story.

To explore the question of municipal aesthetic standards in a multicultural setting, we will turn to the question of noise, long a bone of contention in urban environments. Noise issues illustrate some of the difficulties experienced by municipalities as they try to update and modernize the old and very subjective notion of "public nuisance," for centuries the main legal tool to regulate all types of urban disorder from begging to nasty smells. The noise section includes both empirical findings about enforcement and recent case law. We will then return to the question of weeds in front yards and tell the story of how huge amounts of time and effort were devoted to reforming the rule of the compulsory front lawn—only to end up with a bylaw that still imposes the nineteenth-century English ideal of gardening on the whole population of Toronto. But first a brief interlude about another historic source of urban complaints, namely smells, will highlight the cultural politics of local law.

"Whose Nose is the Reasonable Nose?" Private Nuisance and Cultural Difference

In industrializing nineteenth-century cities, there were few codified rules, local or national, targeting urban problems such as factory smoke or smells. Such annoyances could only be policed by mobilizing the private-property rights of competing owners through private-nuisance actions.[7] Today, even public-nuisance law is rarely used, since most municipalities have codified rules that name every possible risk, making generic public-nuisance powers redundant. But nuisance law still exists, and both public- and private-nuisance charges are possible. A lawsuit concerning Chinese cooking practices in an inner-city area will be discussed here to demonstrate that private citizens with special legal ingenuity and/or resources can still mobilize the ancient legal machinery of private nuisance to engage in fights about cultural norms. In general, old legal forms are rarely struck off the books as new ones (e.g., property standards rules) are invented, and the private-nuisance case discussed here illustrates the eclectic character of the local legal arsenal.

In 1999, there was a bitter dispute between two neighboring households in a downtown street, just a few blocks from the heart of Toronto's best-known, oldest Chinatown. Two couples of different races had lived beside one another for about a decade, when, for some unexplained reason, the English-speaking, two-lawyer household of David Martin and Elizabeth Magner decided that the fumes being emitted from their next-door neighbor's Chinese cooking constituted a nuisance.

As is the norm, the Martin-Magner household first approached the municipal government. An inspector was sent to investigate the complaint. In keeping with the dispute-resolution approach that the Municipal Licensing and Standards department has maintained for many years, the inspector attempted to mediate, rather than to determine whether any law had been broken. In response to pressure from the inspector, the Chinese couple did some renovations and changed the fume hood in their kitchen. This did not suffice, however, to appease Martin and Magner. Unhappy that the city was no longer engaged in policing the smells next door, they decided to launch a private-nuisance lawsuit for $20,000, $10,000 in nuisance damages and $10,000 in punitive damages.[8]

The papers filed claimed that the cooking smells were not only unpleasant but potentially carcinogenic (a typical legal maneuver, since one's case is stronger if environmental or other physical-risk arguments are added to aesthetic complaints). However, rather incautiously, Mr. Martin also added a rather racist warning to the effect that the Chinese couple ought not to bring up their lack of English language skills as a defense, since, in Martin's opinion, the immigrants should have learned English. Not surprisingly, the Chinese couple then turned to a lawyer from within the Chinese community. No doubt disturbed by the comments about English, the Chinese couple (or their lawyer) decided to shift legal gears entirely, serving notice that they would make a complaint of racism against both of the Anglo lawyers before the self-regulation body for the legal profession, the Law Society of Upper Canada. The *Toronto Star* (Canada's largest daily) sent its "diversity reporter" to investigate:

> Tung Chu Huang can once again look forward to stir-frying in her wok to her heart's content. . . . The family and their lawyer, Roslyn Txao, have filed a complaint against Martin with the law society, accusing him of being unprofessional and acting in a discriminatory manner.
>
>   The complaint raises a letter Martin wrote to the Huangs where he warned them not to use their lack of English to seek the sympathy of the court because "you have chosen not to learn English despite living in Canada for many years."[9]

Some of the neighbors then decided to wave the diversity flag. They held a news conference to say that the "suit stinks of cultural intolerance," in wording that cleverly turned the fumes complaint on its head. The Chinese Canadian National Council also became involved. Council president Philip Tsui complained about the racial bias of the lawsuit with a comment raising the issue of the cultural bias of the "reasonable person" standard of law. "Whose nose becomes the reasonable nose?"[10]

The fact that a national organization jumped into the fray of a local dispute about stir-frying smells might have made some people cease and desist. But in the case of Martin and Magner, the intervention had the opposite effect. The lawyer couple took their time—and in the meantime the private-nuisance lawsuit was settled out of court, with the details remaining out of the reach of news media. But three years later Martin and Magner sued the Chinese Canadian organization for "defamation" and the Chinese couple for "libel."[11]

The moral of the story, in terms of the local politics of diversity, is that Martin and Magner had shown no hesitation in objecting to the fact that their neighbors spoke little or no English, and in alleging in their initial lawsuit that Chinese cooking smells are carcinogenic. But when the people involved, some of their mutual neighbors, and a national ethnic organization all mobilized to complain about the racist slant of the nuisance lawsuit, the lawyer couple counterattacked. Being called a racist, even when there are good reasons to do so, is now grounds for a defamation and libel lawsuit.

The stir-fry fumes incident received a great deal of coverage in part because the situation lent itself to clever headlines and in part because it is so unusual. But it serves here to illustrate that private law tools (such as nuisance actions) can still be used to address matters that one would have thought are amply covered by municipal rules of general application. As in the case of the condominium exception to the Ontario-wide ban on laundry-line local prohibitions, we see that private law is still relevant in studying urban governance. But it is now time to turn to the heart of the chapter, which concerns municipal codes.

From the Common Law of Nuisance to Municipal Codes

There are two types of legal tools that enable municipalities to police the bête noire of modern urban living, noise.[12] First, cities can and do use hard-and-fast rules that apply to everyone equally. Some are numerical, such as those setting maximum decibel levels. Other hard-and-fast rules consist of blanket prohibitions on certain types of noises in certain zones—for example, no car horns near hospitals, no truck traffic on residential streets.

However—and this is where the story gets interesting—such objective rules are supplemented by a vast array of necessarily vague standards through which noises are rendered illegal because they are, as Ottawa's noise bylaw states, "unusual, unnecessary, or excessive." Every municipal code I have examined featured a combination of objective rules and standards that, while not necessarily "subjective" in the sense of arbitrary, require enforcers and adjudicators to make certain judgments about what is normal and what is excessive, what is reasonable and what is not.

Those keen to promote cultural diversity might think that the solution to the problem of cultural bias in municipal law is to eliminate "reasonableness" and similar standards, and use only objective rules. But any effort to consistently enforce objective rules leads necessarily to paradoxes and absurdities (as will be seen in regard to New York City's new rule limiting the barking of dogs to ten minutes, during the day, or five minutes, at night). In those situations both law enforcement personnel and courts abandon the objective rule and fall back on the "reasonable person" legal tradition. And in the local governance context, the question of whether a reasonable person would tolerate a disturbance because it's part of the urban fabric is addressed through the ancient legal machinery of nuisance mentioned in the Chinese-cooking case.

Nuisance is an intrinsically relational notion. Even the foulest smell is not a nuisance if, to paraphrase the philosopher George Berkeley's comment about trees falling in the forest, there are no neighbors to be bothered. But whereas private nuisance requires an actual neighbor to complain—the Anglo lawyers, in the case discussed above—public-nuisance charges do not require an actual complainant. The municipality can prosecute before anyone has been actually bothered. Public-nuisance charges are rarely used today, given that most nuisances have been codified; but the logic of nuisance undergirds the whole machinery used to regulate noise, smells, and sights. Tellingly, the term "nuisance" often appears in court decisions even when the municipal code section in question makes a point of avoiding this rather vague word. Similarly, when enforcing nuisance-type rules, cities resort to the ancient legal argument that noises or smells ought not to exceed what the "reasonable person" would expect (although often avoiding the use of the words "reasonable person"); and courts do likewise.

Many people, when first introduced to the figure of the reasonable man/person, dismiss it as a ridiculous invention of judges. Social scientists are particularly apt to get outraged. How can courts take "the reasonable man" as a standard, when they don't even know what the average person thinks, since they don't read social science research? However, judges do not simply make up random stories about what the reasonable man tolerates. For each area of law, there are leading cases that set out some parameters for reasonableness. These may not be known to city inspectors; but they are certainly known to the city solicitors who would have to pursue a formal prosecution, if the matter went that far. And observing municipal inspectors at work, one sees very clearly that the reasonable person—who also goes by the name of "local custom"—is invisibly perched on their shoulders, as they decide when to let things go, when to issue a written warning, and when to lay a charge.

The reasonable person of municipal law is a rather conflicted figure. In municipal law, it has long been acknowledged that the "tranquility" and "quiet enjoyment" so often mentioned in bylaws and nuisance decisions are unachievable in urban environments. On numerous occasions courts have said that a noise that someone has complained about would be acceptable to "the reasonable person," and is therefore not illegal. In nuisance law, judges do defer to middle-class, middle-aged, single-family-detached sensibilities; but they have also dismissed some complaints as neurotic—as happened to the elderly lady bothered by the "manly" sport of cricket being played in front of her house, who did not find much sympathy in an English court.[13]

The myriad numerical rules set out in Toronto's building code, noise

rules, and property standards bylaw, therefore, can never completely eliminate flexible terms such as "excessive noise." That's a key reason why the
enforcement of local law is necessarily full of ironies and paradoxes.

Whose Tranquility Counts? Noise Complaints and the Hierarchy of Citizenship

An inspector specializing in noise complaints explained to a researcher
that what he called "quantitative" noise complaints are straightforward,
since there is an objective technical standard of eighty-five decibels. Enforcing this objective bylaw, however, is another matter. The Municipal Licensing and Standards department (MLS) has very few officers trained in
the machines that measure decibels, and police officers are neither trained
to measure noise nor motivated to spend time doing this kind of work.
Unusual pressures—usually political—have to be deployed in order to
draw regulatory resources to this area.

In the summer of 2004, repeated noise complaints by the residents
of Ward's Island (a somewhat countercultural, nearly all-white group of
people living in a car-free small island off Toronto's harbor) succeeded in
mobilizing unusual enforcement resources from both the city (MLS) and
the police. The source of the objectionable noise was a large bar located
on the waterfront, The Docks. The island community's ability to get attention from MLS was increased by the fact that the establishment was
already in trouble with MLS managers due to management's persistent
refusal to ask for the necessary permits for objects and activities in need
of permission, from billboards to playing amplified music after 11:00 p.m.
The MLS officer we will call Frank had trained the Toronto Police Service
Marine Unit to measure decibels, so that they could send officers out on a
boat, in the evening, to see whether the sheer quantity of noise emanating
from The Docks infringed the maximum-decibels-at-night section of the
bylaw. But on the evening in question, no police were to be seen, marine
or otherwise (in keeping with the usual police disdain toward municipal
bylaws). Instead, one MLS officer went to the island to listen for the noise,
while another remained on the mainland. The noise from The Docks was
barely audible across the water on the island, however, so nothing much
happened, on that evening.

The island community's success in having MLS send not one but two
officers, and in the evening (when overtime pay would be accrued), was

due in part to the fact that Municipal Licensing and Standards had its own reasons for pursuing The Docks' owner. It was also due to the political and cultural capital enjoyed by island residents, who had waged a long and eventually successful battle to secure their private-property rights in the face of a policy to preserve all of the islands as pure parkland. In addition, the savvy residents mobilized regulatory resources from other levels of government, finally striking pay dirt when they succeeded in having The Docks' (provincial) liquor license suspended because of noise and other complaints.[14]

The throw-the-book-at-them approach evident in The Docks situation is highly unusual, however. A very different way of deploying regulatory resources—still in the area of noise problems—was observed during a more routine evening shift in which the MLS noise expert, our friend Frank, spent several hours with a local community association, helping them to ensure that the noises emitted during their street festival did not get "too loud." Incidentally, working with or even for a group is not un-usual, at least for the noise expert. When a film is being shot on location, a common occurrence in Toronto streets, Frank is often paid to be "on call," we were told, even if he just sits in a hotel room until he's needed to ensure that the noise of car chases or other film actions does not breach the bylaw. Another officer, whom we shall call Tony, remarked: "He (Frank) even gets to attend the parties and hang out with the actors!"

But on this occasion, Frank and Tony were called not by a commercial firm but by a community group wanting to appease the local city councillor and those residents who had in the past complained about excessive noise. What they did on arrival was not to measure noise, however, but rather to show a volunteer from the group how to operate the decibel reader. Frank, who loves to tell war stories about how decibel levels had to be calculated with complicated algorithms before the machine was invented, used a lot of technical language to explain how it works. But learning to work the machine seemed easy—until Frank mentioned that the decibel counting machine does not measure bass. The bass element in music has to be mea-sured by ear and by feeling the vibrations, apparently. This would clearly pose problems for a group hosting a rock band performing outdoors; but since the festival in question featured mainly acoustic music and jugglers, the technical abilities of the group's volunteer were never tested.

Frank concluded his exchange with the community group by waxing eloquent about the city of Toronto's philosophy of bylaw enforcement. He wanted "everybody to be happy," he said. Therefore, he encouraged the organizing group to respond quickly to any complaints, whether the noise was illegally loud or not. Ideally, one shouldn't have to actually enforce the bylaw, he added. The municipal inspector is there mainly to make sure that people get along and to be what Tony calls "the voice of reason" in disputes that threaten to breach the civic order.

Interestingly, in regard to the reasonable person standard, the "voice of reason" theme appeared several times during other observation sessions (ride-alongs). Officers in another district, for example, job-shadowed by another research assistant three years later, took pride in criticizing what they called the "Robocop" mentality of a few overzealous officers. Clearly, the officers dealt with the problem of discretion by seeing themselves as "not-Robocops"—that is, as reasonable people who use common sense and do not try to enforce laws to the letter. But back to noise complaints. Enforcement is complicated by the fact that according to inspectors, the majority of noise complaints reported to police or to municipal inspectors do not concern sheer quantity of noise, but rather quality. Frank told a researcher that what he called a "qualitative" noise complaint, such as a truck picking up garbage during the night, is handled differently from reports about extremely loud noises. First, for these qualitative, nuisance-style problems, only complaints reported by at least two and preferably three independent people are taken seriously—otherwise, Frank explained, MLS staff would do nothing but attend to noise complaints. Secondly, the noise must be one that persists over a long time or recurs frequently. Citizens who phone in complaints are told to keep a noise diary for at least twenty-one days. Only after the offending noise has been documented for that period of time will the inspectors initiate enforcement action.

Having explained this screening mechanism to the researcher while in transit, Frank arrived at an office where someone had complained that trucks were picking up garbage from a business before 6:00 a.m., making a lot of noise. Getting out of the city vehicle, Frank walked around the building to see where the garbage was stored, but was unable to find any bins. He then went to the front of the building and up a flight of stairs into an office, which turned out to be a publishing business. Frank (who, like most MLS inspectors, does not usually wear his uniform) flashed his badge at a woman behind the desk. She looked confused and asked: "So you're with the city?"

Frank explained his presence. The woman replied that she had never heard about the issue, and that she is never there at 6:00 a.m. so could not confirm whether noise is a problem, but added that the property managers had just sent out a memo with new instructions about garbage disposal. Having ascertained that it's the city, not a private contractor, which is now picking up the building's garbage, Frank was relieved: "Oh, that's easy, then. All I have to do is call the Works department to tell them to send the trucks a little later in the day."

An hour later, Frank went to a different office building on the same main street to respond to a very similar complaint. The researcher asked whether noise diaries had been kept by several independent citizens, as per departmental policy. Frank responded that they had not yet kept a log, which meant, he explained, that he was on a "courtesy call," not doing formal enforcement. In this building there was a private company picking up the trash, not city trucks, and so Frank told the property manager of the building to call the company and ensure the pickup was done after 7:00 a.m.

One might well wonder why a cash-strapped municipality that only has about 150 bylaw inspectors serving a population of over two and a half million people wastes resources sending officers out to make "courtesy calls" in person over rather trivial matters. And the two incidents just described are by no means untypical; in over one hundred hours of ride-alongs, some of which were at night and thus represented greater resources (overtime pay), there were only a handful of potentially serious or risky situations.

Why many rather trivial matters attracted significant regulatory resources remained a mystery in the initial period of research. But after other facets of the research project had shed light on city governance, the mystery began to clear up. In regard to noise complaints, the approach taken to enforcement is very similar to the process used for other matters. While some citizens with no particular connections with city hall or with the local press do sometimes get "service" from MLS inspectors, for no reason other than their name and address was given to the local manager, the "generalist" officers who were job shadowed spend half or more of their time responding to complaints that are channeled through the councillor's or the mayor's office.[15] The complaints that get priority are those that come "from above" (Frank's term), a phrase which meant not the inspector's immediate supervisor but rather the local councillor or the mayor's office (or sometimes, as in The Docks case, the top boss of their department).

Apart from the automatic priority given to complaints coming from a councillor or from citizens via their councillor, another principle, spontaneously generated in the local subculture of bylaw enforcement inspectors, is used to prioritize complaints. This is the distinction made between homeowners and tenants. One would think that both noise complaints and property standards complaints about deteriorating buildings would be more common among residents of cheap rental high-rises. But only two high-rise rental buildings and one public-housing complex were visited by inspectors during the research period, by contrast with dozens of single-family homes and an equally large number of businesses. And while complaints by public-housing tenants are considered valid, and not dismissed out of hand, one officer attending to a public-housing tenant complaint about cockroaches told the researcher that he "can't just go around ordering them to fix everything," because there the housing company has a limited budget and "almost everything" is in need of repair in the city's decaying stock of public housing. Thus complaints by public-housing tenants, this officer explained, are handled differently than complaints against private landlords.

Another officer explained that tenants in general are known for making frivolous complaints. Maybe they owe back rent (he speculated), and so they file a complaint to get back at a "nagging" landlord. "Tenants often use these tactics to get out of paying rent or to receive a free apartment make-over," he added. An officer from a different district of the city held similar views. Tenants are not really paying property taxes, he said (which is untrue, since the rents paid to landlords include an unitemized portion used to pay property taxes). He waxed quite indignant about having had to respond to a call from a rental building in a poor part of town: "These people living in the apartment building across the street are complaining about the condition of a house? Why do they even care about the paint job? If they don't like it, they should just move."

The actions of a different officer who responded to two different noise complaints in a single shift illustrate a similar enforcement bias. "Vito" went to a home on a busy arterial road in north Toronto to investigate a complaint about factory noise. The factory turned out to be somewhat distant from the house, and when standing in front of the house, all the officer and the researcher could hear was the roar of traffic. The complainant was not at home, but the next-door neighbor was a "nice lady" (in the officer's description). She explained that the noise would become unbearable when tanker trucks deliver fuel to the factory, several times a day. Vito was not impressed by this—perhaps because he thought someone living on a very busy arterial road was being unreasonable in complaining about noise. So, instead of following up on the industrial noise, he began to cast his practiced eye over the complainant's own backyard. (Later, he told a researcher that inspectors, who are legally not allowed to enter a home without the owner's permission, often end up investigating the complainant's own property, since they have been given access to that for the purpose of making the complaint against someone else—an interesting enforcement move that he called "the can of worms effect.") He opined that the lady's fence was too high and that the shed might not be legal (that is, might lack a permit). As he began to jot notes to take action, the "nice lady," perhaps wanting to divert the regulatory gaze elsewhere, volunteered the information that the absent complainant was a heavy drinker, had a criminal record, and had been in jail for nine months. Vito then told her that if the factory were to hire a lawyer, the lawyer would bring up the criminal record to discredit the complainant. As Vito and the researcher left, they noticed railway tracks nearby. Vito explained that between the criminal record, the fact that the factory was some distance away, the fact that the complainant lived on a busy arterial road, and the complicating factor of the train tracks, the factory noise complaint did not rate as what he called a "noticeable nuisance in the community."

Later the same day, Vito visited a town house where people had complained about loud music from the neighbors. The complainants, a white well-educated English-speaking couple, were home, and were able to produce the required written noise log. Vito looked through the log, seemed pleased with it, and promised to send a warning to the offender. If the warning did not result in less noise, then the city would prosecute, Vito explained, and the complainants would be called as witnesses. On leaving, Vito explained to the researcher that these people were "more credible" because they had no criminal record, no alcohol issues, and furthermore had a small child whose sleeping was disturbed by the noise. They seemed "respectable," and Vito explained that he would put in the time and effort to ensure that the matter was resolved.[16]

The process of investigating and enforcing—and not enforcing—municipal rules about noises and other disturbances clearly has the unintended effect of creating differentiated forms of local citizenship. The differentiation is not a direct effect of class and race privilege, since all citizens who persists in calling the local councillor will likely get their complaints at least investigated, if not pursued further; but political capital, while not directly proportional in any mathematical sense to wealth and other sources of privilege, is not unconnected to the usual sources of social inequality. Tenants, most notably, while not always dismissed, do not get consistently treated as the citizens that they are. This discrimination is ubiquitous in North America. As Sally Merry found in her influential study of small-town Massachusetts in the 1980s, owning property, but especially owning a home, "is a culturally valued avenue to honor and prestige."[17] Furthermore, the fact that one inspector explained that tenants are not taxpayers (which is incorrect, but is a common misperception) underlines the point that citizenship practices at the local level are fundamentally mediated through property.

The Contradictions of Objective Rules and the Eternal Return of Flexible Standards

Let us look at a recent noise-related case from Ottawa in which neither diversity nor inequality is mentioned, but which perpetuates the idea that citizens are not all equally entitled to being legally protected from nasty smells and sounds.[18] This case involved a bar called Maxwell's, which persisted in playing amplified music late at night in contravention of a bylaw prohibiting amplified sound played between 11:00 p.m. and 7:00 a.m. on weekdays, and up to 9:00 a.m. Saturdays and noon on Sundays. (The cultural bias of the Sunday-morning lie-in went unmentioned during the challenge, incidentally.) The restaurant's lawyer claimed that the noise bylaw was illegal because it "lacked an objective standard." It did impose a single, objective rule about hours; but this was followed by a clause reflecting the second source of municipal noise-policing powers, namely the reference to people behaving "so as to disturb the peace and comfort of any person in any dwelling house."

Counsel for the city argued that the "disturb the peace" element of the bylaw did not amount to vagueness and arbitrariness, but rather flexibility and responsiveness to local specificity. Essentially arguing that Ottawa's municipal inspectors should just be trusted not to overenforce the admittedly vague law, the lawyer added that a certain amount of discretion in enforcement is necessary. Why? First, because some complaints might be trivial; and secondly, because, "tolerance to noise will vary from community to community depending on the make-up and characteristics of the community residents involved" (*Ottawa v. Freidman*, par. 9).

Going deeper into the question of demographics and noise tolerance, the judge took up the idea of differential protection from noise introduced by the city's lawyer: "An inner-city community as opposed to a suburban community, or again, a community of predominantly retired residents as opposed to a community of predominantly university students may tolerate a very different standard of what are reasonable night-time noises" (par. 23). Therefore, Judge Linhares de Sousa concluded, the bylaw is upheld, since even though the wording ("disturbing the peace") seems vague, a "flexible standard" makes sense.

The notion of flexible standards for noise thresholds is an integral part of the long history of nuisance law, which, as mentioned earlier, continues to provide much of the content as well as the logic of current municipal law (both municipal codes and judicial decisions). No city law would say explicitly that poor neighborhoods have to put up with garbage and noise; but in a less direct manner, when nuisance law or nuisance logics are used to regulate urban disturbances, the result is often the institutionalization and naturalization of existing inequalities. Those who cannot afford to buy a house or pay the high rents demanded by luxury apartment owners are imagined by law as either not deserving protection from noise or as culturally predisposed to minding noise less. The notion of locally variable, "flexible" standards allows courts as well as municipal inspectors to avoid the embarrassing situations that could arise if courts demanded to know whether cities officially believe, and can prove, that the protection of noise codes should be differentiated by class, geography, or housing tenure.

Flexible standards that are responsive to local cultures are of course not inherently problematic. Indeed, they are key tools in the contemporary trend toward "smart regulation." And it is probably true that university students living in residence do have a higher tolerance for noise than retirees. However, what the judge failed to mention is that in the case at hand there was no evidence at all about what the actual locals thought or felt. There was no evidence that the neighbors were all elderly or otherwise particularly susceptible to noise. And there was no evidence that families that rent apartments mind noise less than families that own homes. It was the court's own assumptions about the ability of municipal staff to use their "commonsense" knowledge of demographic differences that mattered. The judge concluded that the law need not be revised because he was prepared to trust officers to classify complaints as either frivolous or credible.

It is important to emphasize that inspectors and other city officials, at least those observed in Toronto, do not set out in the morning to protect wealthy homeowners. Local law enforcement is not biased in that overt sense. But the findings of our job-shadowing research, as well as the numerous descriptions of municipal enforcement found in the case law, suggest that enforcement work is full of culturally laden assumptions about who has the right to what level of "tranquility" and about who is a credible complainant.

Blindly trusting municipal inspectors' commonsense knowledge about which noises are or are not bothersome to which microcommunities was exactly what the Supreme Court of Canada, or at least a majority of the court, also decided to do in adjudicating a challenge to the Montreal noise bylaw, one similar to the one in the Ottawa dispute.[19] The Montreal case does not focus so much on differences among urban communities, however, as on the question raised early in the chapter of whether objective rules are better, in municipal legal regulation, than older, more subjective, relational categories, such as "nuisance." The decision starkly shows why the utilitarian modernist project of replacing flexible legal standards such as "the reasonable man" (or "the reasonable nose") by objective rules is bound to fail.

The main Montreal noise bylaw states that regular noise (also called "environmental" or "background" noise) is not actionable; only unusual noises distinguished from the background are actionable. As we have already seen, however vague the notion of "disturbance" or "unusualness" might be, this language is a common feature of noise bylaws. But in addition to this old-fashioned, nuisance-style provision, the Montreal bylaw also contains an objective rule prohibiting all amplified sound that is generated indoors but heard outdoors. This was the clause under which a strip club engaged in a war for customers with a neighboring strip club was prosecuted. Because of the hard-and-fast wording of that section of the bylaw, the city could prosecute the club without offering any argument about disturbance, either actual or hypothetical.

The majority of the court agreed that article 9(1), the ban on amplified "noise" leaking out of buildings, was very broad, and did indeed constitute an infringement of the club's free speech. But in keeping with the deference to municipal paternalism mentioned at the outset of the chapter, they decided that the bylaw should not be read literally. Whatever the text said, the city really meant to ban only disturbing noises. One has to trust municipal officers to be sensible:

> The history of the by-law shows that the lawmakers' purpose was to control noises that interfere with the peaceful enjoyment of the urban environment. It is clear from the legislative purpose that the scope of article 9(1) does not

include sounds resulting solely from human activity that is peaceable and re-
spectful of the municipal community. [headnote]

In a powerfully worded dissent, however, Justice Ian Binnie cast ridicule
on the majority's efforts to save the Montreal city council from its badly
drafted bylaw by pretending that the objective rule was really a flexible
standard:

> Article 9(1) imposes a general ban on noise classified only by source and in-
> cludes noise which is not a nuisance. . . . The legislative power to define and
> prohibit nuisances conferred to City Hall by the Charter of the city of Montreal
> 1960 does not extend to defining some activity or thing as a nuisance. . . . Noise
> is not by nature a nuisance. . . .
>
> Read in its ordinary grammatical sense [as opposed to in the creative man-
> ner employed by the majority], art. 9(1) would . . . catch people who can only
> make themselves heard using "sound equipment," such as Dr Stephen Hawk-
> ing, who . . . can only communicate through a voice box . . . art 9(1) would
> preclude a Montrealer sitting in his garden listening to Mozart playing softly
> through an open window from a kitchen radio. (par. 45)

We can see that when municipalities try to remedy the legal problems
plaguing the subjective standards contained in such phrases as "disturbing" or "unusual," they can easily fall from the constitutional frying pan of
vagueness into the fire of absurdities caused by inflexibility. The Montreal
bylaw aimed at amplified noise attempts to carve out one particular kind
of noise, mainly issuing from bars and commercial establishments. But in
its attempt to be objective and to provide certainty (so that Montreal citizens will know in advance if they are breaking the law, unlike those whose
municipalities have nothing but vague nuisance rules), the city can then be
accused, as it was by Justice Binnie, of governing too much, or governing
the wrong things. While Justice Binnie is certainly not saying that a municipal inspector would be likely to charge Stephen Hawking, he believes
that the letter of the law matters.

The Montreal case goes to the heart of the eternal dilemma of the
form of municipal law. Faced with criticisms from both citizens and courts
complaining about "flexible" standards that make room for a great deal
of discretion on the part of enforcement officials—a discretion that will
inevitably open the door for culturally biased judgments about who needs
to be protected from what nuisances—municipalities have tried to use

objective rules that leave little room for interpretation. But setting out narrowly tailored, more objective bylaws that use hard-and-fast rules does not eliminate the subjectivity and discretion that was thought to be the problem in the first place. A Montreal municipal inspector who decided to enforce the law to the letter and lay charges against citizens listening to Mozart while sitting on their balconies would likely be disciplined, if not fired. If the inspector laid charges against a club whose loud rap music disturbed Justice Binnie's classical-music hypothetical, however, that action would likely meet with greater approval. It is clear that replacing standards by objective rules does not necessarily help to make the everyday work of noise policing more rational and less subject to the systemic cultural prejudices that shape the everyday work of policing urban disorder.

The Aesthetics Beat: Regulating the Look of Private Yards

Neighbors' front yards generate a steady stream of complaints to "city hall," and one particular shift in the summer of 2007 was exclusively devoted to this type of issue.

In an MLS district office serving a very socially mixed area in west-end Toronto, an officer whose "beats" included complaints about long grass/ weeds and debris on private property, along with noise and signs complaints—the aesthetics beat, one might say—explained to a researcher that his day's agenda was the product of an e-mail from the councillor listing a series of properties in need of inspection, homes that "could benefit from a little homeowner pride."[20] At the first address, on a socially and ethnically mixed street of century-old houses, the front yard looked (to the researcher) somewhat run down, but without serious infractions. The back yard had some litter and a few weeds growing through the patio bricks, as well as a shopping cart placed next to a clothesline with laundry drying. Officer "Cris" (an Italian-Canadian young man) took a digital photo of the supermarket trolley and another one of the front of the house. An older Asian woman then came out of the house and lit up a cigarette on the porch, looking somewhat concerned to see strangers in her yard. (The officer was not wearing his uniform.) Cris tried to explain what he was doing, with some difficulty due to a language barrier. She explained that she was a tenant, not the owner. Cris then took down the landlord's phone number from a For Rent sign and went on his way.

The next address was a few doors away. The front porch was full of bins and old, yellowing newspapers. Cris took photos and moved to the backyard. The garden had not been maintained and the weeds were over a meter high. There were also piles of cardboard boxes and garbage bags. As Cris was performing his inspection, the next-door neighbor, an older Italian man engaged in tending his backyard tomatoes, approached and started to talk with the officer, in Italian. Cris apologized for not speaking Italian as the neighbor self-righteously pointed to various offending items in the "problem" backyard—a shed whose roof was caving in, the boxes, and garbage bags. The Italian neighbor said, "Chinese," pointing to the house with the problem yard. Without challenging the "Chinese" comment, Cris explained that he would issue a warning about the unsafe accessory building and the debris in the backyard. It is unclear whether the Italian gentleman understood the process.

Cris then looked at his list and went to another house nearby. This had some lumber and a ladder in the backyard, but in Cris's opinion these things did not amount to illegal debris, so he decided not to open a file. There was a house next door, however, that was an obvious eyesore, including very long weeds on the front yard. When asked why this one was not on his list, Cris mentioned that because enforcement is complaint-driven, it is rather random: some people get very "nitpicky," he said, about some of their neighbors, while other properties go unpoliced due to the absence of complaints. The local councillor often sends MLS officers to investigate the messy front yards of properties that either are, or he thinks are, rooming houses, according to a different officer.

As the shift wore on, Cris pursued three other complaints of debris. He explained that illegally dumped garbage is a very difficult issue for police given that officers rarely if ever catch someone in the act. On occasion special groups of officers have been sent to alleyways and parks known for illegal trash dumping; one police officer zealously opened up garbage bags to see if he could determine the source: "Sometimes you can find junk mail with an address," he proudly said.

Most of the complaints about the properties on Cris's list appeared to be unfounded, which casts an interesting light on the councillor's method of drawing up his hit list. One property, however, which had been the subject of earlier action, appeared to still have the same garbage as it did before. In this case, Cris decided to call the contractors who do junk removal for the city to begin action. (The cost of the removal is put on the owner's property tax bill.) This was the only enforcement action taken during the eight-hour shift.

This day in the life of an MLS officer, a fairly typical one (for summer-time shifts), shows that even though enforcement action is rare, yards are a frequent subject of complaint and an equally frequent target of inspection activity. One reason for this is that MLS officers can easily enter yards or at least see over the fence into them, unlike the inside of buildings, which are not legally open to them unless they are invited. City inspectors can and sometimes do gain access if accompanied by a fire marshal. But fire officials are reportedly less than willing to have their legal powers to enter private property "borrowed," as it were, to enforce nonfire bylaws, since, as one MLS manager told me, fire folks feel superior because "fire kills, but zoning doesn't."

Thus, most of the time, their weak powers of entry mean that MLS inspectors have difficulty in determining whether a house is being illegally used to run a business, or whether a large Victorian home is or is not a rooming house. By contrast, yards are legally as well as visually avail-able—and because the yards are equally visible to the neighbors, they generate numerous complaints.

Weeds as Speech: A Legal Reform Story

Repeated complaints about a yard by a persistent neighbor was in fact the spark that started a (very rare) major campaign in which citizens spent time and energy finding out about a bylaw and doing something to reform and update it. A key point is that the campaign was not a Tea Party–style effort designed to get government off homeowners' backs. Challenging the city's power to set aesthetic norms for private property, or challenging neighbors' rights to mobilize the city's resources to have their neighbors' yards inspected, are notions that do not cross the mind of law-abiding Torontonians. The campaign in question was merely a modest effort to change the weeds-and-grass part of the property standards bylaw so as to allow environmentally conscious people to fill their yards with native plants rather than with lawns and store-bought flowers.

Sandra Bell, a homeowner living in a socially mixed, partially gentrified east-end neighborhood, took the unusual step of simply refusing to cut the weeds in her front yard when told to do so by municipal inspectors. As seen in the "day in the life of an inspector" just recounted, inspectors rarely bother to regulate the appearance of yards unless a complaint has been made: in Bell's case, her next-door neighbor, visual artist Hyla Fox, made repeated complaints. The voluminous press coverage generated by this dispute and the subsequent legal challenge revealed that Ms. Fox objected to Ms. Bell's cats, Ms. Bell's child, Ms. Bell's boarder's dog, and various other things. But the only entity that was legally actionable was the weed-filled yard.

In the mid-1990s, the bylaw made lawns and/or flowers compulsory for front yards. In addition, "excessive" growth of grass and weeds was said to be illegal. Whether motivated by environmental concerns or by sheer dislike of her obnoxious neighbor, Ms. Bell decided to go public and complain that Ms. Fox and the city were imposing on her their own preference for what she called "industrial monoculture"—that is, the classic suburban lawn.[21] The local environmental movement mobilized around Ms. Bell and organized a conference focusing on the question of the effect of municipal rules on the environment.

Since at the time there was also a nationwide movement advocating that municipalities flex their legal muscles to ban aesthetic pesticide use, a movement that became visible as high up as the Supreme Court of Canada, the result was that whether or not Ms. Bell's gardening habits had been originally politically motivated, by the time the conflict jumped from the microscale of neighbors' disputes to the scale of nationwide environmentalism her weeds had acquired a strong political identity. Her weeds then went on to also acquire legal personality: the lawyer hired by Ms. Bell and her supporters decided that since a direct challenge to the city's power to set aesthetic standards would not succeed, given the strength of the municipal paternalist tradition, the best strategy was to construe the weeds as "expression." If the weeds were the expression of a political point of view—a concern for the environment—then the higher-level law of the Charter of Rights (whose section 2 guarantees freedom of expression) could be mobilized to trump the municipality's extensive powers to regulate taste. And while such free speech claims, when made by strip clubs and porn shops in the United States, have generally failed to trump cities' powers to arrange and regulate urban space, the wholesome character of Ms. Bell's expressive activity could be expected to help her get past the legal hurdles.

In the meantime, the city council debated reforms to the bylaw several times. The council considered and eventually rejected a possible new law that would allow "naturalized" gardens but require that such gardens be framed, literally, by a strip of conventional lawn, just to make it clear that culture, not nature, was responsible for the yard in question. (Such ordinances exist in some US municipalities.) Throughout, right-wing councillors who opposed the environmentalist argument simply because it was coming from the left wing of the council complained that lazy homeowners who let their properties go to rack and ruin would be able to use the environmental exception as a loophole.

After various debates about nature and culture, the council eventually passed an amendment that attempted to make the bylaw more defensible in court by replacing the venerable nuisance-law term "excessive" by an objective numerical rule, namely ten centimeters. But this shift from standards to objective rules did not suffice to save the bylaw. In court, gardening experts poured scorn on the idea that all plants in a front yard should be subjected to the same Procrustean height rule, and the judge who heard the case spent little time on this last-ditch effort to save the bylaw by modernizing it.

In the main part of his decision, the judge departed from the usual judicial practice of deferring to city fathers' supposed knowledge, and instead adopted the unusual weeds-as-speech argument put forward by Ms. Bell's lawyer:

> The appellant challenged the validity of the by-law as a violation of the Canadian Charter of Rights and Freedoms. . . . The appellant's garden was found to violate the by-law simply because of its appearance, and not on the grounds of any health concerns, fire hazard or other nuisance . . . Section 7c of the by-law was found invalid, both because it was void for vagueness and uncertainty and because it unjustifiably violated the freedom of expression guaranteed by section 2 b of the Charter. While some of the goals of the by-law were sufficiently important to justify overriding a constitutional right, the objective of creating neat, conventionally pleasant yards did not warrant a complete denial of the right to express the values and beliefs reflected by naturalistic gardens. (*Bell v. Toronto [city]* [1996] OJ No. 4156, par. 22)

In Canada as in the United States, courts rarely use their power of judicial review to strike down bylaws. The standard generally used is that any bylaw that is not patently unreasonable and that was passed "in good faith" will stand, even if the regulation in question is unnecessary or inefficient or draconian. But in the *Bell* case, the lawyer was able to mobilize two very powerful discourses to have the bylaw struck down. First, as mentioned above, the plants in Ms. Bell's garden were construed as speech, and political speech at that. But that would not have sufficed, since the voluminous case law regarding billboards and other signs is clear that as long as municipalities do not completely ban either community-produced posters or commercial billboards, their location can be very stringently regulated.[22] In respect to front yards, with the exception of official election signs, homeowners are simply not allowed to put up large signs on their front lawns, whether these are commercial or not.

Freedom of expression is thus not an all-powerful legal weapon, therefore. But Ms. Bell's lawyer had another equally powerful weapon at his disposal, and that was the locally hegemonic ideology of "diversity." And so Judge Fairgreave was able to see Ms. Bell's pursuit of environmental gardening as an example of diversity, and hence as an activity in need of legal protection, even though diversity had not been mentioned in the city council debates.

> I have no difficulty thinking that in 1968 when the [weeds] bylaw was passed, at a time of greater conformity and homogeneity, perhaps there would have been no confusion as to what the word "excessive" conveyed in the context. In the more diverse, pluralistic, and accommodating society of the 1990s, however, I do not think that it is so easily ascertained. Even if a preference for the typical suburban lawn remains prevalent (and I am sure that it does), I think we have all become accustomed to accepting that not everyone shares the same tastes, and that the differing practices are no less valid or tolerable because they deviate from the norm. (*Bell*, par. 44)

The sentiments of this paragraph are nothing but the conventional local wisdom. Torontonians are very proud of the fact that their city scores extremely high on the "tolerance" index used by urbanist Richard Florida. But as we see in this passage, a tolerant attitude toward minorities and their cultural habits does not mean that majority tastes are displaced. Judge Fairgreave states as a fact that the "typical suburban lawn" remains the cultural preference of the majority; he regards Ms. Bell's naturalized garden as a minority taste that, however peculiar, should be given a (small) place in the sun in a tolerant, diverse city.

But the judge made sure that the city did not lose the traditional paternal power to force people to follow English middle-class norms that demand that proper homes be surrounded by strips of land and that those strips be gardened. Ms. Bell's challenge succeeded because, in his view, a consciously planned environmentally friendly garden was "distinguishable from the uncontrolled weed patch that one might associate with an abandoned vacant lot or a yard completely neglected by its owner" (*Bell*, par. 28).

Diversity discourse thus saved Ms. Bell and other environmental gardeners from being prosecuted; but diversity discourse also ensured that their practices, their tastes, were firmly relegated to the margins, to the realm of a minority taste that a "pluralistic and accommodating society" needs to tolerate—without the toleration ever going as far as to make the majority question its tastes.

The city council, forced by the judge's decision to change its bylaw yet again, followed Judge Fairgreave's version of diversity very precisely. In keeping with recent American ordinances, the council passed an amendment that, without challenging the hegemony of the weed-free lawn, provided a new exception that would be available to that group (construed as a permanent minority) which subscribes to the ideology of compulsory gardening but chooses to do it somewhat differently. The new exception to the lawn-and-flowers rule comes in two parts. The first part (the kind of objective, hard-and-fast rule that as we saw in the case of noise bylaws municipalities feel they must have to prevent "void for vagueness" challenges) simply bans all the "noxious weeds" that are already recognized in the provincial Weed Control Act. But in addition, the local bylaw also bans, for purely aesthetic reasons, any plants that grow on their own, without gardening. Toronto front yards must not have any "growth which does not form part of a natural garden that has been *deliberately implemented* to produce ground cover" (City of Toronto, Bylaw amendment 1997–0037, emphasis added).

To make the insistence on human management of nature even clearer, the new bylaw insists that in order to be protected by the exception, the nature-lover's ground cover needs to include: "one or more species of wildflowers, shrubs, perennials, grasses or combinations of them, whether native or non-native, consistent with a managed and natural landscape other than regularly mown grass." How a "landscape" could be both "natural" and "managed" is not explained. But it is clear that the bylaw expresses a deep fear of uncontrolled nature that is no doubt connected to the fears about rooming houses and ethnic groups supposedly prone to messy yards documented in the previous section of this chapter.

Both nature and human nature, then, require wise city councils to pass laws regulating taste and imposing gardening as a norm—even if in diverse Toronto, tolerance for gardens designed according to environmental rather than traditional criteria is now the law.

A few years later, a man named Mr. Counter who planted a "natural" garden on the city-owned strip of land between the sidewalk and yard in front of his house, a garden designed as a memorial to his late wife's life, attempted to take advantage of the *Bell* decision to fight against the city's efforts to force him to cut down the vegetation. City-owned strips of land bordering private property are customarily treated by both citizens and city officials as quasi-private property; owners are allowed and even encouraged to tend these green patches as if they were their own. So the city did not try to use its rights as formal owner to impose its norms. And, perhaps due to the publicity garnered by the *Bell* case and subsequent bylaw change, officials were careful not to talk about unkempt weeds and neglected yards; instead, they mobilized the legally more powerful discourse of utilitarianism. The naturalized garden interfered with the sight lines of drivers emerging from driveways, the city argued in court. This argument was successful, so that Mr. Counter was obligated to cut down his vegetation.

Mr. Counter attempted to use the same freedom of expression argument that had been successful in the *Bell* case, but both the trial court and the Ontario Court of Appeal concluded that while the garden was definitely expression (unlike Ms. Bell's, it featured a sign with text explaining who Mrs. Counter had been and why the garden had been planted), the city's order to cut the vegetation was not an unreasonable infringement of freedom of expression.

Interestingly, the city did not introduce any expert evidence to show that the vegetation in question really did pose a safety hazard. In keeping with the numerous US and Canadian court decisions in which municipalities have been exempted from having to provide either firsthand or expert evidence to justify their regulations, Judge Pitt said:

> Here, it is not appropriate to require the municipality to scientifically prove every inch of sight line from every direction for every individual. The [plant] height restriction imposed by the City is based on sensible driver sight line estimates, and still permits generous natural growth. Therefore, the minimal impairment [of rights] requirement is met. (*Counter v. Toronto [city]* 2002 33MPLR [3d] 109, par. 33; the appeal is *Counter v. Toronto [city]* [2003] OJ No. 1940, 39 MPLR [3d] 308)

Conclusion

The legal systems of the English-speaking world share a fundamental liberal belief in individual freedom. As John Stuart Mill influentially argued, governments ought to use coercive law only to ban what is harmful to others. Governments can try to encourage good citizenship through schooling or tax incentives or other means, but for Mill and for later advocates of liberal legality, questions of taste are not the proper domain of coercive public law. If one looks mainly at the "higher" reaches of law—the legalization of abortion and homosexuality, for example—one could say he won the war. Free speech and privacy doctrines have made legal room for all sorts of activities that many people find offensive or in bad taste or immoral, but which are no longer illegal.

Municipalities, however, continue to actively regulate taste and culture. They regulate taste not only by banning certain sights and sounds and smells but also—in contrast to John Stuart Mill's theory of law—by using law to compel people to maintain aesthetic standards, not only in public spaces but even in their own private property. Aesthetic standards are obviously culturally specific (and to some extent also generation- and gender-specific). And yet, the most striking fact revealed by my study of Toronto's aesthetic bylaws and their enforcement is that diversity talk is almost invisible in this area of local law. The comment quoted at the beginning of the chapter about the nonenforcement of the antivegetable rule in Italian areas is one of the very few times in which city personnel directly acknowledged the cultural bias of many of Toronto's bylaws. And as we have seen, even when citizens care enough to fight to reform antiquated aesthetic bylaws, the reformers talk about values such as environmentalism and keeping public space free from commerce—but not about multiculturalism.

But that does not mean that diversity is not constantly being managed, minimized, channeled, and/or remade through these bylaws. Diversity is constantly produced, or swept under the rug, through the bylaws themselves, in the court decisions that justify or reform them, and by the daily work of municipal inspectors deciding whether a plant is an illegal weed or a legal shrub and whether a noise is one of the "normal neighbourhood annoyances" that urbanites must "suffer" stoically,[23] or whether it is a "disturbing" and excessive noise.

CHAPTER 4

City Bureaucrats and Village Elders

The Dysfunctional Dance of Local Governance

Permits for Walking?

O n a crisp autumn day in 2009, some seniors participating in an organized fitness class were taking a walk in a lakefront park. A municipal inspector drove into the park with his city pickup truck, began to take pictures of their walk, and asked the group if they had a permit. The seniors (or at least those who spoke to the press) were outraged. What they did not seem to know is that their fitness instructor, who was leading the walk, had been in trouble with the city for a year, since she had consistently refused to obey the bylaw requiring for-profit businesses that use parks to obtain a permit, at $28.65 per hour.

Some of the subsequent media coverage gave the impression that it was the seniors, not the fitness entrepreneur, who were subject to law enforcement—an impression that the city councillor heading the parks committee, Paula Fletcher, attempted to dispel. Fletcher clarified that while she agreed that the seniors' group should have been left alone, the city's policy was not unreasonable: "Some people do use parks in a major way, and should be having a permit," she said. "They're making a lot of money while they're in the park."[1]

Mark Grimes, city councillor for the area, initially responded by trying to explain the bylaw to the seniors and to the public at large. Appearing on local television, he stated that the issue was not the seniors but entrepreneurs who use public facilities to make a private profit. He reassured his constituents that "all residents and visitors are welcome in our parks and green spaces" but added that "permits and processes are in place to ensure equitable and safe access to all those wishing to enjoy our park space."[2] Reportedly, Grimes's executive assistant also tried to explain to constituents who called that the instructor was already facing charges for previous attempts to run for-profit fitness programs out of public parks.

The city's policies on parks use were not given much airtime, however. The image of seniors harassed by bureaucrats while taking a walk was so irresistible that after a few days of coverage making city staff look like the KGB, Mayor David Miller felt compelled to issue a public statement calling for "discretion and flexibility" in bylaw enforcement. The local councillor also began to change his tune. Instead of explaining the issue of for-profit businesses using parks, Grimes took up the position of a village elder defending his villagers against the big bad bureaucracy, stating: "They [the seniors] won't be paying to walk in a park in my ward, and shouldn't have to pay in any other ward, either." The seniors who met with Grimes in turn told the press that "he told us all that we won't be hassled again."[3]

Citizens, in Toronto as elsewhere, are sometimes subject to capricious or simply stupid bylaw enforcement. But while overaggressive local law enforcement does exist, especially in regard to street vendors and taxi drivers, respectable citizens such as the seniors in the incident generally experience city law enforcement as characterized by mediation and conflict resolution.

Ordinary citizens encounter mindless city bureaucrats who insist on enforcing stupid rules, or enforcing reasonable rules stupidly, only on rare occasions. But these occasions are consistently remembered and told to others, often in a one-sided manner. By contrast, ordinary prudence and common sense garner no attention. A story circulating among Municipal Licensing and Standards inspectors is a good example. On a researcher's first day of job-shadowing, the inspector being shadowed chose to explain the department's philosophy by recounting a legendary story featuring an overzealous colleague who charged a group of children running a lemonade stand with the offence of vending without a permit. The lemonade-stand story was presented as a cautionary tale highlighting the reasons why the department makes a point of *not* enforcing the letter of the law in what one of the inspectors called "Robocop" fashion. But the commonsensical officials who refrain from busting kids operating lemonade stands get no media coverage.

Events that garner publicity precisely because they are unusual are, in this as in other spheres of political and social life, the ones that people hear about and remember, the ones that are told and retold, often with some exaggeration or distortion, and that will thus shape the public image of institutions and persons in lasting ways. This affects politicians as much or more than it affects civil servants. However, civil servants are relatively powerless to try to save their own reputation by speaking up in public, especially if that would involve criticizing a colleague or a boss. They might distance themselves from overzealous colleagues, as was done by the inspector recounting the (perhaps mythical) story of the lemonade-stand bust; but they cannot speak to the press, and they cannot directly challenge either their bosses or the politicians.

This puts the bureaucrats at a disadvantage in the never-ending game of political tennis that has long pitted city officials ("the bureaucracy") against local politicians. A backbench member of the national Parliament will occasionally speak up on highly local matters; but on most issues they have to be careful to not stray from party policy. Toronto city councillors are not bound by party discipline, however. And unlike in Vancouver, where the custom is to have two competing groupings, each featuring a slate of candidates united by a platform, Toronto local politics has traditionally had only the weakest of left-wing and right-wing groupings. Councillors are individually elected and pay for their expenses individually. Their electoral campaigns usually feature only one or two local issues on which they express definite views (usually, against something). Voters have to essentially choose the person they trust the most. If they watch local news or read the local press they may know what this candidate thinks about one or two immediate issues; but they will be very unlikely to know how that person is likely to vote on the majority of issues.

The ward-based electoral system and the absence of parties or slates are meant to encourage independence and prevent the emergence of party "machines" such as Chicago's Democratic establishment; but the political system strongly encourages seat-of-the-pants decision-making and a reactive style of governance. Each issue comes into visibility as a distinct agenda item, and positions are taken on the fly, without being grounded in long-range plans or overall political platforms. The system pushes councillors to quickly respond to any discontent among his/her constituents by taking the side of the "small people" against any threat. The threats to local community that give councillors the opportunity to become local heroes can be external (e.g., the province imposing a power plant) or can consist simply of what is perceived to be a sloppy or stupid bureaucracy. Given the prior existence of a negative image of "city hall" as a bureaucratic, unfriendly labyrinth—an image that certainly has a foundation in fact, but is distorted by media coverage practices that emphasize scandals and stupid decisions while ignoring commonsensical decent decisions—it is easy for populist anger to have the effect of pushing even the most sensible of city councillors into the familiar narrative in which the councillor plays David against a bureaucratic Goliath.

There is nothing wrong with defending one's constituents. However, when the political-administrative structure is such that councillors are pushed into playing the local champion role as a full-time job, and city staff are prevented from explaining their side of the story to the public, other important functions and tasks that are not easily slotted into the David versus Goliath narrative will be neglected, to the detriment of the local civic fabric.

The Dialectic of Bureaucracy and Local Populism

The political effects that the seemingly trivial seniors' walk incident had over the following week shed much light on one of the key dilemmas of local government. To understand it we first need to note that, on top of the usual evils of red tape, in the early years of the twenty-first century, the machinery of Toronto local government was hobbled by the sudden and forcible amalgamation of six Toronto-area municipalities rammed through by the provincial government in 1998. One of the many negative effects of the amalgamation was a serious staff morale problem: while mass layoffs did not take place, many employees had to reapply for their own jobs, and in many cases only a few former managers survived the process.

The problems created by the top-down amalgamation that created a "megacity" of two and a half million under the same name as the old city of less than seven hundred thousand were compounded by the province's simultaneous decision to download responsibility for many social services and all public transportation to municipalities.[4] Low morale, constant fear about one's job security, and cynicism about public service work were particularly acute at the time of amalgamation, but were still major factors ten years later.[5] Thus, amalgamation put a great deal of pressure both on the bureaucratic apparatus and on local politicians (whose numbers were at one fell swoop cut in half, and who were suddenly all forced to be part of a single unified city council). But as amalgamation receded into the past, during the period of this study, it became apparent that the pressures of amalgamation had not so much created new problems but rather made structural governance dilemmas that plague local government generally more apparent and more serious.

Governance systems are usually described as static structures, with social scientists often drawing diagrams of informal as well as formal power groups. Governance is an open-ended process in perpetual motion, however, and so it is best described dynamically—even a diagram in which authors insert arrows is too static to be accurate. The "dysfunctional dance" phrase used for this chapter's title is meant to give a sense of how a key element in the governance process (the relationships between elected officials and public servants) works—or fails to work. The purpose of the chapter is thus not to try to draw a static diagram but rather to identify common "dance moves," that is, the interactions and strategic responses that make up a good part of the city's governance habits but whose final result, in each particular story, can never be predicted with certainty.

The basic components of what I call the "dysfunctional dance" of local governance are as predictable as those of a ballroom dance—though one that results more often in vicious circles than in pleasure and beauty. The dynamic goes as follows. First, arbitrary or uncaring law enforcement (or arbitrary decisions by city committees)—often compounded by misleading and uninformed retellings, as in the seniors' walk story—fuel the populist distrust of "city hall" that has long existed in North America and that has been regularly featured in "Tammany Hall"–style stories.

Then, faced with a negative reaction from the media, the public, and/or local politicians, "city hall" goes into defense mode. To appreciate what lies behind the move that looks like mere defensiveness to outsiders, however, it is important to understand that public servants at all levels of government are largely unable to respond publicly to media stories, public complaints, and accusations made by either citizens or politicians. Only some very senior bureaucrats can speak to the press, and even they do not feel that they can directly criticize either other managers or the councils that appoint them.[6] The simmering popular discontent and mistrust that seem to have become the normal political attitude of urban citizens thus combine with the often defensive silence of city staff to create an instant market for champions who can and will speak up for "the little people" and for common sense, champions who think about their careers, rather self-servingly, in terms of telling truth to power. The market need for champions is usually filled very quickly by the local councillor—not surprisingly since the councillor's (or sometimes, the local activist's) political capital depends on responding to local anger much more than on anticipating longer-range and larger-scale problems and taking steps to prevent them.

That longer-term, policy-driven activity by either councillors or public servants is only occasionally covered by the local media, and that citizens are far less likely to become passionate about long-term or geographically dispersed problems than about immediate threats, are two key reasons why the dance of local governance, even in a large cosmopolitan city, takes place largely at the geographic scale of the neighborhood, and at a temporal scale that is reactive rather than future-oriented. "Save X" is the most common rallying cry of local politics, with the X rarely being something that all citizens of a large metropolitan area enjoy (such as affordable public transit).

For the most part, then, the role assigned beforehand to the local champions in this civic game is not to be leaders of the city as a whole, and not to become knowledgeable about longer-range problems, but rather to act defensively and reactively to defend their village against perceived immediate threats—or, even worse, to defend those villagers who make their voices heard, and who are therefore, by definition, not representative. This dynamic is worth exploring in some detail. It is one of the most important issues in local governance, and yet it has not received serious study, whether in official reports or in scholarly work.

Before presenting empirical findings, a note on that much-used, pejorative term "bureaucracy" is in order. That much of what citizens and local politicians think of as the personal stupidity of bureaucrats is a product of structural factors inherent in the very form of bureaucracy is not a new idea; its germ is found in the influential analysis provided in the seminal work of German sociologist Max Weber. Early in the twentieth century, he noted that a key feature of bureaucracies is that they expand by intensification, that is, by giving themselves additional work and new rules, more than by expanding their geographic or jurisdictional reach. As an example, Weber noted that the ancient Egyptian bureaucracy charged with managing the risks of Nile River floods decided to intensify its work—and perhaps justify obtaining a larger part of the state's budget—by designing and building pyramids. These served no useful purposes but required great managerial skills, which led Weber to conclude: "The causes of bureaucratization . . . lie much more in the intensive and qualitative expansion and internal development of the range of administrative tasks than in their extensive and quantitative growth."[7]

Bureaucratic intensification—which includes the multiplication of protocols, policies, and internal rules, as well as the tendency to add more and more tasks to the already ambitious agenda of an institution—is probably the most important feature of bureaucracies at all levels. However, intensification takes a particular form in local government, given the specificities of governance at the local scale. A federal tax inspector, for example, would be extremely unlikely to actually see a lemonade stand during his workday, and would thus not have the opportunity of considering laying tax-evasion charges. And even if he did happen to see such an activity going on outside of his house, he would be unlikely to be thinking of the nearby sidewalk as his responsibility. For someone whose remit is the nation, the sidewalk across the street is not particularly visible.

The differences between local and state ways of seeing are not simply a result of different geographic scales, however. What sociologists of knowledge call "knowledge formats" also differ by scale and by jurisdiction. In general, higher levels of government prefer to rule through preprepared forms and through formal written reports, not by direct, visual inspections.[8] In addition, government departments are physically as well as administratively (and often legally) separate from both politicians and citizens. By contrast, the bylaw enforcement inspector who drives down the street looking for bylaw infractions is in close contact, physically as well as politically, with the residents and with the local councillor. While in theory administrative law doctrine requires that at the local level as well as nationally the legislative function be kept separate from particular administrative decisions, in practice local governance often ignores the doctrine of the separation of powers.

The close (in every sense) relationships of local governance mean that it is crucial to examine not so much one institution but rather the relationships among the various "stakeholders" in urban governance. And what we see in local government if we look at the relationships of governance is that as bureaucracy gives itself further rules, further powers, and further agenda items, a reaction against this intensification will set in, and champions will emerge to defend the local, the customary, the everyday. Such champions, be they residents or politicians, speak in the name of unwritten tradition and common sense—everything that bureaucracies notoriously lack. However, the local champions would not come into being if the "bureaucracy" had not provided the occasion for their rise to prominence; hence, the role of local champion is more of a product of the "dysfunctional dance" than a preexisting identity. The common sense associated with local living and with citizen participation in local government (the form of knowledge eulogized and to some extent practiced by Jane Jacobs) emerges as a distinct entity only by contrast with "red tape"—red tape in general, not just its excesses. Bureaucracies standardize situations and administer rules impersonally; the local champion of common sense, reacting to this actual or perceived coldness, will instead seek one-off, highly local solutions.

Now, one might think that the accumulation of one-off compromises, exceptions to the bylaws, agreements about a park or a restaurant patio, and so forth would create such a regulatory anarchy that the dancers would start to move in the other direction, and people would develop a desire for rules of general application that are enforced evenly and fairly. However, the push in the direction of rationalization and standardization seems to be rather weak, not only in bylaw enforcement but even in the sphere most closely associated with overall, rational, bureaucratic, modern plans: the planning department itself. Today, planners describe themselves as unable to actually plan and as crushed under the weight of one-off arrangements and more or less arbitrary exceptions to the rules. In planning circles the current trend is known as "let's make a deal planning."

Case Study: Civic Action and the "Adult Entertainment" License

To pursue the story of village elders whose political capital is derived in large part from successfully fighting bureaucracies, let us now turn to a story that took place in the summer of 2008.[9] The area in which a locally contentious strip bar was located had been a solid blue-collar suburb with numerous industrial jobs; but in keeping with the loss of industry in the region, the area had declined from the 1960s onward. In the 1990s, however, Toronto's condo boom extended across the old city boundaries. Soon, the first glimmers of gentrification could be discerned in the small area of the former municipality of Etobicoke known as "New Toronto." The proportion of households earning over $100,000 doubled from 2001 to 2006, as middle-class people who could not afford a house closer to the downtown but who did not want to live in the suburbs bought homes in previously blue-collar streets.

It was the newer, white-collar residents of "New Toronto"—but mainly those living in detached or semidetached homes, not in condos—that decided to take action when, in May 2008, a local country-and-western bar on the Lakeshore put up a large sign on its window proclaiming that it would soon become a "gentleman's club" (i.e., strip bar). The sign featured a scantily clad woman with come-hither eyes. Residents, seemingly upset more by the actual sign than by the business it advertised, contacted the local business association (Business Improvement Area, or BIA). The association responded that it could not intervene to tell the bar owner to change his sign since the sign was on his own property—and, perhaps more to the point, he was a dues-paying member of the BIA. The residents, who organized themselves via an online petition, then contacted the councillor, Mark Grimes. He personally asked the bar owner to take down the sign, but the owner refused. The neighbors continued to pursue the campaign, and the councillor made it clear that he was on their side.

In keeping with what researchers doing ride-alongs with bylaw enforcement officers observed, Grimes responded to the residents' moral concerns by pressuring city employees to send inspectors of every kind—fire inspectors, public health, and so forth—to the bar in question. "They gave me thousands of dollars worth of work orders," the owner explained.[10] The representative of the strip-club ("adult entertainment") industry stated that while every single commercial property on that section of Lakeshore Boulevard had graffiti somewhere on the rear of the property, only the strip-club owner had been told (just before a long weekend) that he had to immediately remove the graffiti or face prosecution. It was clear, then, that diverting a significant amount of regulatory resources in the direction of the strip club was a move designed more as a message to the residents that the city was on their side, rather than as a rational solution to the problem of graffiti.

In the meantime, the councillor and the residents found out that the transformation of the bar into a strip club had been approved by the Municipal Licensing Tribunal. They seemed very surprised to find out that during the previous winter, the tribunal had given the bar an "adult entertainment" (i.e., strip-club) license. Such a license would not have been granted for a new establishment, since the zoning bylaw does not allow for a strip club on that location. But the licensing tribunal treated the application as the continuation of an old license—the club had been a strip bar decades earlier—and so, as a manager of licensing tried to explain to the citizens, it was "grandfathered" as a "legal nonconforming use."

There seemed to be no way of preventing the club from opening, therefore. Thus, having finally finished all the repairs, cleaned the graffiti on the back of the building at his own expense, and so forth, the owner opened the strip club. The residents turned up to demonstrate but there were no incidents.

The matter might have ended there (it is common for "land uses" that are highly contentious before the fact to quickly become an accepted part of the scenery as soon as they open), but it did not, mainly because the capable leaders of the residents' group now turned to their member of Parliament, then Liberal leader (and global intellectual) Michael Ignatieff, who did not intervene personally but who reportedly loaned them a lawyer. The lawyer quickly discovered that the licensing tribunal should not have granted the bar the adult entertainment license, since the bylaw clearly states that a nonresidential use cannot be legally "grandfathered."

The result of this discovery was that the anger that had been previously directed at the bar was now redirected toward "the city" and augmented by a feeling that the residents had been somehow duped. The tribunal members were not directly accused of corruption, but resident leaders interviewed in 2009 uniformly portrayed the tribunal as either incompetent or uncaring or both. Perhaps understandably, resident leaders made no distinction at all between the tribunal and the bureaucracy. In fact, the licensing tribunal is an arm's length quasi-judicial body that had for years disregarded the views of the licensing bureaucrats; but, perhaps because the licensing manager who met with the residents did not distance himself from the tribunal, the residents (and the councillor's executive assistant) treated "the city" as an undifferentiated unit, and one characterized by deception.

An interesting feature of the situation is that the councillor as well as the residents seemed to think that they had a statutory right to be notified about the business licensing hearing. In numerous statements posted on the councillor's website and made to the local media, they expressed as much or more outrage at not being consulted as they did about the outcome. The councillor no doubt knew that the business license was a matter for the licensing tribunal—which is not subject to any community notification process—rather than a matter for zoning hearing, which does have public participation processes. But he did not dispel this misconception, or at least not successfully, hence adding fuel to the residents' anger toward city employees.

Throughout the summer of 2008, the councillor and his very able executive assistant acted as champions of the locals in their fight against "the city" in general, the big bad bureaucratic city.[11] And in taking on the champion role, they had no qualms in diverting numerous inspectors away from other work so that they could say that they had thrown the book at the strip-club owner. The opening of the strip bar was thus repeatedly delayed. However, it could not be stopped, since the licensing tribunal had used its considerable discretion to approve the adult entertainment license. In the wake of this failure, the group that had arisen to fight the strip club decided to turn its accumulated political savvy to a new, more positive campaign to revitalize the main street and encourage locals to shop there instead of in nearby malls.

What lesson can be drawn from this mini-campaign? The licensing tribunal had certainly made the wrong legal decision; the lawyer loaned to the civic group by the local member of Parliament's office was probably correct. However, this would not justify the devious motivations imputed to "the city" by the outspoken locals. As I knew from my earlier study of the tribunal, the licensing tribunal members are extremely unlikely to have been acquainted with the 1994 zoning bylaw that applied to that specific district. It's likely that they simply did not know that an adult entertainment license previously held by a past incarnation of a bar could not be resurrected as a legal nonconforming use. But, not being familiar with the often cavalier and not always legally accurate processes of the city's quasi-judicial tribunals, the residents never contemplated the possibility that neither the licensing tribunal members nor the inspection personnel actually knew what the relevant law was.

The broader implication of the story is that the sheer complexity of the existing creaky, jerry-built municipal legal edifices—whose creakiness is compounded in municipalities that have undergone major geographic and jurisdictional changes—creates a high risk of legal mistakes on the part of rank-and-file employees and even adjudicators. But residents do not appreciate the situation of city staff and low-level adjudicators. Decisions that are either illegal or unpopular can thus be represented as the result of conspiracies—rather than the accidental product of some combination of overly complex rules, inattention, incompetence, and lack of knowledge.

The combination of opaque bureaucratic processes and a hopelessly byzantine legal structure thus creates opportunities for both self-appointed civic leaders and local politicians to seize the position of local champion, a position that by nature encourages one-off solutions that, while satisfying people in the short run, may well create future governance problems. Furthermore, this dysfunctional "dance" is not merely repeated; the moves become increasingly extreme, as it were, as decisions that are opaque or even illegal but not devious create a backlash of righteous anger. The combined legal-administrative system ends up creating an increasing demand for commonsense representatives of local custom who can "cut through red tape."

Reactive Law Enforcement and Municipal Political Capital in a Downtown Ward

It was mentioned above that during the Lakeshore strip-bar controversy, the local councillor made sure that every kind of municipal inspector descended upon that particular property looking for bylaw violations, thus forcing the owner to spend considerable sums on such things as cleaning up graffiti. This is in keeping with the findings on the work of "generalist" inspectors discussed in the previous chapter: most "generalist" bylaw enforcement is complaint driven, and a good proportion of the complaints come via the local councillor's office.

A series of conflicts that developed over the course of two or three years in the so-called Entertainment District reveals both the pros and the cons of having an enforcement system that is so disproportionately weighted toward complaints (rather than proactive enforcement) and that puts the local councillor in the crucial position of broker of scarce regulatory resources.

The "Entertainment District" emerged in the 1990s. A nineteenth-century district that had housed numerous small workshops and light industries (especially related to textiles) saw factories and warehouses converted to new commercial and entertainment uses, especially after the opening of the "SkyDome" stadium, which motivated many entrepreneurs to open bars and restaurants in the nearby area. At the same time, a very rapid process of "condofication" was taking place in the adjacent neighborhood. By 2006, the King-Spadina Residents Association, whose members are overwhelmingly condo dwellers, claimed to represent about ten thousand people. No doubt those who bought condos were in part drawn by the bars and restaurants that had sprouted in the loft-style buildings of the nearby former textile and fur district. But as leisure entrepreneurs realized that profits could be maximized by enlarging their premises, keeping later hours, and having dance music that would cater to a largely suburban and much younger demographic, conflicts quickly emerged.

These conflicts could have been foreseen by city staff, especially given that a radical, unprecedented planning-policy decision was taken in 1996, one abolishing all density controls in that area and allowing all uses except heavy industrial. Some white-collar businesses and light industrial uses did move into the five- and six-story nineteenth-century buildings formerly occupied by textile industries; but lofts and condos proved more profitable than offices, and, without density controls, developers engaged in an orgy of condo building construction. Up to this time residential high-rises were generally in the ten- to twenty-story range, but in the King-Spadina area buildings of forty stories became the new normal.[12]

In 2005, in response to complaints about noisy and drunk young people interfering with the "quiet enjoyment" of the newly arrived condo dwellers, then–local councillor Olivia Chow had pushed for an interim control bylaw prohibiting new clubs in the now formally designated "Entertainment District," for one year.[13] After the one-year moratorium, new permanent rules were instituted, in the form of a special "club" license. (Prior to this time, clubs had generally operated under a restaurant license, offering dinner in the earlier part of the evening, prior to turning into dance clubs.) The new license required clubs to hire security staff to police the sidewalk lineups and the sidewalks adjacent to their properties, and imposed stricter noise controls.

Even with the new controls, however, conflicts continued. When elected in 2006, Councillor Adam Vaughan took on the same champion of the local residents role previously played by his predecessors, Olivia Chow and Martin Silva, but with even greater zeal. The group that he clearly felt accountable to was the King-Spadina Residents Association; neither club owners nor customers figured as citizens in the subsequent regulatory battles. The *Toronto Star* described the King-Spadina residents' group as follows:

> Initially created because of noise complaints due to club sound systems, the group is now firmly entrenched and is at least partly responsible for bylaw changes, such as the new business designation for night clubs in 2006 that includes more stringent security and noise requirements. It also keeps tabs on the 88 clubs in the area, as well as neighbourhood controversies, of which there seem to be no end.[14]

A police officer interviewed by the reporter said, "We have a strong relationship with the residents' community"—though he quickly added that the police also have a good relation with the businesses, organized under the Toronto Entertainment District Association.

A few months later, in the middle of the summer—which is when To-rontonians, suburban and young or not, linger on sidewalks at night—a researcher was given permission to go on several ride-alongs with two Municipal Licensing and Standards (MLS) officers working in the Enter-tainment District. Her observations shed much light on the "local cham-pion" role described earlier in relation to Councillor Mark Grimes. The officers, who we will call "Jane" and "Doug," explained that their night shifts were the city's response to the advocacy efforts of the residents' as-sociation. They said that their managers (who were no doubt under pres-sure from politicians) would be happy to see some of the clubs be charged with violations of the new 2006 rules, but that as frontline enforcers, they much prefer to mediate and problem-solve, without going on to charges. In addition to their philosophical preference for conflict resolution rather than prosecution, they pointed out that if they were to lay a charge, it would not go to court for several months, and in the meantime, the owner would have no incentive to turn down the music or otherwise make things better for residents; and their own safety might suffer too, they suggest. (Although the researcher did not witness any harassment of officers by bar bouncers, the officers claim that this happens.) Warnings and informal discussions are much more effective, according to Jane and Doug.

On one summer evening, Jane and Doug left the office at 9:00 p.m. and proceeded to the local police division. There, the police notified them of potential "gang" and drug-selling activity in particular bars. Jane and Doug explained to the researcher that both the police and their own man-agers wanted to ensure their safety, and so they were instructed to end their shift at 2:00 a.m., just before the district becomes "overrun," as they say, with closing-time crowds. Doug then added that a particular club was off-limits to MLS officers because it was deemed too dangerous, having been the site of a recent fatal shooting. (In fact, after the researcher had gone home that evening, there was a fatal shooting at one of the bars vis-ited on the ride-along.)

After the police meeting, the officers went on to the district, in an un-marked vehicle. They had no weapons (no MLS officers carry any weap-ons), but they had cell phones and BlackBerrys. It was about 11:00 p.m. and the streets were fairly quiet. Loud music emanated from one club, so the officers got out of the vehicle to speak to the bouncer. A radio-station van parked outside the club was contributing to the noise. The officer asked the bouncer if he could shut the club's door to minimize the noise heard outside. The owner came out to the sidewalk and agreed to the request. It is difficult to say whether the officers were purposively wasting time policing the establishments that least need policing.

The next club had its doors wide open, contrary to the rules of the special district law, and the music was blaring. When informed that city inspectors had arrived, the two owners appeared, and they too responded quickly to the request about closing the door. One of the owners flirted with Jane. Going to the next club, Jane mentioned that clubs were not doing as well this year as the previous year, perhaps because club owners, unhappy with the constant regulatory efforts being made by the city, were moving elsewhere. (In fact, by 2010 the center of bar and club activity had shifted a couple of kilometers west, to smaller establishments in the Dundas-Ossington area.)

The owners of the next club to be visited were not as friendly as the previous ones. One of them looked annoyed as Doug asked them to shut the main door to minimize noise. However, the other owner began to chat with Jane about her hobby—it was clear that he knew her well. The less friendly owner was in the meantime expressing his frustrations with the residents' association to Doug, saying, quite reasonably, "If they don't like the noise, why are they buying condos in the Entertainment District?"

Walking to the next club, Doug and Jane both commented that residents often make trivial complaints. They suspected that some of the complaints are fabricated to put pressure on the clubs and eventually force them to close. At the next club, Doug and Jane got upset on seeing that several police officers were standing around outside without paying any attention to the fact that loud music was emanating from inside. This prompted them to launch into a speech about how police could do much more to enforce bylaws, including noise bylaws, than they do, but they feel such things are too trivial for them.

As the night wore on, it became clear that the particular list of clubs on the agenda for that evening was largely if not wholly the result of citizen complaints. It also emerged that someone—perhaps the city councillor— had given the individual officers' e-mail addresses to the residents' association. Officers picked up messages not only at the office, before their rounds, but even as they walked their beat; that was why they had Black-Berrys, it seemed. Even more surprising is the fact that after they investigated complaints, they took the time to report to the complainant or to the residents' association, in person ("unless it's too late at night," one officer adds). A complaint made late the previous night—when the officers had already ended their shift—had to be attended to the next evening, with the officers dutifully reporting not to their boss but to the residents.

This kind of service no doubt makes the residents feel empowered; but, as in other situations described in this book, the "people" to whom the city officials and councillors are accountable are not all the people. The condo residents are probably ethnically diverse, given that the vast majority of the condos in the area are populated by young urban professionals. But they are not very diverse socioeconomically, by household composition, or by housing tenure. The term "yuppie" is often used merely as a term of abuse, but in the case of this microneighborhood—in which over 4,400 condo and loft units were built in a five-year period, and in which children make up only 4 percent of the population—the term may indeed be justified as an accurate descriptor.

That the local councillors who have over the years represented the area—all identified with the council's left wing—see nothing wrong with diverting so many of the city's scarce regulatory resources in the direction of the King-Spadina condo residents and other "squeaky wheels" of the ward is what is most interesting about the city's order efforts. There are numerous immigrant families living nearby—most in private homes, some in a public-housing complex a few blocks north of the district. Their views were not canvassed, much less taken into account, in local media coverage, among city inspectors, or on the local councillor's extensive website. (This is in keeping with findings from other parts of the research project.) And although left-wing councillors sometimes promote environmental measures or affordable-housing developments without deferring to the local squeaky wheels, the "local champion" role is one that councillors of all political stripes embrace wholeheartedly, as the club district example shows.

The local champion role was historically associated with the more or less corrupt practices of favors and patronage known locally as "ward-heeling," which is very similar to the American "Tammany Hall" tradition. Observers of municipal government agree that today there is far less corruption and favoritism than in the past. Nevertheless, the rarity of out-and-out, money-for-votes corruption masks the fact that Jane Jacobs–inspired champions of local neighborhoods sometimes reenact—in a less corrupt manner—ward-heeling practices, such as diverting the city's regulatory resources to small groups of homeowners or even to individuals. A senior city employee working in a research capacity (and thus entrusted with serving the whole city rather than a ward) told me: "Amalgamation was supposed to have promoted a larger, more integrated view, and to have put an end to 'ward-heeling.' But it hasn't. Ward-heeling is alive and well."

Whether we call it ward-heeling or whether we more charitably call it being responsive to local issues, we can see that using the city's regulatory resources in response to complaints that by definition reflect the needs and views of a small proportion of citizens is seen as routine and appropriate. A councillor responded to an interview question about the unrepresentativeness of the people to whom he responds by shrugging his shoulders, as if to say, "that's the way things are."

But some readers may think that the situations described thus far are unusual and unrepresentative, in that they received at least some, and in some cases, a great deal of news coverage. Let us therefore now have a look at a few instances of complaint-driven regulations that could not be said to be publicity driven, since they consisted of much more mundane, under-the-radar conflicts.

During the summer of 2004, the city of Toronto experienced a scare about West Nile virus infections, which affect humans but are carried by mosquitoes. The MLS officers in a relatively poor inner suburb had been told by their managers that they should check for stagnant water and ensure that residents removed anything that might encourage mosquitoes to breed. On a routine day in August, however, officer "Robert" ended up devoting only about twenty minutes to West Nile inspections. About an hour of his time was spent checking up on a variety of disparate complaints, or checking that certain warnings that had been issued earlier had indeed had the desired effect. But the main events in his day were two meetings that he called "site" meetings. A "site" meeting is one convened to mediate a dispute between neighbors not in a community center or city office but on the property that is the bone of contention.

While driving to the first site meeting at 10:00 a.m., Robert explained that a plumber doing work in a basement had accidentally caused a leak in an oil pipe. The oil seeped into the front yard. A city official with responsibilities for environmental issues had requested that the owner, who was trying to sell the house, prove that the soil was no longer contaminated. But the next-door neighbors were apparently not mollified by this. Arriving at the site, the researcher noticed a crater in the front yard with exposed piping; an excavator and a bobcat were parked on the street. There were eight people standing on the driveway: the property owner, his lawyer, the neighbor and his lawyer, a building inspector, the contractor, someone from the environmental-assessment firm that was doing the work required by the city, and an engineer. Presiding over this driveway courtroom was the local city councillor, whom we shall call "Mr. Chevy," an old-fashioned local leader known for his fiscal conservative outbursts on the city council and his blue-collar, even redneck style.

The lawyer representing the owner stated that the owner had paid for the environmental assessments and that he was now seeking the city's permission to go ahead and put the earth back in the hole so that he could sell the property. But the lawyer representing the next-door neighbors argued that the assessment was not conclusive and that further tests were needed; he also argued that his clients were seeking compensation for the decrease in property value caused by the oil leak. The MLS officer then intervened to try to separate the issue of a potential lawsuit among neighbors from the question of complying with city bylaws. The hole in the front yard is the only issue that the city is concerned with, he said, since the environmental assessment seems satisfactory.

The two lawyers then started to argue—until Councillor Chevy, who has an imposing physical presence, spoke up, at which point everyone else became silent. "I don't care about your private issues," he said, telling the feuding neighbors to go to civil court if they want to pursue their fight. He added that the neighbors and their lawyer were "holding the hole as hostage" to pursue their civil suit, and that he doesn't like this. The city simply needs to see the hole covered up and the chain-link fence around it removed. He pointed to a neighboring lawn and said, "I want to see grass just like that on top of the hole in two weeks! If it's not done, everyone will start to get fined." The lawyer representing the property owner was rather pleased, and was quick to say, "Thank you, Councillor Chevy." The second lawyer, perhaps cowed by Chevy's rough justice, followed with a similar remark. The city councillor then left the site, accompanied by the MLS officer and the ride-along researcher.[15]

Two hours later, Robert and the researcher attended another outdoor meeting convened by the same councillor. Here, the site was a low-rent strip mall of mixed-use buildings, with businesses on the ground level and apartments above. The residents had apparently complained about chronic problems with garbage disposal and garbage dumping. When Robert arrived, two representatives of the fire department were already there, looking at the buildings and paying particular attention to the vents protruding from a restaurant. As mentioned earlier, fire marshals do not always cooperate with MLS, in part because they feel that bylaw inspectors often want to "piggyback" on the greater powers of entry and inspection that fire regulations give them; so the presence of not one but two fire inspectors at this nonurgent meeting is an indicator that the convener of the outdoor meeting—Councillor Chevy—holds considerable sway. To confirm this, the fire inspectors told the researcher that Councillor Chevy often asks them to drop whatever work they are doing to attend to a complaint by one of his constituents.

After a few minutes, it became apparent that the garbage complaint had managed to garner a very large quantity of regulatory resources: two fire inspectors, an MLS officer, a public health official, and a building inspector all left whatever other work they were doing to attend Councillor Chevy's strip-mall quasi trial. (It may be useful to remind readers that the MLS department only has about 140 officers of Robert's type, for a city of two and a half million.) While the fire inspectors looked at vents, the public health representative looked at the garbage bins. However, the councillor, having called a considerable number of well-paid city officials together, had not seen fit to show up. The officials nevertheless tried to be useful and stood around discussing some grease and paint stains on the ground, wondering in whose jurisdiction these objects might lie. Robert told the other officials that there might be a public health or a fire issue, but that his own department was not concerned. He thus left—without expressing any frustration or even surprise at the fact that the councillor who had called people away from their jobs had not shown up.

The same shift (in August 2004) also featured yet another councillor-initiated enforcement action. The complaint was that vehicles without valid stickers were parked on a property (meaning that the vehicles might be abandoned). Robert arrived at the property, checked and saw that there were four vehicles, all with valid stickers. He thus closed the file. However, in an instance of what an officer quoted earlier called the "can of worms effect," Robert then noticed that the neighbor (who might well have been the source of the original complaint) had a car parked on the driveway that had neither a plate nor a sticker. The teenager who responded to the knock on the door of the house with the illegal car was warned and told that if the vehicle did not have a valid plate and a valid sticker then it would have to be disposed of. Robert even wrote up a formal "Infraction Notice" (somewhat unusually for the situation). Only after this protracted incident did Robert return to his regular scheduled rounds. By then the shift was nearly over.

The department's priority for that time period had been said to be the West Nile virus. However, about half the shift was taken up with attending Councillor Chevy's "site meetings." A significant portion of the rest was devoted to investigating a councillor's complaint that turned out to be quite unfounded. And the rest of the shift (about three hours) was taken up enforcing a truly obscure bylaw: one that requires that citizens empty and deflate inflatable children's plastic pools as soon as they are not being supervised (whether or not the pools are accessible to passing children). Of course, leaving water in the pool over a number of days could increase the risk of West Nile transmission; but once turned into a "property standards enforcement" matter, the public health aspect disappeared. Robert is an experienced officer, but he had to call the office to get the details on the precise wording of the bylaw about inflatable pools; apparently, if they have less than two feet of water then they are not subject to the pools bylaw. Clearly, stagnant water that is less than two feet deep could still breed mosquitoes, but the officer chose to enforce the bylaw to the letter rather than shift to a public health logic. None of the stay-at-home moms who got the warnings about the pools showed signs of resistance, but the visits from the MLS officer could certainly have prompted much neighborly gossip about the stupidity of bureaucrats who waste time measuring the height of water in kiddie pools.

We see, then, that during a randomly chosen day in the life of a city inspector, a great deal of time was spent enforcing extremely petty rules (about stickers on vehicle plates, about children's plastic pools). But a roughly equal amount of time was spent participating in "site meetings" convened by the councillor, meetings which represent a very serious investment of municipal human resources. It may be that such "site" meetings help to coordinate actions across a notoriously fractured bureaucracy and are thus helpful in "cutting through red tape." However, these meetings are necessarily random; given the size of each of the forty-four wards into which Toronto is divided and the tiny size of the MLS enforcement labor force, only a tiny fraction of disputes and problems and bylaw infractions can possibly be attended to. But more important from the governance perspective, site meetings such as the ones described give an inordinate amount of political capital to an individual who may well be more concerned with winning the next municipal election than with ensuring that the regulatory resources are used in a rational manner.

"Site" meetings convened by city councillors are common occurrences throughout the city, incidentally, not only in wards with populist or colorful councillors. One issue that illustrates how the deficiencies of existing bureaucratic mechanisms create a space for the champion of the local to impose an extralegal solution that ends up having the force of law concerns restaurant and bar patios.

A councillor's assistant explained that if a restaurant proposes to have a few tables and chairs on the sidewalk, the city's rule is that residents within a certain distance are polled to ask them if they support the patio or not. However, for some mysterious reason, the information is sent not to the householder but to the person listed as the property owner, which means that renters are not notified (unlike in planning consultations). In addition, the real estate ownership lists are often out-of-date. There is thus a very low response rate. Nevertheless, the rule is that if an application does not get at least a 25 percent response rate, it will be denied.

Even if all householders were informed, however, the vast majority of residents do not bother to respond to notifications about community developments unless they have objections. This means the process is structurally biased against businesses both because the list of those consulted is inappropriate and because of the 25 percent response rule. In addition, it does not say much for the "Diversity is our strength" city motto that the 50 percent of the Toronto population that rents a home is excluded from this (admittedly not very significant) polling process. Thus, the process subjects individual small-business owners, however inoffensive, to a process that is neither bureaucratic nor democratic, but rather combines the worst of both worlds.

Given the completely dysfunctional system for patio permits, it is not surprising that both residents and business owners end up circumventing the formal process and resorting to informal, one-off deals. In one quite typical case, a councillor held several meetings with residents upset about late-night alfresco dining at one local restaurant, and spent something like the equivalent of a full working week to reach a solution by which the restaurant agreed to reduce the number of outdoor chairs from eighteen to twelve. Similarly, residents' complaints about music are sometimes addressed by forcing the restaurant to stop playing music at a certain time of the evening or to build more walls or other enclosures around the patio.

A councillor's assistant explained that her particular boss (representing a ward with numerous restaurants and bars) decided that since the routine bureaucratic notification process did not work, they (the councillor's office) would get "more hands on." By this they did not mean that they would work to reform city hall's processes—but rather that they would undertake their own, ward-specific supplementary process. The process instituted in that ward was (and may still be) that the councillor and his/her staff informally poll the neighbors—rather than using the official list of property owners—and if they detect a strong feeling one way or the other, this is then brought to "community council." This body has limited formal power (since it is not a formal part of Ontario planning law or municipal government), but it happens to have jurisdiction over outdoor patios. The councillors that constitute this body (despite the name, the community councils have no community members) can overturn the results of the (official) patio poll. This is important because while councillors usually do whatever the loudest homeowners want, councillors also need to pay some attention to business interests.

That the rather trivial issue of outdoor patio permits sheds much light on some of the key contradictions in urban governance is illustrated by a long-running conflict between condo dwellers (not necessarily owners) and a pub:

> For almost five years, Robert Costelloe has been trying to get a modest patio approved for his pub in the Beaches. And for five years, the same 14-unit condo building two doors away and the same city councillor have stood in his way. Costelloe, owner of Kitty O'Shea's Irish pub since 1999, has agreed to reduce the size of the patio from 20 to 16 to 12 seats. He's agreed to close at 9 pm—two hours earlier than his competitors—and agreed not to pipe music outside the pub at Queen St. East and Beech Avenue. He's reinforced the ceiling to prevent noise problems for tenants above. . . . "We're squeaky clean, we've never had a charge or complaint in the five years we've been here from police, liquor, or the noise bylaw inspectors. We don't even have complaints on Saint Patrick's Day here."[16]

Despite his good behavior, the pub owner was unable to persuade the local councillor, Sandra Bussin, to support his application for a patio permit. The association of condo dwellers and the councillor opposed the patio application at community council, and it was duly defeated four to two.

The *Toronto Star* noted that "even Bussin's allies on council are urging her to seek a compromise" (since, as we saw earlier, it is common for councillors to mediate and broker deals that give each party some of what they want). Given Bussin's disregard for the unwritten law of mediated solutions to patio disputes, the councillor for the neighboring ward (who also sits on the same community council) broke with the usual cabinet-solidarity practices of councillors and told the *Toronto Star* that she had urged Bussin to reconsider her opposition. Such public comments are highly unusual, as a councillor from the other side of the city—who would therefore not be called upon to vote one way or the other on the issue—resignedly observed:

> Councillor Joe Mihevc (Ward 21, St Paul's) said a community council would have to have a "very strong case" before it would overrule a local councillor's wishes. "The general rule of thumb, if you want to put it negatively, is it's feudalism. If you want to put it generously, it is that we have respect for the councillor," Mihevc said.[17]

As we have seen and as Councillor Mihevc confirms, for issues considered as involving only a single ward, the councillor can simply decide to oppose a rezoning application or to oppose a patio permit, and other councillors will defer.[18] This "feudal" system works because the councillors who put common sense aside as they defer to their colleague's whim or their colleague's pursuit of certain votes can confidently expect that when they decide to take a stand on some local issue they will in turn be supported. That a whole lot of micro-local decisions that are rubber-stamped by fellow village elders end up creating precedents and policy by default is widely admitted to be true; but the councillors, who are the only ones who could change the system, are unlikely to give up any of their quasi-feudal powers willingly. And it needs to be stressed that a councillor's position on the left-right spectrum makes no difference in this particular game.

Grassroots Champions of the Local

The local champion role is one that can be played by private citizens as well as politicians. Often such volunteer champions are not known beyond a single street or a single residents' association, but the councillor and her/his assistants make a point of knowing who these people are, and not only at election time. Playing the role of micro-local champion is time-consuming, which may be a reason why this role is generally played by people with few work and child-care responsibilities. While becoming a grassroots champion of the local does not require being wealthy or even being a homeowner, certain skills are crucial: knowing something about city hall, having some acquaintance with the planning process, being confident and articulate, and, last but definitely not least in a city where half the citizens were born outside of Canada, being articulate in English. In my own neighborhood, for example, there are a number of such micro-local champions. One of them is a Chinese immigrant, who often brings groups of older Chinese people with her to meetings and translates for them (she speaks at least two Chinese languages). But most of the other local leaders encountered repeatedly during the research—about half a dozen—are white native speakers of English, and, judging by their speaking styles, have enjoyed a good education.

The work of my particular local champions will be described in some detail in the chapter on community consultations that follows. Here we will feature someone from the opposite, west end of the city who, unusually, has gained some citywide fame. His name is Misha Glouberman, and his reputation was built to some extent on the strangely contentious, recurring issue of restaurant patios. Glouberman lives in a neighborhood that has seen second-generation gentrification. The original run-down artists' area of Queen Street West became gentrified in the 1990s, driving the artists somewhat further west. Soon, an area that had long been considered impervious to gentrification, due to the presence of the province's largest mental hospital and the attendant population of former psychiatric patients, began to gentrify as well.[19]

Glouberman is the founder and head of the Queen-Beaconsfield Residents' Association. He is self-employed, undertaking such pursuits as the organization of "hipster lecture series" and "alternative workshops."[20] He says that his leadership has been questioned because he rents an apartment over a trendy clothing store, rather than owning a condo or a house; but while his tenant status makes him unusual among residents' association leaders, his civic activities are not. Glouberman was personally responsible for brokering a compromise with a local restaurant: the restaurant was able to obtain a patio permit, but, in keeping with what councillors do elsewhere in the city, the patio is smaller and closes earlier than the owner had planned. This compromise required a huge expenditure of volunteer resources (skills as well as time) and city staff time. Glouberman is quoted as follows: "We came to a happy conclusion and that's wonderful. But it's also fair to say it took like six to twelve months of work by about half a dozen neighbours who were working really intensely, the bar owners, and much more work from the city councillor's office than it should have done."[21] A *Toronto Star* feature on him two years after this incident opens with the following description:

> Walking the three blocks of Queen Street that separates the Gladstone Hotel from the Drake Hotel [both renovated to serve an artsy /fashionable clientele],

Misha Glouberman points out the bars that have opened or at various stages
of construction. "The density of bars in this neighbourhood is incredible," he
says.

That this local champion is not universally popular becomes clear as the
journalist continues his walk on Queen Street with Glouberman: "As he
continues strolling along Queen, a man walks purposefully by without
making eye contact. 'That's Richard Lambert, who owns "The Social,"'
says Glouberman. 'He doesn't like me very much.'"

After describing the details of a current rooftop-patio application by
a bar owner, while also reminiscing about the earlier patio war on which
his political capital was initially built, Glouberman feels compelled to tell
the journalist that he could have bought a property, but he simply did not
think it was a good use of his money: "I put money into dot-com stocks
that went way up in value and I got out before everything crashed."[22] Having financial independence allowed him to spend large amounts of time
acting as the local village elder.

The people who buy or rent condos or houses in gentrifying neighborhoods, and who have the time and the interest to reach an agreement
with a bar owner about the precise number of chairs that can be placed
on an outdoor patio, are undoubtedly sincerely committed to improving the quality of life and to exercising their citizenship at the local level.
But one wonders why it is possible to get volunteers to work on this kind
of project while it is so very difficult to mobilize the same people on a
citywide scale, to work on systemic improvements. The neighborhoods
in which poverty has been not only increasing but also becoming more
concentrated have other concerns, many of them of a much more pressing character. And residents' associations are much weaker in areas with
a majority of immigrants, not only due to language and cultural barriers
but also because more immigrants live in rental housing and few renters
become involved in local civic politics. Some of the unfashionable areas in
which low-rent high-rises dominate the landscape do produce grassroots
activists who speak for the vast number of Torontonians who live in drab
high-rise apartments on arterial roads and whose lives are utterly different from those of Misha Glouberman and his downtown artist friends; but
such local heroes (a couple of whom ran, unsuccessfully, for city council, in
the October 2010 elections) are the exception that proves the rule.

A governance process that depends largely on receiving complaints by
groups and individuals with the resources and the know-how to get atten-

tion (from either city staff or the city councillor or both) will be necessarily biased in favor of the largely white, well educated, and mostly gray-haired folk who already feel a sense of civic entitlement, and whose claims to urban citizenship are confirmed and reinforced by the village-elder political system that has been documented in this chapter.

Conclusion

Deploying city employees charged with enforcing bylaws to respond to councillor (or councillor-brokered) complaints is a regulatory strategy that makes many people feel that "the city" is listening and is responsive. And in some cases letting the councillor simply impose a mediated solution (e.g., the pub owner can get his patio, but will close it at 9:00 p.m.) produces results that satisfy the parties involved and take less time and trouble than going through a bureaucratic process. However, this governance system (if one can call it a system) has a number of inherent, structural effects. First, from the point of view of efficiency, there are obvious problems with prioritizing tasks depending on whether they have immediate, short-term political traction. One former senior manager, for example, explained that at one point a councillor got upset about the proliferation of charity drop boxes in his ward and insisted that MLS staff do an investigation, write a report, and come up with a system for enforcing the permits that such boxes require. Responding to that request meant dropping other work of greater importance.

The "common sense" in whose name citizens, and their champions, rise up is inherently fuzzy and undefinable; but its outlines emerge as the latest "red tape" disaster tale is disseminated. "They" are bungling; "they" do things like ask seniors if they have a permit to walk in the park, or go around measuring the water in kiddie pools. Since "the city" is clearly stupid and bureaucratic, "we" must therefore be sensible.[23]

The local champion—a generic and highly symbolic figure that is produced by the governance structure as much or more than by individual effort—is structurally compelled to act as the defender of "the community." It is difficult if not impossible to mobilize citizens in favor of long-term improvements that benefit the whole city (such as a more inclusive local political system). But it is relatively easy to whip up the simmering resentments against "city hall" by attacking something that threatens to take away people's (often rosy-colored) sense of micro-local community

peace. Busy tending to local resentments, the local champion will be unlikely to have the time or the encouragement to proactively work on systematic reforms of the rules. Neighborhood groups have no permanent
staff, no researchers, and thus very little capacity to engage in anything
like systematic planning. Local councillors have some administrative and
research support, but they devote far more time to responding to local
crises or outrages than to either policy or planning. Even mayors, who are
accountable to a large and diverse population rather than to highly local interests, are not immune from the logic of reactive nay-saying. John
Sewell, a noted figure in local politics who rose quickly from community
worker to alderman (councillor) to mayor, and who may well have been
the most left-wing mayor Toronto has ever had, gained his stripes in purely
defensive fights to preserve existing neighborhoods against developers and
against freeways.

While on occasion a champion of the local can end up "jumping scale,"
as geographers say, to higher levels of government, by and large the local champion or village elder is characterized by a highly limited spatial
scale. He (or she, but it's usually a he, Jane Jacobs notwithstanding) also
typically uses a very limited temporal scale. Energy is spent fighting fires
rather than contemplating policy alternatives for the future. This is not
necessarily a matter of choice. The one fight at a time, one property at a
time character of councillor action is to a large extent the product of the
existing system for managing conflicts, which over time has clearly shaped
the expectations of residents and makes it difficult for any councillor to
pursue a more long-term and less micro-local agenda. All councillors try
to generate improvements in their specific area, and they appear to devote much more time and energy to this ward-based work than to citywide
work. Even when participating in citywide committees, councillors often
leave the room for long periods of time, only to reappear when an item
concerning their area is on the agenda. And when citizens make deputations, councillors often leave their official seats to acknowledge people
they know, with these disruptions being regarded as normal.[24]

Councillors and local civic leaders may not be provincial in their views;
they may want to encourage local citizens to expand their horizons, instead of caring only about whether their particular street has potholes or
whether the dogs in the local park are on leashes. But this kind of nudg-
ing toward a broader sense of citizenship will always be an uphill battle,
especially in municipal governments that have no political parties with
governing programs and political platforms. The vast amount of time de-

voted to brokering one-off solutions to patio disputes is by no means an unusual occurrence: one city councillor told me that the conflicts between dog owners and parents about the proper use of tiny local parks was, at the time that we talked, taking up more of her time than any other single issue.

In conclusion, everyday conflicts and disputes in a large cosmopolitan center turn out to be governed by dysfunctional, often spiraling interactions between two kinds of authority: bureaucratic organizations in "city hall," on the one hand, and local champions, including councillors, on the other. Outdated, overly complicated bureaucratic rules, enforced by a very small body of officials who are constantly engaged in responding to squeaky wheels, necessarily create a need, indeed a market, for informal mediation. But such village-elder politics often favor those who are already privileged, who already feel entitled, and thus unintentionally work to the detriment of local democracy, diversity, and inclusion. Village-elder politics, finally, may perhaps be appropriate in actual villages; but the village-elder approach is wholly inadequate to address the citywide problems affecting large metropolitan and cosmopolitan urban centers.

CHAPTER 5

Law without Rights

Zoning, Poverty, and the Normative Family Home

Introduction

Housing issues have long been central in urban life and have played a key role in stimulating urban civic movements, as Manuel Castells's magisterial, transnational study of urban politics points out.[1] In some jurisdictions, municipalities have exercised a strong, direct role in regulating housing—for example, by imposing strict rent controls and/or providing large amounts of public housing. In many North American cities including Toronto, however, a combination of weak legal powers and a political culture wary of anything like a municipal welfare state has long limited cities' ability and willingness to regulate either the physical features of houses or the economic and social relations of housing. The city does on occasion flex its legal muscle; for instance, it is legally difficult to convert rental apartment buildings into more profitable condominiums. In addition, the city has also run and managed a public-housing program, though one that is small not only in comparison with Britain but also with those developed in Chicago and New York. But the city does not have the power to put in rent controls, for example.

Weak legal powers could nevertheless be exercised in a coordinated and coherent manner. But when exercising its meager legal powers, Toronto has never had a coordinated long-term housing policy. An Affordable Housing Office was set up at city hall only in 2003, and its role is very limited. This does not mean there have been no rules and policies and innovative experiments, but rather that housing policy has been made across a large number of different and uncoordinated sites, including a significant nonprofit housing sector. Activists from the nonprofit housing sector as well as city officials readily admit that much if not all of their work is reactive, localized, and lacking in overall perspective. But the general feeling seems to be that one might as well do something, and if overall change is not in the cards, small changes are better than nothing. Thus, some people (inside and outside city hall) know about public housing and do their best in this area even though there is no new money for public housing, or even an adequate budget for repairs; other folks know about and work on regulating rooming houses; on their part, planning- and zoning-law specialists pore over plans and bylaws with little thought about such issues as affordable housing. In the meantime, experts work hard on very specific campaigns: in 2009–10, these included a bedbug epidemic, the intricacies of using section 37 of the Ontario Planning Act (which allows what is usually called "bonusing") to induce developers to add a few units of affordable housing to condo buildings, and the structural and environmental deficiencies of 1960s "tower" apartment buildings.

This chapter will analyze the legal and governance dimensions of a series of local housing-related issues, but without trying to discern some implicit overall policy, since the research has persuaded me that there is no overall plan, explicit or implicit. Taken together, the mini case studies suggest that neither good intentions on the part of some city officials and/or councillors, nor continued passionate activism on the part of the city's housing activists will suffice to change a system that is structurally flawed, a governance system (or rather nonsystem) in dire need of radical overhaul. As we shall see, efforts are regularly made to use local regulatory tools to make up for the obvious market failures that plague the city; but these reform efforts have been, by and large, as particularistic and fragmented as the rules they attempt to change.

The fragmentation of the field studied is thus reflected in the episodic structure of this chapter. But as the reader goes from one story to another, it will become apparent that some of the underlying governance problems plaguing housing issues are already familiar from previous chapters. In particular, the prevailing village-elder local political style is totally unsuited to deal with the fact that while many groups and many city areas are doing just fine, taken as a whole the city is in dire need of regulatory innovations to provide an array of housing options. The city's diverse population desperately needs decent housing options for the down-and-out singles who use rooming houses and shelters; it also needs large numbers of rental apartment buildings in good repair, as well as a supply of affordable owner-occupied homes. But the private sector only finds it profitable to provide either bourgeois family homes worth half a million dollars or more, or else, small condos not suited for families whose mortgages also run into the hundreds of thousands.

Housing is one of the areas in which boom conditions do not bring benefits for all—indeed, boom conditions can exacerbate existing inequalities, inequalities across socioeconomic groups and across neighborhoods, as New Yorkers know.[2] The financial crisis that has sent real estate prices plunging in many US cities has certainly underscored the need for better state regulation of both the financial sector and the housing market. But a booming real estate market does not distribute benefits equally. The long boom of the urban Canadian real estate market (which was barely affected by the 2007–8 downturn in the US housing market), while a great boon to developers, real estate agents, and homeowners who sold up and moved out of the city, is increasing the severity of the problems caused by the city's—and the country's—continued failure to actively regulate housing markets.

Making the process by which housing is governed more just, equitable, and reflective of the city's diversity would require a radical overhaul of the same dysfunctional governance processes that afflict other areas of municipal activity. Since the focus of this book is not the increasingly unequal social structures, but rather the legal and governance structures, we begin not with aggregate numbers but with a vignette that simultaneously casts light on the governance of housing in one neighborhood (South Riverdale, where I happen to live) and on citywide efforts to reform the law.

The Eternal Return of the Rooming House Bylaw: The Difficulties of Legal Reform

"Pedro" was one of the first people I met when I started doing research for this book, in the spring of 2004. An exceptionally knowledgeable young man of Latin American descent, he was then—and still was, as of 2010—employed by the WoodGreen Community Services, a venerable emporium of social services and community development in Toronto's southeast. As I write these lines I can see the original site of WoodGreen's network if I lean out of my study window. The appallingly ugly piece of postwar institutional architecture I see housed, until recently, WoodGreen's main office and many of its staff, as well as three stories' worth of tiny apartments for hard-to-house singles. The head office is no longer there, however: its

TABLE 1. **Neighborhood gentrification**

Occupational type	1996	2006	Percentage change
Professional	8,625 adults	10,535 adults	22.1
Art, culture, recreation	1,760 adults	2,500 adults	42.0
Sales and service	5,545 adults	5,205 adults	− 6.1
Blue collar	4,220 adults	3,095 adults	− 26.7

move was prompted by the rapid gentrification of the area ("we wanted to follow our clientele," a staff person told me). And sure enough, walking on the sidewalk across from the WoodGreen building one day, I heard two of the old down-and-out inhabitants complain to each other about "yuppies having $50 breakfasts." My neighbors anticipate that a loft-style condo building—with a ground floor devoted to a trendy bar or a specialty shop, such as the "dog spas" that have mushroomed in recent years—will soon be replacing the neighborhood's social service mecca.

Postindustrial South Riverdale, now home to the city's thriving film industry and to the bistros and lofts associated with it, was for about a century the preferred home of largely poor immigrants from Ireland, both Protestant and Catholic, and their descendants. When I moved to the area, in 1991, I missed the roti shops and Portuguese corn bread I had enjoyed in the more ethnically diverse west end. No espressos were available anywhere on the local main street. Instead, a large Colgate factory loomed over my tiny backyard, and many small workshops and industries operated nearby. But in a sign of things to come, the Colgate plant was demolished in the mid-1990s, replaced by "infill" privately owned town houses; in subsequent years most of the industrial properties, including a large art deco Wrigley chewing gum factory, were turned into lofts and condos.

There are many disputes about how to define and measure gentrification, but local demographic data fits well with all definitions, even if one looks only at changes over the ten years preceding the 2006 census (see table 1).[3]

In this context of rapid gentrification, it is important to pause to consider the forces and resources that work to preserve and support economic and social diversity, and WoodGreen Community Services is probably the most important one. The agency owns about half a dozen low-rise buildings providing four hundred "supportive-housing" units, as well as apartment complexes without direct social worker support but with subsidized rents. It also provides employment services for local youth and a variety of programs for seniors and for newcomers (many offered in Chinese languages). It also runs eight day care centers, most of them in schools. The organization, whose work is spread out over twenty-five sites, employs over five hundred staff, and trains and uses a large body of volunteers.

Like other agencies rooted in the Jane Addams "settlement house" Progressive era tradition, most of WoodGreen's services are localized. In general, community agencies tend to work at a different scale than state agencies, with the target populations being defined either as local residents or people of a particular ethnicity or language. But community agencies sometimes take up citywide roles as well. One example is that, by contrast with most of his fellow workers, Pedro had, in 2004, an important citywide responsibility: he was the guy to call if there were any emergencies in rooming houses anywhere in the city. When I first met him, he showed me a pager that would ring if a city inspector decided that a particular licensed rooming house was uninhabitable (an extremely rare occurrence) or if there was a rooming house fire. If any such "de-housing" took place, the Red Cross and the Salvation Army were to be notified and their emergency services activated, in keeping with a protocol developed after a notorious rooming house fire.

Pedro came to the interview armed not only with his pager for rooming house emergencies but also with a bulky bundle of photocopies. This turned out to contain the rooming house licensing bylaw of the old city of Toronto and an excerpt from the "Etobicoke code." (Etobicoke is one of the inner suburbs amalgamated into the "megacity" in 1998.) The code excerpt looked as if it had been retrieved from an ancient archive, and the content was equally quaint, beginning with the definition:

> LODGING-HOUSE. Any dwelling in which the proprietor supplies for compensation, with or without meals, and with or without communal cooking facilities, accommodation for more than two (2) lodgers. A lodging-house shall include a rooming house, a boarding house, a rest home or retirement home, a transitional residence, a dormitory and premises operated as a lodging-house by social clubs, fraternal societies and religious orders for their members, but shall not include a hotel, hospital, one-family dwelling as defined in the Zoning Code, student housing operated by a college or university group home, home for the young or institution which is licenced, approved or supervised under any General or Special Act.

After a few pages of details about bathrooms and kitchens, one finds yet another blast from the past, in the subsection on homes providing personal care: "The operator shall ensure that, prior to admission to the lodging-house, each resident has had a recent tuberculin test or chest X-ray and further tests thereafter as required by the Medical Officer of Health."

Pedro's photocopy of chapter 166 of the municipal code of the (defunct) city of Etobicoke was my first encounter with the shadowy legal entities I came to call "ghost jurisdictions," that is, entities that have been politically abolished but some of whose legal rules continue to be in force. While ghost jurisdictions exist at other levels—for example, the Ottoman land code still governs rural properties in Israel—legal ghosts of political entities past can play an important role in urban governance. These ghosts make local law much more obscure and inaccessible than necessary, and they cannot be easily exorcized if the city's legal machinery does not keep pace with political changes. The rooming house bylaw is one example, but most of the ghosts of dead political entities are to be found in zoning processes: planners, lawyers, developers, and planning adjudicators have to repeatedly conjure up ghost jurisdictions such as the nonexistent "Etobicoke" of Pedro's photocopied law as they do their daily work.

That the existence of ghost jurisdictions makes local law inaccessible and obscure is corroborated by the fact that the Official Plan drawn up by the city of Toronto's planning department in the late 1990s was appealed to the powerful Ontario Municipal Board by numerous property owners and interest groups, and, as a result of this long-running appeal, during the period of my research both "the old plan" and "the new plan" coexisted at planning hearings. In other areas of law, new laws replace old laws, but in the case of urban municipalities that are subordinated to state or provincial planning authorities, cities do not have the final word, and so old laws can continue to linger.

As if the simultaneous existence of two official plans were not enough of an administrative law headache, the forced 1998 amalgamation of six municipalities including the old city of Toronto was not accompanied by a harmonization or merger of the zoning rules developed over many years by each of the former municipalities. The new city posted the rules that were in place for each of the former municipalities on its single website; but the laws were not merged or reconciled. Even in 2010, twelve years after amalgamation, citizens needed to know which former municipality had previously existed at the address in question before they could locate the relevant rules.

The rooming house licensing clause had not been included on the official website, however, since the city's licensing bureaucracy was hoping that city councillors would soon pass a harmonized rooming house licensing bylaw covering the whole "megacity." That was the rather complicated reason why Pedro had to resort to photocopying.

Six years after I first saw the quaint photocopied codes, the affordable-housing community and the officials in the licensing department were all still waiting, Godot-style, for a rational, unified rooming house bylaw. Legal rooming houses exist only in the old city of Toronto and in parts of Etobicoke. Everyone knows that rooming houses exist de facto everywhere; but in most of the city's territory it is not possible for them to get a license, so they exist in a state of a-legality. Officials and fire marshals are unable to supervise and regulate them, and indeed even to count them.

Bureaucrats and representatives of the nonprofit housing sector meet regularly in the "Rooming House Working Group," whose chief goal has been to create a unified and sensible licensing and inspection system. But nothing much has happened. The harmonized zoning bylaw, which managed to squeak through city council in the summer of 2010 (only to be quietly repealed in 2011), does not include anything about rooming houses. When asked about this omission at a public meeting, the chief planner stated that rooming houses were "left to a separate policy process," despite the fact that during the official hearings about the comprehensive zoning bylaw, the head of the Ontario Human Rights Commission made a detailed presentation about zoning and human rights in which she said, among other things, that "we encourage you to allow rooming houses in all residential areas."

The lack of fit between law and reality has become more stark in recent years due to the gentrification mentioned above, which is very stark in my neighborhood but affects large areas of the older parts of the city. In the 1970s there were around two thousand licensed rooming houses in the old city of Toronto, but the numbers had dwindled to below five hundred by 2004, Pedro told me. The fact that low-income housing, in general, has moved away from the gentrified areas of the downtown and to the "inner suburbs" is well known in civic society as well as in city hall. But the law has not changed.

Opposition from suburban councillors reluctant to acknowledge the existence of rooming houses in their areas was in the past, and remains, a major factor in resisting reforms that would allow law to catch up, at least in part, to reality. But due to the recent election of a progressive mayor and council majority in 2003, in 2004 there was hope in the air for the reformers. The plan supported both by city hall and by activists was to extend the old city of Toronto's provisions to the whole territory of the megacity. Extending licensing would have immediately empowered city inspectors to investigate reports by tenants or neighbors about rooming houses that had failed to get licensed. Enforcing housing standards can backfire, as Robert Fairbanks's detailed study of a type of rooming house shows;[4] but the Toronto licensing authorities' reluctance to prosecute financially pressed landlords would likely have resulted in pressure to plan for necessary repairs and updates, but without regulatory zealousness causing a loss of housing.

Extending the existing old-city rules to the whole megacity appeared as the obvious solution to the problems caused by the extreme legal fragmentation of rooming house licensing. However, a closer look at how the dwindling number of legal rooming houses in the old city of Toronto are actually regulated reveals that the licensing system has very troubling features. These have the effect of turning rooming houses into political footballs in ward-politics games in which low-income tenants generally lose (if they even get to play), which in turn suggests that the plan of extending the existing license system everywhere is not without its flaws.

In the space previously occupied by the former city of Toronto, a rooming house is defined as a building which is not a hotel and which contains separate "dwelling rooms" for three or more persons that can be locked and that have either cooking facilities (in practice, a hot plate) or a bathroom, but not both. (If a "dwelling room" had both kitchen and bathroom facilities it would be a bachelor apartment, and if there were no locks on the rooms then it would be a single-family home, regardless of the relationships among the people living in it.) The definition is similar to those in other municipal codes, with one interesting exception, which is that in Toronto there is no maximum number of rooms or tenants set out in the code. In local parlance a rooming house means a largish house that used to be a single-family home but has been split up. But the unusual absence of an upper limit for the number of "dwelling units" means that something closer to an institution or a hotel can also be licensed as a rooming house. For largely commercial reasons few private landlords run large rooming houses (though some run-down hotels, often also featuring strip bars, serve this market); but charitable agencies such as the Salvation Army do run midsize housing developments for singles that are legally designated as rooming houses and that elsewhere would probably be "SROs" (for single-room occupancy).

The lack of an upper limit for the number of rooms is a useful regulatory feature for landlords and tenants alike: it allows landlords, particularly nonprofit landlords, to take advantage of economies of scale in serving the bottom rung of the housing market. The second useful feature of the rooming house category is that, while subject to inspection and, as we shall shortly see, interference from the local councillor and middle-class homeowners, rooming houses can be legally located anywhere in residential areas, as long as the size of the building fits within the relevant zoning rules. As stated earlier, only a portion of the city can contain legal rooming houses, but that's a product of the lack of licensing in most areas, not zoning restrictions. Group homes, nursing homes, and shelters, by contrast, are subject to special zoning rules.

Drawing Moral Lines with Zoning Numbers: Separation Distances

Among the zoning rules that hamper the provision of urban housing for down-and-out singles throughout urban North America, a key local legal tool is the "separation distance." Municipal codes routinely state, without justification, that group homes, shelters, and sometimes rooming houses as well have to be more than X distance away from one another. The separation-from-one-another rule is used to govern all manner of businesses and types of nonfamily housing—buildings that perform a variety of functions, but which are lumped together in planning-speak under the offensive acronym LULUs, for "locally undesirable land uses." Since separation distances are only used in respect to spaces that are unpopular, one could argue that imposing a separation distance, no matter what the number, is a way of enshrining moral judgments in law.

If requiring that similar businesses or types of housing be located a certain distance (often, one thousand feet) away from each other, for fear of moral or social contagion, is a legal tool that clearly contradicts principles of equality and diversity, then another set of numbers often found in sections of municipal codes applying to rooming houses, porn shops, and other unpopular buildings in turn force these LULUs to be located not only away from one another but also from "good" buildings. For example, porn shops typically have to be at least one thousand feet from any church, school, or community center. (Forcing certain "bad" buildings to be away from one another but also away from "good" buildings is logically contradictory, of course; but the illogical combination of rules embodies the long-standing municipal indecision as to whether it's best to let "vice" be restricted to a single area or whether it's best to make it less visible by scattering it.)

If these separation rules are problematic, from the free speech perspective, as they apply to businesses, the use of separation distances to govern where certain kinds of people can or cannot live is even more questionable. But even cities that pride themselves on diversity rarely think about abolishing the moralistic separation distances that have for decades worked to keep the type of housing associated with nuclear families away, physically and morally, not only from bars and shops but also from nonfamily housing such as group homes or nursing homes. And courts are unlikely to find such rules unconstitutional. As the Supreme Court of the United States put it, in an important decision empowering municipalities to use zoning rules to draw moral lines,

> There are some [land] uses which, because of their very nature, are recognized as having serious objectionable operational characteristics, particularly when several of them are concentrated. . . . Special regulation of these uses is necessary to insure [sic] that these adverse effects will not contribute to the blighting or downgrading of the surrounding neighbourhood. (*Young v. American Mini Theatres*, 427 US [1976])

Separation distances are accepted as "the way things are." Fights about particular separation distances do occur, of course, when some groups demand greater or lesser distances. But the idea of using separation distances to shape the moral order of the city spatially is never questioned in these battles about whether 250 or 500 meters is the "right" separation distance. At one public meeting concerning zoning rules, I tried to open the black box of separation distances by suggesting that instead of targeting group homes, separation distances could perhaps be imposed on Starbucks outlets or McDonald's restaurants; but everyone treated this as a mere joke.

The myriad separation distances found in municipal codes are unlike building codes numbers, since they are not based on expert studies. Neither are they based on public opinion polls. The numerical format is hence quite misleading.[5] For example, when I began this research project I came across a Toronto bylaw with a very peculiar separation distance, something like 321 meters. The rule seemed bizarre, so I asked an experienced planner about the origins of the number. I imagined that documents would be produced, since the bureaucracy seems to have several background documents for every occasion. But that was not the case. "Oh, it's just that we had to translate feet into meters, back when Canada went metric," I was told.

The separation distance numbers have been rounded either up or down over time, and the rounding conceals their arbitrariness: a 500-meter distance appears as more rational than a 321-meter rule. But none of the myriad separation distances found in municipal zoning codes have any objective factual basis. Certain numbers are used simply because other municipalities have used them.

Whatever its origins, the technique of using numbers to make a moral judgment appear objective is given new life as legal rules come to be debated by planners and by fractious councils. When councillors fight about separation distances (usually for "land uses" that raise social-moral concerns, such as shelters), planners often come up with a new number that is "in between," thus using arithmetic to effect a political compromise. For example, in Toronto, the Ontario Human Rights Commission and some affordable-housing advocates had complained about the discriminatory effects of separation distances governing nonfamily housing several times during the process when a comprehensive zoning bylaw was being elaborated, in 2009–10. As a concession, the planners revised the proposed harmonized (that is, citywide) group home separation distance, decreasing it from 300 meters to 250 meters—a small "technical" concession that had few if any practical effects but which successfully foreclosed any discussion of why certain kinds of "uses" are regarded as inherently undesirable, the implicit assumption grounding all separation distances.[6]

That the main function of separation distances is to create a moral hierarchy of housing types is corroborated by the fact that, in practice, "undesirable" types of housing and social services for the poor usually end up congregating in certain neighborhoods, despite rules about separation from similar "land uses." This can happen legally because in some areas of inner cities there are few or no middle-class neighbors to raise vocal opposition if housing providers ask for zoning variances to have these homes and institutions be located closer together. Also, residential uses predating the relevant zoning rules are usually "grandfathered" and treated as "legal nonconforming uses." Social service agencies such as WoodGreen are more likely to be located in the inner city, and so the buildings they operate often enjoy the curious combination of legality and illegality that is the planning-law term "legal nonconforming use."

To reinforce this dynamic, once a particular street contains numerous such "uses," planners and local politicians are more likely to allow even greater concentrations, no matter how many variances are required, since "the character of the neighborhood" is a key principle of planning law. That the "character of the neighborhood" legal principle, which promotes homogeneity, flatly contradicts the dispersal principles embodied in separation distances does not seem to bother any of the stakeholders. As mentioned above, consistency has never been valued in municipal law. Whatever may be happening on the ground, then, the separation distances remain in the books. Thus, the legal rules, including separation distances, make it necessary for affordable-housing and social service providers to jump through legal and political hoops to obtain the required exceptions and permissions.[7]

That separation distances, especially when they apply only to certain types of housing, have the effect of discriminating against the poor, and often against the disabled as well, has certainly been noted. However, the lines drawn on urban space by means of zoning numbers are not reflective of these interests alone. They also target those people who do not live in family households because they do not live in a family; unlike race or disability, household composition is not a prohibited ground of discrimination in municipal law. In most North American municipalities, six or seven friends sharing a house run the risk of being charged with keeping an unlicensed rooming house and/or being accused of a breach of codes that set a maximum number for "unrelated adults" living together. Single people are not discriminated against in a direct manner: a rich single banker can live in a family-oriented suburb if he wants. But if you are not rich and need to share a home with others, or if you advocate and practice communal living, you may well be in legal trouble.

The planning literature does not seem to have acknowledged that the key term "residential," in municipal law and municipal practice, means "family living," with other types of households being tolerated only if they can prove that they resemble or emulate a nuclear family. The US Supreme Court 1926 decision in *Village of Euclid*—a hugely influential decision that confirmed that municipalities can impose general zoning rules, and not only in regard to noisy or smelly factories or shops—declared very clearly that local law can be used to import the moral ideal of the nuclear family into law. *Euclid* was and remains the key legal text allowing municipalities to impose very serious restrictions on private owners' ability to extract profits from their properties by restricting nonfamily housing (which, depending on local markets, can be more profitable than family housing). Even middle-class apartments for singles and childless couples, when they first became popular, gave rise to much anxiety about the decline of the nuclear family. The 1926 *Village of Euclid* decision expressed the still prevailing view that "residential" refers paradigmatically to single-family homes, since in its text apartments are explicitly counterposed to "residential" districts:

> The apartment house is a mere parasite, constructed in order to take advantage of the open spaces and attractive surroundings created by the residential character of the district. Moreover, the coming of one apartment house is followed by others, interfering by their height and bulk with the free circulation of air and monopolizing the rays of the sun which otherwise would fall upon the smaller homes . . . thus depriving children of the privilege of quiet and open spaces for play . . . until, finally, the residential character of the neighborhood and its desirability as a place for detached residences is utterly destroyed. Under these circumstances, apartment houses, which in a different environment would not only be entirely unobjectionable but highly desirable, come very near to being nuisances.[8]

In Canada as in the United States, "single-family detached" is universally the most privileged category of zoning, labeled as A1 or R1.The phrase "single-family detached" creates a slippage between the building and the household, and obscures from view the fact that a family with ten children will always be a legal household, no matter how overcrowded the space, whereas a perfectly orderly household of six adults will often be in breach of local law.

The welter of restrictive rules concerning the types of housing used by poor people and/or people who do not live in family households differs in its details from one municipality to another, but the moral-legal hierarchy that puts nuclear families living in single-family detached homes at the top is the same.

Empowering the Nosy Neighbor and the Moralizing Councillor

As already mentioned, rooming houses are not subject to separation distances in Toronto (unlike in many other municipalities). But they are subject, by law, to moral regulation by middle-class nosy or prejudiced neighbors.

Just north of where I live, on a block that is more run-down than the surrounding, largely gentrified area, there is a rooming house operated by the Salvation Army. Designed for a Victorian bourgeois family with servants, the home used to house single pregnant women. But while a facility for male recovering alcoholics was being rebuilt, the Salvation Army moved some of those men to this house. One evening, one of the male residents was returning home, and mistakenly went to the house next door. Whether or not he was intoxicated, there is no disagreement that he did not cause any disturbance, once he realized he was in the wrong house. But over subsequent weeks the neighbors became agitated. Via the city councillor, they found out when the rooming house license under which the home operated needed to be renewed, and they made sure they were present at the licensing hearing. In this case the councillor did not oppose the Salvation Army's license renewal, despite the sudden appearance of a lawyered-up "Riverdale Community Safety Committee" (which, like other similar misnamed committees, disappeared from view once the specific issue had been resolved). The license was, however, given conditionally, for only six months—a decision that meant that another opportunity to complain would be automatically provided. The municipal code states that notice of an application for a rooming house license shall be given to the local councillor, and that the license will be issued only "if there are no outstanding complaints with respect to the rooming house or objections to the application."

Thus, if I have a noisy family living next to me, there is little that either I or city officials can do. But if the people next door are singles receiving welfare or disability payments and living in a legal rooming house, then I have an automatic right to voice my opinions about them to officials who hold the all-important threat of denying the proprietor a license renewal. In other words, neighbors wield a power that—especially if their feelings about rooming house tenants as a class are shared by the local councillor—can deny housing to those who are already less empowered and more marginalized not only economically but from the point of view of citizenship.

The final feature of the rooming house licensing system that is relevant to questions of diversity and justice concerns the fact that the empowerment of intrusive and possibly class-biased neighbors that is effected by the bylaw can happen even if the property in question is not in fact a licensed rooming house. An example will illustrate that a law can wield power even when it cannot be used.

At one Committee of Adjustment (board of zoning appeals) meeting, in August 2005, an owner (an Asian man) showed up to try to get a variance allowing him to create a new second-floor apartment over the one-story half of a building in which the other half was already two stories. This kind of request is routinely granted by the committees (especially in a street which, like the one in this case, is a major road with a bus route on it, since "densification" along transit routes is a major policy objective in local planning). But at the hearing, five neighbors, all white, appeared to complain. Their spokesman said that he and the other neighbors wanted to ensure that what was approved was a "single-family unit," not a "dwelling." In the past there had been a rooming house in the lower part of the building, he said. The chair of the committee expressed some concern that this fear was not really a zoning matter. But he got drawn into the objectors' discourse and proceeded to cast a suspicious eye over the plans. He then agreed with the white neighbor that the proposed bedrooms seemed larger than the living room, which to him (the chair of the committee) was an indication that a rooming house was being contemplated. Another member of the committee—a former city councillor—added that the plans (which she had not examined until the objectors drew her attention to them) "look like dorms, not an apartment." One of the neighbors attending began then to talk about the building having been used as a "crack house."

The committee then took a quick vote and turned down the application. Only then did the owner point out that he had not been given any chance to refute the objections or explain his plans. The committee realized its legal mistake, so it reopened the discussion. The applicant then tried to use a kind of cultural defense, stating that "most oriental homes" have smaller living rooms and larger bedrooms, and added that he was trying to provide rental housing for "recent immigrants to Canada who have larger families than most Canadians." The neighbors were unpersuaded by the "larger Asian families" arguments. Without entering into debates about family sizes and ethnicity, they said that the property had been a problem for sixteen years. The committee then concluded that the applicant had brought up "some good points"—but it denied the application one more time.

Throughout, nobody noted that in the area of the city in which the property was located (East York), there was and is no provision for licensing rooming houses—which means that if the owner wanted to rent out individual rooms rather than the apartment as a whole, without a license, this would not be illegal.

In the case of the Asian man wanting to build an apartment with larger than average bedrooms, there was no evidence that the local councillor interfered to support the white neighbors. But councillor meddling was very evident in another situation in which the specter of the rooming house loomed large.

During a ride-along with a research assistant, in July 2007, a municipal inspector doing routine inspections in an older downtown neighborhood commented that the Municipal Licensing and Standards (MLS) department does not want to close rooming houses, legal or illegal, and throw tenants on the street; but they do want to make sure that greedy landlords don't let their properties run down. One rooming house inspected the previous week due to a complaint about sewage flooding the basement was revisited. "Last week, there were needles floating on the sewage," the inspector said. The place still looked dirty but somewhat improved, so the inspector moved on to another rooming house. There, the owner had mowed the grass, as per instructions given by the inspector the previous week. Asked by the research assistant whether grass was a real priority, the inspector explained that the local councillor notes every unkempt front yard that he thinks belongs to a rooming house and calls MLS to demand regulatory enforcement. He added that inspectors resent having to pursue those complaints, since they feel they do not have enough time to deal with serious health and safety hazards as it is.

The harassment of both actual rooming houses (e.g., the Salvation Army case discussed above) and suspected rooming houses by nosy or prejudiced neighbors and by moralistic councillors sheds new light on the rooming house licensing-bylaw project with which this chapter began. Reformers such as Pedro want to extend the existing licensing provisions to the whole territory of the city in order to facilitate better supervision of a type of housing in which tenants are especially in need of consumer protection. And it is clear that the present situation is wholly dysfunctional, since rooming house–type housing has been moving to the less gentrified areas of the city, mainly in the inner suburbs, which means that the existing geographically limited licensing is becoming irrelevant.[9]

But is the current system worth extending to the whole city? The current provisions for community notification and input are particularly problematic, since neighbors who do not object are highly unlikely to show up, phone, or e-mail either the licensing authority or the councillor, whereas those who harbor fears and dislikes based on prejudice are much more likely to make their voices heard. Like zoning rules, licensing provisions are often waived or modified; but having to ask permission is time-consuming and expensive, and in addition the process exposes vulnerable people (and providers of low-rent housing for singles) to attack from both officialdom and neighbors.

The next section will take up the same issues, but in the context of public housing. Public housing is not, thankfully, a zoning category. Whether a house is owned by the city or by a private owner is not relevant from the planning-law point of view—in theory. As we shall see, in practice public housing is treated as if it were an "undesirable land use" that should be allowed only if it happens to be tolerated by those who feel that they own the neighborhood, not just their actual homes and businesses.

Napier Place Becomes Don Mount Becomes Rivertowne: Micro-Urban Renewal

In 1964 the newly formed Ontario Housing Corporation formed a partnership with the city of Toronto and the federal government in order to raze about eight acres of an old neighborhood of small nineteenth-century houses on the edge of Riverdale, in order to build a spanking new public-housing development. Napier Place, shown on a housing company map as a block on which both sides of the street were uniformly colored black (which the map legend explains means "houses in poor condition"), was to disappear completely, as were substantial numbers of houses on nearby blocks. The supposedly stigmatizing name of "Napier" was erased completely (and does not survive in local memory, as far as I have been able to ascertain).[10]

The design for the new development followed international trends. Narrow Victorian streets, widely regarded in those pre–Jane Jacobs days as breeding grounds for crime, were eliminated with a stroke of the planner's pen, with little regard for the traditional social uses of the street. Similarly, the front stoop, that key site of housewives' social interaction, was also banished. The new buildings would not have either private or communal front doors on the street. Instead, a series of low-rise complexes, internally linked by elevated concrete passageways (much like council housing estates in urban England), provided an infrastructure that was thought to be conducive to healthier and purer living.

In Don Mount Court (as the new community was baptized), these architecture and urban-design choices would soon be found to cause an array of both practical and social problems. First, the development stood out as "public housing" a mile away. A more immediate problem was that most residents had to walk a considerable distance before reaching a proper street sidewalk, much less a grocery store or a pub. Expanses of grass and parking areas stood between the front doors of units and the street; and units on the second or third floors were reachable only via outside staircases. Residents complained that it was difficult to phone for a taxi or get a pizza delivered—which may sound somewhat trivial, but which reveals some important consequences of the design choices made by the bulldozer-happy urban renewal experts of the day. The design meant that it was not easy for residents to interact with neighbors from the surrounding, non-public-housing blocks. I experienced this personally: when my son was young, his best friend lived at Don Mount, and even though for a couple of years that family and ours were regularly in and out of each other's homes, I often got lost in the bleak concrete walkways when picking up or delivering children.

The no-streets plan also made it impossible for police cruisers to include Don Mount in their regular rounds (as was later pointed out in meetings of the Metropolitan Toronto Housing Authority, in the 1970s and 1980s).[11] Not surprisingly, the concrete walkways became, at one point, a haven for drug dealers, as the tenants' representative testified at a planning hearing held in July 2005, when Don Mount was about to be replaced by mixed housing. ("We just got together and drove them out," she said proudly, when asked by the adjudicator whether they called the police.)

By the time Don Mount was built, in 1968–69, the slum clearance–urban renewal movement had already come under considerable critical scrutiny, by writers such as Jane Jacobs, as well as by local activists. One could therefore say that Don Mount was outdated even before it received its first residents. But however late the timing of its opening, everything about it—from its physical look through its economics to the social problems caused by the design choices—was borrowed from the work done by city governments and public-housing authorities elsewhere.

Don Mount was an initiative of the local government, though not of the city but rather of the second-tier "Metro Toronto" created in 1957, whose boundaries were those of the current amalgamated city. Documents in the city archives reveal a great deal of squabbling between the province and Metro—but, in a testament to the power of welfare state ideas then, the squabbling happened because both levels of government wanted to control public housing (unlike today, when no level of government is happy to fund it). In January 1966 the Ontario Housing Corporation went as far as to publicly call for Metro to get out of the public-housing business. Interjurisdictional fights reached new heights when the working-class homeowners who were being expropriated claimed that Metro was not paying them fair value for their houses and attempted to appeal to the federal government (since it was providing some of the funds). Don

Mount Village (later Court), a medium-size public-housing development containing (by the end of the twentieth century) 232 units, was not born under a lucky star, obviously.[12] And bad luck continued to plague it. Only a few years after opening its doors to residents, serious structural problems were found and the project had to be largely rebuilt.

If Don Mount's birth was simply a local example of international trends in public-housing design and public-housing governance, so too Don Mount's death—in 2007–8—was also a local example of an international urban-governance trend, namely, the sudden enthusiasm for using public-private partnerships to redevelop aging social housing. The biggest and by far best-known such development in Toronto is Regent Park, which is a few blocks closer to downtown than Don Mount and much larger: Regent Park had ten thousand residents at its height, whereas Don Mount never had more than about a thousand. (As of this writing there is no published information on how the locals feel about the newcomers; but a young man who has lived with his African immigrant family in Regent Park since they came to Canada in the mid-1990s said to me: "Now we see white people in running outfits going out and running on Saturday mornings. We never go out running.") But Don Mount's redevelopment, which began before the Regent Park one, was the first public-private partnership in social housing in the city, which makes its legal story worth telling.

By the end of the twentieth century, when new structural flaws were found, the community was being run by the city's public-housing authority. The expense of fixing the problems was cited in official reports as the reason for the city to seek a partnership with a private developer who would build private condos and rebuild the public housing on the same site with the proceeds from the private homes. But an official told me that the cost-benefit analysis was not quite as clear as the official story would have it: repairs would have been extensive and costly, but, from a purely economic perspective it would have been appropriate to fix the problems, he said.

The choice made to not fix Don Mount Court but rather tear it down and replace it by the spanking new public-private community that would go under the pretentious, faux-antique name of "Rivertowne" was as much ideological or cultural as financial, according to this official. By 2000, the consensus throughout North America was that the postwar approach to public housing was plain wrong, and that integrating private and public housing was the way to go, and not only for fiscal conservatism reasons.

The legal basis of the Regent Park redevelopment was laid without any legal or political hitches. If there were complaints from neighboring homeowners, these never reached the stage of formal legal proceedings.

However, in Don Mount, a group of hostile neighbors appealed the city's Rivertowne plan all the way to the Ontario Municipal Board (or OMB, a quasi-judicial planning tribunal whose decisions are usually final, since judicial review is very limited). A brief look at this appeal will shed light not only on public-housing issues but also on how the public-consultation mechanisms pioneered by Jane Jacobs and her friends are now used.

I became involved in the Don Mount/Rivertowne OMB appeal more by accident than by research design. The housing company had set up a "regeneration committee" including tenant representatives and home-owners from the immediate area. The housing officials attempted to use the committee to get the two groups to understand one another and to contribute ideas for the design of the future community. The housing com-pany approached the principal of the local elementary school to seek the school's support and, by acclamation, I ended up representing the parents' council on the regeneration committee. In that capacity I participated in meetings but also followed the lengthy OMB appeal process.

Several people told me that in its early days the committee had been very fractious. But by the time I joined, however, the group had settled down. The main tenant representative—an older, large, very funny woman with a strong West Indian accent, whom we shall call Phyllis—raised ten-ant issues vocally several times in my presence; but on the whole she went along with the housing company's proposals. And the representatives of neighboring homeowners who were still participating on the committee had also come to be supporters of the city's redevelopment plan. They even seemed comfortable enough to make jokes; one teased Phyllis by suggesting, in jest, that she might get a Jacuzzi in her unit as a special favor from the housing company, for example.

When I began to participate in the regeneration committee I did not yet know much about planning law, but nevertheless I quickly realized that the complaining neighbors who were seeking to stop the develop-ment or introduce major modifications by appealing to the OMB would get nowhere, legally. Indeed, I was surprised that a full hearing took place (in July 2005), since at the pre-hearing, on March 4, 2005, which I at-tended, it was patently obvious that the group (Riverside Area Residents Association, or RARA) was very small, unrepresentative, and lacking in both legal advice and planning advice. It was also very clear that the hous-ing company had already consulted widely, and indeed, had drastically changed the initial design (which had been for one very tall tower) in re-sponse to consultations.

The RARA leader, a middle-aged white professional woman I will call

Maureen, did not seem very familiar with the planning process. At the OMB hearing her strategy was to put forward every possible objection she could think of, from potential seepage from the nearby Don River, to architectural choices that she claimed would promote crime, to street widths that were insufficient for fire engines, to a claim that the local city councillor had a conflict of interest because she sits on the board of the housing company. (The city's lawyer had to explain at some length that this did not constitute a conflict of interest.)

But in a prior publicity campaign in the neighborhood, the group had clearly decided to focus not on the project's possible technical flaws but rather on the emotional and environmental value of the trees dotting the property. "Save the trees" became the rallying cry of RARA, disseminated in letters to local media and in leaflets distributed door-to-door. The objectors, familiar with the local ethic of diversity, could not directly attack public-housing tenants, so they spoke in defense of trees instead. And because Don Mount was the pilot project in the city's grand plan to redevelop Regent Park and other larger public-housing communities, the housing company took the opposition more seriously than was perhaps warranted and made great efforts to "save the trees," or at least to be seen to be saving the trees.

Some trees were indeed cut down; but several quite large ones were moved, at considerable expense, to the grounds of the local school, and planted there in a ceremony attended by housing company officials and the city councillor. (I attended, on behalf of the regeneration committee, and was urged by the councillor to be the one photographed as if I were planting the trees myself, no doubt to create an impression of community, though I had had no role in the decision to uproot the trees.) Clearly, the trees were not just trees.

But at the planning hearing the adjudicator decided to treat the arguments about trees at face value—even though the housing company had already moved some trees elsewhere and, for the remaining trees, had obtained the necessary "tree permit" that is required to cut down mature trees on private or public property.[13] The housing company's witnesses pointed out that since the tall tower design had been abandoned in favor of town houses, more ground space was required, and hence some of the trees would inevitably have to be taken down. Nevertheless, Maureen, while looking increasingly frazzled and worried as the hearing wore on, persisted, and the adjudicator—who, typically for the OMB, gave her a great deal of leeway in introducing evidence—continued to treat her with great courtesy even after it became clear that she had few legal straws to clutch. After three full days of hearing, however, the adjudicator, instead of deferring the decision to a later date as is the custom, issued an immediate order, so that the housing company would not lose even one more day in its development work.[14]

The best commentary on the appeal process and its undemocratic effects was provided by Phyllis, the tenant leader. At a coffee break during the hearing, she and I and the private-sector developer were sitting with housing company officials. I asked the developer how much he spent on legal bills for the appeal. He responded that he spent over $100,000 out of his own funds, but that the city did most of the legal work. At that point Phyllis joked, "There goes my balcony!"[15]

We all laughed—but it was rather a bitter laugh. Balconies had not been included in the plans of most of the public-housing units, in any case. But Phyllis knew who was really paying the price of "community consultations."

Community Consultations in East Chinatown

Many of the largely Chinese residential areas that now exist throughout the Greater Toronto Area are characterized by relatively high family incomes[16]—but that is certainly not the case in Riverdale's East Chinatown, which appears to be considerably poorer than most other micro-neighborhoods in the rapidly gentrifying area.[17] While many of the cheap Vietnamese and Chinese restaurants of this mini-Chinatown seem to be viable, grocery and other "ethnic" shops go out of business with regularity, unable to compete with a new, large-scale Asian supermarket a short distance away.

Over the past fifteen years, many Chinese immigrants with professional degrees have moved into the area, but only temporarily. A Chinese immigrant who has chosen to remain in the area told me that the norm for her fellow Chinese immigrants is to live for a few years in cheap rented accommodation near the Chinese businesses but to then buy a home in a "better" area, often in suburban municipalities, thus doing in a few years what the postwar Italian and Portuguese immigrants usually did in a generation.

Some of Toronto's commercial ethnic enclaves manage to survive even after suburbanization—Little Portugal and Little Italy, in the west end, remain lively commercial areas to which suburban middle-class "ethnics" will travel on weekends to shop and eat. But East Chinatown has the feel of an area that has been left behind, economically and socially, as Asian immigrants and their children gravitate to flashy Asian malls. In 2005 one researcher counted sixty-five such malls in the region, including the gigantic Pacific Mall, which has over 350 stores and is North America's largest Chinese space of consumption.[18] The dozen or so rather run-down herb and tea and grocery stores of East Chinatown look like remnants of the past.

While the political economy of microneighborhoods does not determine the shape of local politics in any direct manner, when trying to understand the passionately felt resentments that erupted in the summer of 2005 in regard to a supportive-housing project in the area, it is important to keep this socioeconomic context of decline and marginalization in mind. The proposed development, to be located on Gerrard Street at the edge of East Chinatown, was very small. Taking over an existing four-story apartment building located above a bar, a local Chinese agency serving people with mental health issues partnered with an old Catholic agency to provide bachelor apartments for twenty-five people with a history of homelessness and drug or alcohol dependence.

While the initial proposal called for an extra story to be added, which would have helped with economies of scale as well as providing a little more housing for a desperate sector of the population, the project managers quickly modified the proposal so that the built form would remain the same. This meant that the development was now "as of right"—that is, it did not require a zoning variance. (Affordable-housing providers told me that they scour the city for properties that can be used "as of right," to avoid expensive and unfruitful consultation processes, but this greatly limits their choice of properties.) But if the two agencies thought that by proceeding with an "as of right" project they could fly under the neighborhood political radar, they were wrong.

The project had received federal housing funding in March 2005, and for a few months preparations went on with little or no publicity. In July, however, a small group of white middle-class residents living in nearby well-off residential streets joined forces with the East Chinatown business community to oppose the project. A "community meeting" was held on July 27, in which a large number of speakers were mobilized to provide information and context for the upset local residents: six people representing the agencies and their architects, several city officials, the local councillor, a constituency worker for the local member of Parliament, the senior affordable-housing manager for the city, and no less than three police managers—as well as two Chinese-Canadian facilitators.

Local opposition was fueled in part by the fact that the non-Chinese Christian agency involved in the project had already been running a rooming house in the area that was regarded as a source of problems. But promises that the objectionable rooming house would be shut down once the new apartments were functioning did not seem to reassure the participants. Shifting scale from the micro-local to the level of the wider neighborhood, resentments about the second-class status of East Chinatown and the surrounding area rose to the fore. Many complaints were made, by the self-appointed leader of the upper-middle-class homeowners as well as by some of the Chinese business people, about the fact that South Riverdale has a disproportionate number of social services and subsidized housing. An exchange recorded in the official minutes of the meeting was typical:

QUESTION: Councillor, when the proposal came out, were you in favour or not? With fifty supportive residences and 170 shelter beds in this ward, who at Council is responsible for the community as well as those with special needs?

ANSWER: I have not been crazy about this proposal from the start, but I want to wait for further information about the project. . . . We cannot discriminate because someone has a mental illness. You can talk about shadows [shadow impact studies, often used in planning hearings], but not who will live there, or that is discrimination.

QUESTION: Don't we have enough for homeless, young offenders, with Chester Village [a former old-age home] becoming a shelter—when the process was up for approval, how did the Councillor vote? Who is ultimately responsible?

COUNCILLOR: I did not want this in this community. Chester Village is not a shelter.

The local councillor is solidly left-wing and supports affordable housing; but the dynamics by which councillors become hostages to small but loud groups of homeowners and business owners affect all council members.

At a meeting held on August 15 at one of the larger Chinese restaurants on the strip, largely in Cantonese (with erratic translation into English), the (white) homeowners' representative opened by congratulating himself on supporting "diversity." But it quickly became apparent that for him diversity meant being able to patronize nearby Chinese restaurants, not being supportive of the poor and the mentally ill, since he launched into a speech demanding that "the city" put supportive and affordable housing in other parts of the city. After this, a number of very heated speeches against the proposed supportive-housing development were made by Chinese business owners and their allies. A Chinese-Canadian former school principal, whom one would have thought would have authority over a crowd that included many of her former pupils, spoke in favor of the development and attempted to educate the meeting's attendees about mental illness, but her speech (made in English) did not seem to persuade anyone. It was the kind of meeting at which people arrive determined to express their existing views rather than to listen or learn.

While the white homeowner representative and many of the Chinese business owners present at the meeting were speaking against rooming houses and mental health patients, other elements within the Chinese-Canadian community were working, more quietly, to counter the local fears. Interestingly, however, this was not known to many of the white English-speaking activists (including myself) who became involved in the disputes. After the very heated and badly managed restaurant meeting of August 15, one of the few other non-Chinese attendees told me, as a confirmed fact, that "the Chinese press" had been fueling the fire by spreading rumors. And a photocopied sheet purporting to summarize in English articles published in the Toronto Chinese press during July 2005 (given to me at that same meeting) appeared to support the notion that Chinese-Canadians as a group opposed local housing for people with mental health issues. A typical passage, purporting to translate/summarize local Chinese press coverage, read: "Based on numerous researches, it was shown that mental patients are a high-risk group for drug abuse and criminal activities."

However, a detailed study of what the local Chinese press actually published revealed that the press merely *reported* that residents were very upset. Contrary to what I had been told, "the Chinese press" was not fueling the fires of prejudice but rather describing them. And two out of the three articles published in the biggest Chinese local daily, *Sing Tao*, devoted much space to the efforts of several Chinese community leaders (including a renowned Chinese-Canadian psychiatrist) to explain that providing special housing for people with mental health needs actually increases community safety. The Chinese language press also carefully reported that the agencies behind the project had accommodated neighbors' concerns by reassuring them that security would be provided 24/7 and that every resident would be assigned a "support worker."[19]

Just as the white homeowner representative felt he was supporting diversity by allying with the East Chinatown Chamber of Commerce, with no regard for the fact that "diversity" would arguably demand that attention be paid to the needs of mentally ill and destitute Torontonians of all races, so too, some of the white pro-affordable-housing activists, keen to promote diversity on the basis of class and disability, did not stop to question their rather monolithic and simplistic view of "the" Chinese-Canadian community, and of the "ethnic press" in general.

It became clear during that politically hot summer that expressing vehement opposition to mental health patients moving into the area did not count as a breach of the Toronto ethic of diversity. Throughout August 2005, a flyer, in English on one side and Chinese on the other, was distributed throughout the area and twelve hundred signatures were collected opposing the project. The flyer also stated that a public meeting would be held in early September. Notifying neighbors and holding information sessions or public meetings was not legally required, since as mentioned earlier the development was "as of right"; but the political pressures on the councillor—and possibly on the mayor's office as well, since the circulated petition was addressed to the mayor—continued to mount.

The three agencies involved in the project hosted an open house on September 7, in the basement meeting room of a local church, no doubt after some pressure. An experienced housing activist told me that the "open house" format was chosen because if people circulated constantly this would mean people would be free to ask questions and get information from city staff and social agencies, but in a quiet manner, avoiding the rhetorical escalations that often derail public meetings at which people sit in rows of chairs waiting to be addressed.

But the attempt to pour oil on the troubled waters by managing the space and the social interactions so as to avoid harangues proved unsuccessful. The September 7 "open house" degenerated into the single most contentious and least productive public meeting that I attended during the five years of the research project. A neighborhood newspaper, *Etc news*, reported as follows:

> Angry residents and business owners disrupted a community information open house about a housing project. . . . At approximately 6:50 pm, a group . . . entered the basement and denounced Councillor Paula Fletcher for not conducting a proper community consultation process about this project. Paul Lovie, spokesperson for the recently formed South Riverdale Neighbourhood Association

demanded that the project be halted until a formal consultation process takes place and all constituents have an opportunity to make their views on the project known.

"If you look around this room, there are so many discussions happening and so many points of view. We don't know what everyone thinks about this proposal. We should all have a chance to share our views," he said. Lovie then presented a petition with over 1200 signatures to one of Fletcher's assistants. . . . Fletcher was not at the open house when the disruption took place. Once the police completed a safety assessment, she arrived later. Throughout the meetings groups of residents clashed on both sides of the issue. Some held signs that held "stop the dictatorship" while others in support of the project demanded to know why Lovie felt he could speak for everyone in the community.[20]

Tellingly, the South Riverdale Neighbourhood Association that Lovie claimed to represent did not make any subsequent appearances in any local matters. My street, in the heart of South Riverdale, was never leafleted or otherwise contacted by this supposed neighborhood group.

After leaving the "open house," while I was standing on the sidewalk watching people who had also emerged from the church argue with one another, an assistant to the councillor approached me to see if I would be willing to join the "community consultation" committee. My guess was that the councillor was trying to ensure that the committee would not be taken over by those who were adamantly opposed to the project, and from previous experiences she knew me to be a reliable leftist. However, I had been somewhat traumatized by seeing several men screaming and wielding their "stop the dictatorship" signs so close to the councillor's face that it was a wonder she was not physically as well as psychologically injured. And at that moment I formed the opinion that the project should be left to go ahead without any need to consult with, or indeed even to inform, the neighbors. I told the well-meaning assistant that if I moved into a new street I would oppose holding community consultations so that neighbors could "share their views" on my family's propensity to disorder or crime.

Later on, after yet another follow-up meeting (there were at least four major public meetings) that also degenerated into a shouting match, I was again approached to serve on the liaison committee. Again I refused—in part because I did not feel I had the patience to listen to people screaming about mental patients and crime, and in part because of a more principled reason.

Public consultations about specific projects do sometimes promote democracy and help to validate the Jane Jacobs scale of local experience.[21] But at other times (especially when vulnerable populations that have no political power and few resources are involved), they do the opposite. Instead of educating people about the diversity of households and lifestyles that any large city contains, the public meetings I witnessed provided nothing but opportunities for local demagogues to fan the flames of the politics of local resentment.

Later, in June 2006, just before the twenty-five new units were about to receive their tenants, I learned that there had been serious vandalism at the building in the month prior to opening, and that at one point the electricity cables had been cut. These vandalism incidents were not covered in either the English or the Chinese press, however. It was clear that the community agencies were more interested in getting on with the task of housing people than in going public to educate Torontonians about the consequences of prejudice against those who are mentally ill and/or homeless.[22] Since the building opened to house mentally ill tenants, in the summer of 2006, nothing of any note has happened. The absence of crime and disorder, however, has gone unnoticed and unpublicized—it was the dog that didn't bark in the night. Thus, those who fought bitterly against the supportive-housing development have not had an opportunity to learn from experience and realize that their fears were unwarranted.

This is one of many situations that highlight the dire need for a citywide mechanism to guide the process and ensure that public input is based on genuine considerations. At the micro-local scale (the one-property-at-a-time scale of most development processes), there are few if any ways of enabling neighbors and housing providers to learn from collective experiences and use that knowledge to improve local relationships. Some individuals do learn, of course, and bring that knowledge to subsequent consultations, and some housing providers attempt to introduce information from other cases into the room; but the nature of planning law and planning-related consultations is such that the same battles have to be refought from scratch. In many cases housing providers, in a hurry to build and house, end up agreeing to compromise solutions that only perpetuate prejudices. One example among many of the discriminatory conditions imposed on nonfamily or nonmarket housing in the consultation process is that an old-age home was pressured into frosting the windows of its first floor, thus depriving mobility-impaired seniors from looking out onto the street. It was not clear why it would have been so terrible for neighbors to gain a glimpse of the inside of the seniors' home; but such a peculiar decision is an example of what happens when there is no organized way of ensuring that the citywide needs and wishes of those who need nonmarket and nonfamily housing do not take a backseat to the desires of those neighbors who make their voices heard in community consultations.

From Community Consultation to Community Engagement: A Rare Effort to Reform the Rules

A regulatory design with obvious flaws will not automatically cause the officials responsible to change the rules of the game, especially in a regulatory field (such as micro-local planning) in which exceptions and one-off mediated solutions are the norm. But the creation of a new "Affordable Housing Office" at city hall in 2003–4, which was set up outside of the planning department and under the mayor's office—meaning it was relatively independent from both bureaucrats and village-elder councillors—provided the housing activists appointed to the office with an opportunity to adopt a citywide and forward-looking perspective and try to reform the rules for community consultations in regard to nonmarket housing. In June 2006 this office sent out letters to stakeholders announcing that a new "community engagement protocol" was to be developed. The goal of the process, the letter stated, was to create a protocol that

> defines areas of neighbourhood interest and facilitates engagement that will result in good neighbourly relations; allows housing proponents to predict and prepare for the costs of the engagement process; protects the privacy, dignity, and human rights of future tenants; and is affordable, particularly for small developments.

The ideas gathered from stakeholders over the summer of 2006 were then tested out in a real-life situation that, as it happens, was very near both Don Mount and the East Chinatown developments, though in an area that had not undergone much gentrification because it was traditionally upper-middle-class and white. The site in question, on a main road near a subway station, had been in an earlier incarnation a lightning rod for the fears usually generated by nonmarket and nonfamily housing. It had been an old-age home from 1971 to 2000, but the seniors had been moved to another building, and the city had then bought the building and quite publicly contemplated turning it into a shelter for families in need, such as new refugee families and other families seeking emergency housing. Many residents had mobilized against the city's plan, but it is difficult to say whether that was the factor causing the city to abandon the family shelter plan, since at the same time new funding became available for more permanent forms of housing. Be that as it may, the decision to use the building for permanent affordable housing had already been taken at city hall before the new Affordable Housing Office decided to use that building as the occasion to test out a new community "engagement" protocol (incidentally, the choice of the word "engagement," which suggests something more long-term and less reactive than "consultation," is worth noting). Since the basic decision about use had been taken, the consultations would be limited.

The consultation began in March 2007 with an open house. Visitors were greeted with a flyer that clearly laid out what was and was not under discussion. "Some options for [address] are not on the table," the flyer stated. "It will not be sold for a condo" (a statement taking privatization off the table); "It will not be a shelter." Input from neighbors was limited to two issues: (a) the use of the ground floor, which had formerly contained a large dining room and a greenhouse; and (b) the particular population in need of subsidized housing that would be prioritized (e.g., seniors, single mothers, refugee families, etc.).

After the open house, the consultants hired to develop and test a new community "engagement" protocol spent time locating civil-society organizations in the area, such as churches, housing cooperatives, and business associations. Making an effort to locate organizations beyond the usual homeowner-type group was an important part of the process, and one that made it both more democratic (because local citizenship was not being defined exclusively in terms of home ownership) and more likely to be sensitive to diversity needs.

The organizations thus located were invited to a consultation held in late June 2007. There were about thirty people, almost all representing an organization. The church representatives (all white and well educated) played an important role at this meeting in educating attendees (including me, representing a local pro-affordable-housing group) about the fact that although the neighborhood is relatively wealthy, there are soup kitchens and other services for the poor. The representatives of business associations then spoke, but they had less to say about the neighborhood as a whole. The two consultants then went over the city's decision to use the building for permanent housing and explained the scope of the consultation. They then proceeded to use a technique that I had never seen (and have not since seen) used in similar contexts: they gave each participant two red and two green sticky dots, and told us that we had to use them all up. That meant that we had to find two things that we wanted to see in the building—no attendee could express dislikes only. The consultants then took up each of the two matters under consultation and got volunteers to write down all of the possibilities that were mentioned on large white-boards. The board labeled "common space" options included "green-house," "day care," and "store or café." The board labeled "housing," which received more attention, was filled with various suggestions from the floor—seniors, single mothers, youth, refugee families, and so forth.

Then everyone was told to get up, walk around, read all of the suggested options listed on the boards, and use up their four sticky dots. Some of the business representatives got up and quickly put red dots on the "single mothers" option; but since they had to use up their green dots as well, they could not remain purely negative. The favored housing choice was "seniors."

An interesting format difference between this meeting and other similar events was that while the city councillor was present, she was not chairing the meeting, and she was not given any more airtime than anybody else. But councillors seem unable to merely listen, and so she made a speech, in this case one in favor of the "mixed-housing" option—meaning that anybody in need of housing, whatever their family status or age, could become a tenant. The speech had little effect, however, perhaps because the attendees were all experienced in civic politics and so were likely to already know the councillor and her views—unlike in most other community meetings, in which neighbors with little experience treat the councillor as authoritative on all issues from housing to road construction.

The result of the dot process, in regard to the tenant population, was twenty-six green dots for "mixed," forty dots for "seniors," and tiny numbers for each of the other categories (people with mental health problems, single mothers, etc.). The report produced by the consultants did not mince any words about the motivations of those who were keen on seniors only: "Unfortunately, a few arguments in favour of seniors-only housing were frankly discriminatory against other groups."

In regard to the common space, there were thirty dots in favor of a day care center and about twenty for commercial space; as far as I could tell, the business representatives tended to favor commercial space, not surprisingly, whereas the church and community groups favored the day care. It was very clear, however, that it was the population to be housed that was highly politicized, not the use of common space, since the opposition to the "commercial" option seemed to be mainly the result of the fact that people like myself had to use up their red dots somewhere.

A general meeting for any and all residents interested in the project was also held, but this was more of an information session than a structured consultation. The change from shelter to subsidized permanent housing had already calmed some of the fears, it appeared, since the meeting was far less heated than the ones held a couple of years earlier about the potential shelter; but in addition, the consultants showed great skill in defusing negative comments and educating residents about the right to privacy of future tenants and about the city's legal powers to make certain decisions regarding its own property.

The experiment in managing community input into decisions about nonmarket and nonfamily housing differently by abandoning the free-for-all open-floor format in favor of highly structured processes (including such admittedly infantilizing but quite effective techniques as handing out green and red sticky dots) demonstrates that in many situations—especially when the "diverse" tenants of the future do not yet exist, so that it is not possible to involve them directly—it makes sense to design the process so as to limit the opportunities for the airing of prejudices and the venting of grievances that are not relevant to the matter at hand. It is admittedly true that the Affordable Housing Office, or at least the consultants it hired, was limiting "grassroots" input, or structuring it very tightly. But given the long history of residents, especially homeowners with no particular knowledge of community problems, abusing the opportunities afforded by community consultations, whether out of malice or simply out of ignorance, a highly structured process may well be more democratic and more conducive to fostering diversity than a more open format. And in the urban context, diversity and justice are issues that need to be foregrounded even when there are not actual, specific persons being discriminated against. The machinery of civil rights and human rights law requires actual persons to file a complaint. But urban law governs persons only indirectly, by rules applying to properties, buildings, and land uses. It is thus important to think about how justice and diversity can be promoted within the specific legal machinery of local law.

Conclusion: Urban Justice beyond the Rights of Persons

Many students of urban civic life and neighborhood politics would conclude that the situations described in this chapter amount to a problem of rights: some people and groups have too many rights, or claim too many rights, while other groups either do not have rights or are unable to effectively exercise them.[23]

Both the legal machinery of rights law and the broader political discourse of human rights can indeed be very useful in pressuring municipal governments to stand up for the kind of diversity that encompasses not only ethnic differences but also issues of class, housing tenure, mental health, and household composition. For example, locally, political pressure was exercised during 2005–6 at the provincial level by affordable-housing providers who argued that the Ontario Human Rights Code was in conflict with some of the provisions, or at least the effects, of both municipal zoning rules and public-consultation practices. And in the 2009–10 consultations about Toronto's comprehensive zoning bylaw, the head of the Ontario Human Rights Commission (a former Toronto mayor) intervened both in person and with documents to warn that certain practices formerly taken for granted (such as the separation distances imposed on group homes and similar forms of housing) might eventually be found unconstitutional. The Human Rights Commission and affordable-housing providers also took the opportunity to point out that "community consultations" tend to empower the already empowered, and actively disempower those in need of housing who are not yet living in the neighborhood in question.

The impact of all of this agitation on the Toronto zoning bylaw was close to zero. However, at the judicial, or rather quasi-judicial level, an important development took place that points the way to using rights claims to disturb the basic assumptions of North American planning law. In January 2010 the Ontario Municipal Board (OMB)—which, as a planning body, had previously refused to consider constitutional rights arguments put before it by antipoverty and affordable-housing advocates—struck down a municipal regulation designed to stop the "over-concentration of single-person, low-income households" and of "residential care facilities and social/supportive housing."[24] What is most remarkable about this decision is that the city's policies did not specifically name disfavored groups, and thus did not discriminate against persons, technically. There was also no evidence that the poor pensioners, recovering alcoholics, homeless people, and foster children who lived in the households being targeted were disproportionately black or disproportionately disabled, which meant that existing discrimination law did not have much "bite." (Similarly, in the United States, discrimination against poor and nonfamily households in planning decisions can be challenged under the Fair Housing Act and/or the Americans with Disabilities Act if one can prove the impact is disproportionately on groups that enjoy rights protection; but as is the case in Toronto, poor people who are not disproportionately black, or those living in nonfamily households, have little if any legal recourse.)

Generally, only state practices that either single out a particular disadvantaged group or that unwittingly have a disproportionate impact on one or more such groups are subject to rights-based constitutional challenges. And it has been very difficult to use rights law to dislodge regulations governing particular kinds of "land uses," since the fundamental premise of zoning law is that property owners do not have an automatic right to use their property any way they want. The OMB decision in question is thus important precisely because there was little if any evidence of disproportionate impacts on the kinds of groups of people who have traditionally been able to use rights law—people of color and the disabled, mainly.

Putting limits on exclusionary uses of land-use planning and municipal law by resorting to arguments about the rights of persons (as the "right to the city" literature does) is of course a move toward the kind of diversity that is inclusionary. But trumping one kind of law by using a useful bit from another, very differently organized body of law, while strategically useful in particular circumstances, does not help to change municipal law itself. The liberal individualist machinery of "the rights of man" can only reform municipal law at the margins. Municipal regulations that can be shown to have a disparate impact on, say, disabled people, or—in some jurisdictions—people in receipt of social assistance, may be struck down by rights-affirming courts. Rights law can prevent some of the more overt forms of social exclusion through local law; but it cannot be used to reform and reconstruct the highly normative and not at all rights-based edifice that is planning law.

North American planning law has served a wide variety of purposes, from creating proto-environmental regulations to encouraging private automobile transportation; but there is no doubt that maintaining the hegemony of the North American residential ideal—which is, of course, a nuclear family living in a detached home that they own—has been one of its most important, if not the most important, functions.

One can try to make cities a little less unjust by deploying the mechanisms of the rights of persons, as has been done in the United States by housing activists wielding the Fair Housing Act. But that kind of external intervention, which sets some outer limits on what municipal law can do, is no substitute for engaging with municipal law in its own terms. For example, planning law's crucial phrase "the character of the neighborhood" has been interpreted mainly to preserve middle-class low-density family-centered enclaves in splendid isolation. But if the phrase were reinterpreted in such a way as to focus on the value of preserving urban diversity (of income, of stage in the life course, of health status, and of household composition, as well as of race and class), the phrase could become a resource in exploring possibilities for urban justice beyond the rights of persons—though we might need to start talking about "the character of the city" rather than "the character of the neighborhood." The logic of preservation has usually been used to raise legal drawbridges around residential areas that are socioeconomically homogenous; but in cities that have become highly diverse, socioeconomically as well as ethnically, maintaining and supporting that diversity—which may require putting some regulatory brakes on market-led gentrification—is a goal that can arguably be seen as falling squarely within the objectives and customary practices of land-use law, if planning and planning-related decisions took the city as a whole as its object and goal, not just "the subject property" and the micro-local area.

Our urban spaces contain many injustices—geographic injustices, we could call them—that are not easily reduced to a dearth of "rights." There are just and unjust ways of organizing urban space, and we will only be able to begin discussing and exploring them if we lift our eyes from the useful but limited machinery of the rights of persons.

FIGURE 1. Jane Jacobs' street corner in Toronto.

FIGURE 2. A University of Toronto sidewalk with special improvements.

FIGURE 3. As leader of the Street Food Vendors Association, Marianne Maroney became an expert in Toronto's local law.

FIGURE 4. Toronto's "Ambassador" taxi license system has given rise to a race-based human rights challenge.

FIGURE 5. A mosque in Greektown, Toronto.

FIGURE 6. Street scene outside the now old-fashioned, roast-beef-serving Royal York Hotel in Toronto, once the tallest building in the British Empire.

CHAPTER 6

"Putting Diversity on the Menu"

*The Municipal Corporation and the
Micromanagement of Street Life*

The previous three chapters shed light on how cities regulate private property, especially residential property, and explored the implications for diversity and social inclusion. Overall, chapters 3 to 5 show that in regard to the crucial issue of housing, the admittedly limited legal and quasi-legal tools at cities' disposal are very rarely used to ensure that a wide array of housing options remains available throughout the city's area. While cultural and ethnic diversity is celebrated in official discourse, diversity in regard to housing options is invisible at the official policy level and is actively hampered by specific regulations as well as by the planning mantra of "the character of the neighborhood." In a city proud of its diversity, and one that does not share the history of black versus white housing segregation practices of US cities, one nevertheless finds that unattractive rental high-rises peopled overwhelmingly by immigrants are forced to concentrate on arterial roads with no amenities, and are physically separated, by local custom as well as by planning law, from both trendy waterfront condo areas and the leafy streets of single-family homes that are at the top of planning law's moral and social hierarchy.

Turning away from the regulation of private property and housing but still focusing on how some kinds of diversity are furthered while others are blocked, this chapter and the next look at a very ancient area of municipal jurisdiction: the regulation of business and commerce, which, as we shall shortly see, means primarily the regulation of small entrepreneurs, especially those who need to use public spaces to do their work. The bank towers that dominate the downtown skyline are of course regulated through planning and zoning; but the banks themselves, to the extent that they are regulated, fall within federal jurisdiction, while most other corporate employers are regulated by provincial laws governing employment, environmental emissions, and business practices. The city's lack of power to regulate the economic activities that make up its most important economic sector (finance) contrasts sharply with the micromanagement of the smallest and most marginal entrepreneurs.

This situation emerged over time, without any real planning. Before the rise of centralized state regulation of economic matters, municipal corporations had already developed a variety of techniques for regulating business. In medieval and Renaissance urban spaces, municipal corporations monopolized public marketplaces, set strict rules for commerce, and often set rules for craft guilds' productive activity. Today, local authorities play an insignificant role in the regulation of the corporate entities that began to dominate economic life from the mid-nineteenth century onward. But the ancient legal techniques of municipal licensing—which presuppose that trade and commerce and even some kinds of production exist only by special permission from local government—still persist. They are not applied equally to all capitalists, however: they target only the descendants of the hawkers, peddlers, entertainers, booze sellers, and operators of for-hire vehicles that so preoccupied upstanding burghers of yesteryear. A quick look at the range of businesses that requires a municipal license today shows that today's urban regulatory system owes much to the centuries-old struggle to maintain public order and drive out immoral petty entrepreneurs: pawn brokers, peddlers, street vendors, street musicians, taxi drivers, pedicab operators, junkyard owners, X-rated video purveyors, restaurateurs, "exotic dancers," barbers, and beauticians are all subject to municipal licensing. Large restaurants aside, what these have in common is that they're small, often marginal businesses that have historically been regarded with suspicion, for reasons related either to fraud or to immorality (or both). The only one of the ancient municipal sources of regulatory anxiety that got away from cities was the liquor license, which in Canada as in the United States was removed from municipal jurisdiction once Prohibition was repealed and state liquor control was introduced.[1] Only after Prohibition destroyed the capital and the legal rights (licenses) held by bar owners and liquor merchants was it possible for a higher level of government to then seize the field for both fiscal and regulatory purposes, in the process creating large state bureaucracies. All other merchants involved in street vending or in marginal or morally controversial businesses remained firmly under municipal control.

This chapter will shed light on municipalities' unique legal powers by examining a local campaign to "put diversity on the menu"—the menu of street-food vendors, that is—in a larger historical and legal context. Devoting a chapter to a largely unsuccessful struggle to provide pedestrians with a more "diverse" and healthier array of street food is merited because, while the number of people affected by this project was small (by comparison to the numbers patronizing fast-food outlets), the governance process sheds a great deal of light on two key functions of municipal government. First, local business licensing is a legal tool that—like zoning powers—can be used either to promote or to undermine diversity. Second, the diverse-food campaign sheds much light on how both politicians and bureaucrats imagine the paradigm instance of public space, namely the sidewalk. We shall see that the sidewalk is regarded not as public space but as the private property of the municipal corporation.

Street vending may look like a minor issue in advanced capitalist, wealthy cities. And indeed, the hordes of hawkers and peddlers who in the nineteenth century teemed on urban sidewalks all over the world have been reduced, in most of urban North America, to a rather small and docile group. Nevertheless, street vending is very important symbolically and politically, even in places where it is no longer a major economic engine. Highly controlled street vending is, among other things, an important indicator of First World city status. During my research, only one city official was sufficiently bold to tell me that having food other than hot dogs sold on Toronto sidewalks would make Toronto look like a "Third World city." Most other stakeholders would eschew such comments for fear of sounding racist. But the long and involved history of street-vending regulation, and the central role played by the persecution of (usually "ethnic") vendors in the daily work of police and municipal officers, not only in Toronto but also in cities such as London and New York, suggests that a neat and nearly empty sidewalk is a crucial policy goal for municipal authorities. Nicholas Blomley's comprehensive sociolegal study of city officials' quest to micromanage and discipline the public space of sidewalks has amply shown that any interference (or potential interference) with the unimpeded flow of respectable citizens going to work or shopping in proper shops—the only two truly legitimate uses of sidewalks, in the imagination of city officials—has the capacity to strike real fear into the officials' hearts.[2]

The disproportion between authorities' fear, on the one hand, and the actual, rather trivial, risks to be found on North American sidewalks, on the other, is very striking; it may well be due to an unconscious fear of a descent into "Third World" urban chaos. It is not a coincidence that the large and thriving informal street-food economy of Los Angeles is largely Latino, and that even despite the size of the Latino vote, LA officials are only now beginning to loosen up the rules regarding street food and vending carts. And in New York City too, it is notable that the most vigorous recent attack on street vending was undertaken at a time when large groups of African migrants began to sell clothes, purses, and accessories on Manhattan's streets.[3] Unlike New York City, and unlike many European cities, Toronto has not seen any great influx of African (or Mexican) street vendors; but the "Third World city" specter nevertheless looms large in the regulatory imagination.

What the Toronto case shows is that even perfectly legal and highly regulated street vendors who do not belong to racialized, feared groups can still be experienced as a threat to the values and ideals of bourgeois urbanites. For example, long-serving downtown councillor Kyle Rae, often regarded as an emblem of diversity because he was the first openly gay city councillor in the city's history, consistently opposed not only marginal or illegal vending but even well-behaved, licensed, largely southern and eastern European hot dog vendors. An event recounted under the headline HOT-DOG CART CAN'T PASS MUSTER HERE is illustrative.

> Two weeks' notice and a five-minute speech was all Tony Posch was allowed before councillors voted to take away his livelihood. Posch, 64, and business partner Vince De Mercedes-Angelsen, 58, have served hot dogs and cold drinks on Cumberland Avenue in Yorkville for 17 years. The Bloor-Yorkville Business Improvement Area [BIA] is pushing to get rid of the duo as well as another hot dog vendor and a jewelry stand, citing a city bylaw banning vending in parks.[4] . . .
>
> For Bob Saunderson, chair of the business improvement area, the issue isn't a couple of jobs, but the look of the award-winning Village of Yorkville Park, on Cumberland Avenue, which includes a granite wall and fountain. "It should be the jewel of Yorkville," Saunderson said, adding that the vendors detract from that.
>
> "I think it's outrageous," said Nigel Jackson, co-owner of Berson Gifts and Antiques, which is across the street from the cart. "We don't want to be all froufrou and high end. They're part of the charm. They're an asset." . . .
>
> [Upscale restaurant] Sassafraz manager Robin Kemp said he doesn't have a problem with the hot-dog vendor across from his restaurant but said it is

general policy to "support the BIA's position." Councillor Kyle Rae . . . , who pushed to revoke the licences, said, "All I'm doing is responding to the concerns of the BIA."[5]

Councillor Rae was indeed doing precisely what he said. A policy document issued in July 2004 by a different business association in the same area begins with the group congratulating itself on the fact that its association's police liaison committee had helped to pass the province's Safe Streets Act of 1999, an antipanhandling and antisqueegee law. Feeling satisfied that the threat of "aggressive" panhandling had been successfully criminalized, the document proceeds to discuss the not-yet-criminalized threat of street vending.

> Our Association acknowledges that street vendors are part of a vibrant downtown community and can contribute to its vitality. However, they should not interfere with the business operations of retailers . . . and they should not detract from public facilities such as the Village of Yorkville Park.

It then outlines policy recommendations, including that street vendors provide the city with an audited statement of annual revenues, that "major intersections should be limited to one vendor," and that the Business Improvement Area "needs to maintain its right to veto or approve any new vending locations."[6] The phrase "*maintain* its right to veto or approve" is telling: clearly, the local councillor's past practice had been to give the business association—not the city bureaucracy—the "right" to approve specific locations for specific vendors and the right to veto permits and licenses. The legally troubling practice of letting one type of business determine the number and location of competitors is not a local idiosyncrasy; it also exists in many American cities.[7]

Exercising its power to set regulations, the business association demanded a number of new rules. For example, "the city should provide vendors with a standard issue umbrella to cover hot dog carts . . . preferably in a dark colour, not a dirty yellow-and-black umbrella that is littered with advertisements." It further reported that "two board members of the Bloor-Yorkville BIA have met with Councillor Kyle Rae in regards to this issue, and have successfully pushed forward to have two vendors in the area removed, with one remaining."

The irrational fear of street vending is visible not only in the comments made by representatives of upscale businesses but also in the work of the long-dead bureaucrats who designed the relevant application forms. The form for hot dog vendors, for example, is six pages long and includes three "checklists." Check list number 1 begins with the following questions:

- Have you completed the sketch and attached it to your application?
- Have you included the name and side of street, and the tie-in measurements from the curb of the nearest intersecting street for each location you have requested?
- Have you attached a copy of a valid City of Toronto business licence or written proof that you are exempt from requiring such a licence?
- Have you attached a drawing or photograph and included the dimensions of the portable display unit, seat, and waste receptacle?

Six more questions follow—and at that point the applicant is only at the end of the first page. The next page is meant to show that the location meets all the criteria. The first question about the location asks whether "the requested location is on a street or part of a street which appears on the attached Schedule B or Schedule F of the City of Toronto Municipal Code, Chapter 315 (Street Vending)." This is followed by eleven more questions, including whether the proposed location is within twenty-five meters of another vendor, and, last but clearly not least, whether "the requested location is in a Business Improvement Area." The final checklist page asks (at long last!) what items will be available for sale and what will be the proposed hours of operation.

This appears to be the end of the six-page form, but in a gray box, just over where one is to sign, the applicant is warned that certain documents—in addition to the sketches, drawings, and so forth, already requested—are also necessary, including

- A certificate from the Medical Officer of Health which shows compliance of the portable display unit and waste receptacle with the Health Protection and Promotion Act regulations (dated within three months of the application date);
- A propane inspection certificate in accordance with the requirements of the Propane Storage, Handling and Utilization Code of Ontario Regulation 825–82, as amended, from the Provincial Fuels Safety Branch (dated within three months of the application);
- A propane handlers certificate for each person working at the proposed location.

And, at the end, the form asks for "a copy of written consent of the Business Improvement Area's Board of Directors regarding your proposed vending location." This item—which constitutes a major breach of the basic principles of administrative law, since it is akin to telling independent coffee shop operators to ask for prior permission from the Starbucks chain—reveals the quasi-feudal logic that still lurks in many municipal legal processes. Hot dog vendors are forced not only to comply with a long and complicated list of requirements imposed by the public authority, but on top of that, they have to go cap in hand to the locally powerful guild, whose response is highly unlikely to be positive.

Historical Interlude

The important role played by struggles over sidewalk commerce in the shaping of contemporary urban governance can be illuminated by considering a pair of texts, separated in time and place, that in different ways demonstrate the central role played by informal street economies—and the anxieties they have produced—in the life of great cities.[8] A quick look at these exemplary texts will serve as an interlude showing that the story of the "diversity menu" told later in the chapter is not just about hot dogs versus burritos: it is a legal tale that reveals a great deal about how cities use the regulatory tools they have.

The first text is arguably the most thorough study of street vending of all time: English journalist Henry Mayhew's years-long effort to count, describe, and classify the "street folk" of mid-Victorian London, in his multivolume work *London Labour and the London Poor.*[9] Despite Mayhew's political and cultural biases, his work sheds much light on London's thriving informal economy, and thus allows us to consider what was lost as contemporary bourgeois cities used their legal tools to repress the informal entrepreneurs of the sidewalk.

After preliminary remarks that divide humanity into two main races, settled and wandering, and compare the "wandering" street folk to a savage race threatening the very being of the settled, employed "race"—an image that sheds light on the extreme, irrational fear of the homeless that has haunted American cities for several decades now— Mayhew begins, like a good social scientist, by trying to count street vendors. The first chapter of the first volume thus opens with a section entitled "Of the Number of Costermongers and Other Street Folk."

The census of 1841 gives only 2,045 "hawkers, hucksters, and pedlars" in the
metropolis, and no costermonger or street-sellers, or street performers, at all.
This number is absurdly small, and its absurdity is accounted for by the fact
that not one in twenty of the costermongers, or of the people with whom they
lodge, troubled themselves to fill up the census returns—the majority of them
being unable to read and write, and others distrustful of the purpose for which
the returns were wanted.

Mayhew first surveys the relatively new centralized municipal food markets[10] and discovers that about twelve thousand people using temporary
stalls work in these. He then turns his gaze to the streets, and, partly by
personal observation and partly by talking with informants, he generates
estimates: "at least 500 sellers of water-cresses, 200 coffee stalls, 300 cat's-
meat men, 250 ballad singers, 200 play-bill sellers, from 800 to 1,000 bone-
grubbers and mudlarks,[11] 1,000 crossing-sweepers" . . . and so forth.

In all, he estimates that fifty thousand people, including many children,
earn their living on London's streets. And, foreshadowing today's trends,
Mayhew finds that the Victorian informal economy was characterized
by an ethnic division of labor: "the Irish fruit sellers, Jew clothesmen,
Italian organ boys, French singing women, German brass bands, Dutch
buy-a-broom girls, Highland bagpipe players, and the Indian crossing-
sweepers."

Ethnic stratification is a time-honored way to organize labor in the
absence of educational qualifications and other formal ways of sorting
workers into jobs. And from Mayhew's descriptions we gather that London's informal street economy, in the 1850s, was by no means chaotic or
disorganized. Consumer demand for goods and entertainment was met
at low cost; employment was provided for many (especially women and
children, who had few alternatives in the formal economy); and both con-
sumers and merchants enjoyed a lively and diverse street scene. Bourgeois
sensibilities were no doubt offended by the loudness of the hawkers' cries
and by the din created by street performing. Ladies and gentlemen in carriages experienced this kind of street life as an aesthetic affront and an in-
convenience—as today's car-bound enemies of panhandlers and squeegee
people do. But people who did not use carriages, and whose housing was
sufficiently uncomfortable and cold to make the street seem preferable,
seemed to very much enjoy the atmosphere. Mayhew's long interviews
with "costermongers," some reproduced almost verbatim, reveal great
poverty, much crime, and frequent incidents of violence: but at the same

time, and despite the author's intentions, they create a picture of an extremely lively community of smart and resourceful folks.

Let us now turn to late twentieth-century Manhattan for our second text. Published in 1990, this important study of street life was generated with methods that are different from Mayhew's—it is based not on conversations but on detailed, systematic observation and photographs. Its author, William H. Whyte, was, like Mayhew, a popular writer on social issues, one with a keener eye than most academics for the dynamics of street life. His photo-laden, large-format book, *City: Rediscovering the Center*,[12] supports his good friend Jane Jacobs's critique of the evils of suburban life. But while Jacobs came to praise downtown street life, Whyte came to document and measure it.

In painstaking detail, he tells his readers how exactly people use public spaces, calculating, for example, how far acquaintances who meet on the street stand from each other when talking, and how long they talk, on average. (Diagrams are helpfully provided.) He also analyzes the way in which certain architectural details promote or fail to promote street interactions, not through personal experience as Jacobs did but with mountains of observational data. (No university ethics board would now approve the surreptitious photography that gave Whyte much of his data, incidentally.)

Whyte's book tells us that hawking and peddling were still alive and well in Manhattan in the mid-twentieth century, despite the fact that it had by then become almost wholly illegal.

> Whatever the merchandise, the pitch is much the same. It's cheaper on the street. Ten dollars inside. One dollar here. Why pay more?. . . .
>
> Virtually all street vending is illegal. Under the statutes, food and merchandise vendors can be licenced, but that does not exempt them from all sorts of restrictions. Merchandise vendors are banned from the business districts; from areas zoned light commercial; from sidewalks less than twelve feet wide; from crosswalks; from bus stops; from places within ten feet of a driveway, or twenty feet from the entrance to a building. In other words, banned from almost anywhere.
>
> The police do go after the vendors. But not very hard. Cops arresting vendors is one of the standard dramas of the street. Both parties know their parts and they play them cooperatively. When a cop comes up to a vendor and pulls out his summons book, he may say, I got a complaint—that is, this is not his idea. . . . Confiscation of goods is the ultimate sanction, and the police dislike it as much as the vendors do. Periodically, the police will make a sweep, arriving

on the scene with one or more vans in which they proceed to pack the vendors' stuff. These confrontations draw a crowd—from which come boos—and newspaper publicity. And that, to the chagrin of the Fifth Avenue Association, will be that.[13]

Whyte's detailed observations confirm my own finding: namely, that the upscale businesses that push police to harass vendors and push city councils to take away licenses or pass more restrictive rules are not acting out of economic self-interest. Neither Fifth Avenue shops nor Yorkville upper-class restaurants are in danger of losing any profits to street vendors. But high-end shopping districts are always worried about maintaining their cultural distinction, their ability to charge higher prices for the privilege of consuming a whole "lifestyle," not just clothes or a meal.[14] And it is not just panhandlers and homeless people who threaten the identity, the inner essence of the bourgeois shopping district. Even the lowly hot dog of ballpark fame can look like a threat major enough to justify spending considerable political and legal energy.

The political and legal energy aimed at street vendors has a paradoxical form when it focuses on hot dog vendors. On the one hand, they can appear as a threat to gentrified urban order, as they did in the Yorkville neighborhood, and thus give rise to campaigns to make clever use of the city's regulatory tools to drive them out, along with panhandlers and skateboarders. But at the same time, the hot dog is not just any object. The hot dog is the exemplar of the pre-diversity, hygienic, monochrome culture that long characterized North American cities, before recent increases in racialized immigration. For many years, the privileging of Anglo-American cultural preferences in local law went unquestioned, and so hot dog vendors were allowed (though subject to Kafkaesque restrictions) while other kinds of food vendors were not. Given that street food, like all street vending, was bound to be regulated as a special exception to the empty-sidewalks norm, it was "common sense" to give priority to the hot dog (just as it was "common sense" to make "single-family detached" the A1 category of zoning). It is hardly surprising, therefore, that one of the consequences of the validation of ethnic "diversity" in Toronto would be a campaign to diversify street food. But those who valiantly fought to make space for more diverse food did not perhaps appreciate that the basic logic of municipal business regulation is the neo-feudal principle that every kind of trade is forbidden unless it is allowed, only for a particular space and time, through a very specific and hard-to-get permission.

The Law of the Hot Dog

A search of the *Toronto Star* going back to the 1890s using "vendor," "peddler," and "hawker" as search terms reveals that Toronto police have spent an inordinate amount of time, over the years, harassing, ticketing, or otherwise regulating street vendors.[15] In the first half of the twentieth century, when most Torontonians did not have cars, hawkers and peddlers and fruit sellers were very numerous and were tolerated despite the fact that brick-and-mortar retailers constantly complained that such vendors did not pay rent or taxes and could thus undercut them. It was only in the 1950s—when driving to the supermarket began to supersede daily shopping in one's own neighborhood—that street vending became the target of a campaign designed not so much to regulate it but to stamp it out.

The "Metro Toronto" level of government created in the mid-1950s played a key role in this suppression campaign. This was in part because the major roads—the ones on which vendors wanted to locate—were placed under Metro jurisdiction, with the first-tier municipalities responsible only for residential streets. The other change was that Metro was given responsibility for all business licensing, including vending. Given the suburban and automobile-focused culture of the Metro level of government, placing vending within Metro rather than in local municipalities meant that the on-foot shopping habits of inner-city poorer, carless communities would not be valued or taken into account by the regulators.

In 1959 Metro Toronto actually stopped giving out vending permits altogether. Legally cities cannot ban activities absolutely, as we have seen in earlier chapters; but hundreds of small would-be entrepreneurs found that their licenses were useless, since street vending licenses were valid only for particular spots, and Metro (like today's city of Toronto) was not legally compelled to make permitted spots available. In 1986 a spokesperson for the Toronto Street Vendors Association stated that there were 374 licensed vendors but only seventy legal vending spaces. The upshot of the "metropolitanization" process was that sidewalks on the major arterial roads essentially became the private property of the remote Metro authorities. Vendors could occupy a place on the sidewalk only if the spot had been specifically given to them. In keeping with the police-power-of-the-state logic of municipal sidewalk governance,[16] while certain businesses, mainly hot dog carts, are not allowed to move even one foot to get away from the sun or wind (after a 1986 amendment to the licensing bylaw), other food vendors—mainly ice cream trucks, popcorn and peanut carts, and coffee trucks serving construction sites—have to constantly move around the city: the relevant bylaw stated (and still does) that such trucks have to move every ten minutes. (There is no rationale given for either this particular number or the idea that the city has to force food trucks to move.) In Los Angeles, by contrast, hot dog carts have to move every hour. Whatever approach is chosen, the sovereign power of the city is clearly demonstrated by imposing rules that either force movement or prohibit it.

While Metro Toronto could and did use its considerable legal powers to impose draconian temporal and spatial and other conditions on the vending license, the weak legal powers of municipalities meant that relatively low fines were the only punishment that could be meted out. Not surprisingly, in the late 1980s many vendors decided that it was better to pay a fine every week than to try to get legally licensed: one vendor told the *Globe and Mail* that he paid nearly $50,000 in fines every year. Finally, in the early 1990s Ontario cities were given the powers (by the provincial parliament) to confiscate carts and merchandise. As William H. Whyte documented in New York, seizing the merchandise and the cart or truck is an extremely draconian measure, comparable to seizing factories instead of merely imposing safety-related fines, since the goods and the truck are the only capital of street vendors.

Metro Toronto disappeared in 1998 as the provincial government's forced amalgamation created the "megacity." Business licensing—including the licensing of such places as hair salons and massage parlors, not just street vendors—was not significantly affected, since unlike most other functions it had already been under Metro. The fact that the licensing bylaw was one of the few that did not have to be completely redrafted may be one reason why the existing dysfunctional system continued on without any official or public discussion about potential reforms: there were too many other pressing governance problems.

A key feature of the food-vendor licensing system that had developed over the postwar period and that was left intact by the 1998 amalgamation was the compulsory hot dog rule. How can a food choice be made compulsory, one might well ask? The answer lies not so much in the content of municipal rules but in the legal form used.

The rules that had developed during the fifty-year life of the Metro Toronto jurisdiction did not take the criminal-law approach, which would have involved banning dangerous or unsafe products and practices. Instead, the legal form of the licensing department's rules is the same as the legal form used for zoning law. Both departments devise highly specific rules allowing selected activities to be conducted, while leaving everything else in the realm of illegality. Thus, as in feudal times, whatever is not specifically allowed is forbidden. This is not unique to street vending or to Toronto; it is rather a symptom of the pre-liberal or illiberal character of the legal form of the license. When printers needed a royal license to publish books and newspapers, as they did in absolutist monarchies, the press was not free, and neither was the press-reading public. So too, street food is not governed through the liberal principles of individual autonomy, least restrictive regulation, and market self-governance. On the contrary, anything that is sold on the street requires a specific set of state permissions. Some restrictions apply to the person selling (who may have to have a personal license), some to the bit of sidewalk used, which needs to be assigned to the vendor and cannot be used by another vendor at other times, and some apply to the commodity being sold. And in keeping with the "everything that is not specifically allowed is prohibited" logic of the police power of the state, the law stated, until well into the twenty-first century, that all street food was illegal, with one exception: "The only exception is hot dog carts that re-heat a 'pre-cooked meat product in the form of wieners or similar sausage products served on a bun.'"[17]

In the years-long campaign to reform the hot dog exception in order to provide Torontonians with healthier and more "diverse" food, no activist or journalist was ever able to determine who had first decided that "precooked meats in the form of wieners or similar sausage products" should be the only food available from temporary carts. (A few "mobile preparation premises," essentially restaurants on wheels, are allowed, but there are very few legal spots for them to sell their wares.) As I tried to get to the bottom of the compulsory hot dog rule, one public health employee told me that hamburgers would be riskier from the public health point of view. But when asked why products without any meat, risky or otherwise, such as falafels, could not be sold on the street, he simply shrugged, and added that in any case the hot dog rule was provincial, not municipal, and so the provincial parliament would have to change it (as it later did).

One hot dog vendor told me that police officers regularly check one of the conditions of the hot dog cart license; namely, that the hot dogs being sold are precooked and frozen, and are heated on the grill only for taste and color. The condiments, by contrast, seem to draw little attention—perhaps because officers and municipal inspectors do not know that in addition to the provincial compulsory precooked hot dog rule, the city's health department has rules banning mayonnaise and "squeezable cheese." Thus, despite the rules, these and even more inventive condiments are found in many carts. The vendor commented that because there is no variety in the sausages and hot dogs sold, since everyone gets the frozen Italian sausages and frozen hot dogs from the same wholesalers, vendors have to use condiments to increase their market share. The proliferation of obscure condiments creates health risks of its own (or could, if the mayo and cheese were real mayo and real cheese). But in this area, as in the planning law "in action," there is no feedback mechanism through which the creative experiments and evasions of law devised by ordinary citizens and frontline staff faced with antiquated and inefficient rules could be fed back into the policy process.

The Politics of Street Food

In early 2007, a group of young activists launched the "Street Food Vending Project," the first serious, sustained challenge to the compulsory hot dog rule. "Diversity" was a key word in this project's self-description:

> The Street Food Vending project aims to introduce tasty, affordable, healthy, culturally diverse and locally sourced food to Toronto's streets. We will attempt to change current health regulations that limit Toronto's street food to pre-cooked meat on a bun. We'll work to build partnerships between vendors and local farmers, gardeners and kitchens. We'll attempt to reform licensing and permitting regulations to bring street food to neighbourhoods across the City, including those without access to healthy and affordable food.
>
> We'll listen to the experiences of vendors and help them identify possible employment and training opportunities. We will listen to vendor advocates, food security advocates, restaurants, planners, designers, City divisions, and social service organizations in an effort to break down disciplinary silos and encourage innovative solutions to Toronto's vending culture.
>
> Our work will culminate with a street food vending cart pilot project that will be featured in Alphabet City's Food Festival in October 2007.
>
> Why are we doing this? Because we're hungry for better street food. And we want to show that everyday issues and spaces, like street vending and vending carts, are important elements of city life and urban planning.[18]

As the reference to breaking down disciplinary silos suggests, the leaders of this project had many more years of education than the average hot dog vendor (and much better command of English). But they worked hard to talk with vendors and learn from their experiences. More important, the official leader of the hot dog vendors, who was, unusually for the business, a woman, and Canadian-born, continued to work with this group and its fragments for several years. The food-vending activism was thus a rare instance of young urban planning students, cultural workers, and marginal entrepreneurs working together.

In its first year the group spent much time lobbying the councillors responsible for public health rules, so that the city would push the province to legally dethrone the precooked "wieners and similar sausage products." After much positive publicity by the powerful local newspaper, the *Toronto Star*, including a story with the headline "Putting diversity on the menu,"[19] the group met with success. Councillor John Filion, chair of the public health committee of the council, agreed to lobby the province to change the hot dog rule, which, predictably, the province did.

The grassroots group also pursued a parallel strategy aimed at changing the material conditions of street vending. Knowing that even if a variety of foods were legalized, the city would want to micromanage the food carts, the group worked with university instructors to run a competition in which industrial-design students would be given awards for the best street-food vending-cart design. Not wanting to encourage students to openly flout the still prevalent hot dog law, the activists laid out the goals of the competition in careful language that, in a perhaps typically Torontonian manner, managed to uphold the law and challenge it at the same time:

1. Provide a mobile premises to prepare and serve street food;
2. Support the sale of street food that is healthy, affordable and reflective of Toronto's diverse populations;
3. Consider the City of Toronto's vending regulations (licensing, permitting, and health). *Note: you do not need to strictly abide by these regulations. For example, health regulations only permit the sale of hot dogs but we encourage you to consider other foods.* (Italics in original)[20]

In May 2007, two complementary public meetings were held at Ryerson University, at which very tasty and healthy cooked snacks were served, by "ethnic" entrepreneurs hoping to benefit from the campaign. At the first meeting, a design professor explained the vending-cart design competition to the forty or so people present, but most of the meeting was devoted to a discussion of the laws and rules. At the second meeting, two licensing officials spoke to explain the rules and their enforcement. But the speaker who spoke the longest and with the most enthusiasm for his job was a manager from the Public Health Department, a well-meaning, well-educated Anglo gentleman who seemed oblivious to the practical and financial limitations that precarious microbusinesses face. The public health manager assumed that street food should be discussed only from the point of view of health risks.

As he spoke at length about food handling certificates and temperature control, it slowly dawned on the audience that the Public Health Department would never allow the kind of home-cooked snacks that we were enjoying as we listened to the speeches. The department was unlikely to budge from its position that any food sold on streets (other than pre-cooked wieners and sausages, of course) must come from kitchens that were already inspected by them—that is, restaurant or institutional kitchens. When asked to clarify whether this was indeed the case, by a speaker suddenly upset to hear that the meeting organizers' vision of new immigrants using the food-vending program to establish themselves was going up in smoke, the official stated that existing restaurants would not quite have a monopoly, since some noncommercial kitchens (e.g., those preparing "meals on wheels') were already approved to make cooked food as well. But he remained deaf (and blind, given the home-cooked food being served around the room as he spoke) to the criticism that empowering existing restaurants to make more profits was not what the organizers of the campaign had in mind.

The same official was interviewed at length by a *Toronto Star* reporter. The article included a large photo showing a traditional hot dog, on one side, and a delicious-looking dish served on a coconut shell, on the other side, over the forty-two-point headline WHICH ONE DO YOU THINK IS HAZARDOUS?[21] The health official in question, clearly on the defensive due to the wide support garnered by the "putting diversity on the menu" campaign,[22] explained that hot dogs are not the only food vendors can sell. "Prepackaged granola bars," he said, would be fine, as would "prepackaged bran muffins." However, butter could not be provided to improve the taste of the packaged muffin, he added, given that "a muffin by itself won't support bacterial growth from the point of view of pathogens," but "if you take a muffin and you want to put butter on the muffin, butter is a hazardous food."

Obsessed with pathogens, the manager remained oblivious to the reporter's polite criticisms. As a great concession, when asked whether apples could perhaps be sold by hot dog vendors, he graciously agreed that perhaps apples might not be a "hazardous product" to sell on the sidewalk.

Particularly relevant from the sociolegal point of view was the fact that the manager explained that contrary to what one might think from reading the text of the bylaw governing "mobile food premises," a cart, he said, is *not* a mobile food premise. "Premises," in Public Health's view, can only mean "a building or vehicle with four walls and a roof." A cart, selling hot dogs or other things, is "outdoors," he said. The polite reporter did not point out that "outdoors" is not generally provided with a freezer, a cooler, and a gas grill, all mandatory components of hot dog carts.

In any event, the city's request for an amendment to the provincial public health legislation was successful, and it was passed on August 1, 2007. But it quickly became apparent that neither city bureaucrats nor city councillors had any intention of letting "ethnic" gastronomic micro-enterprises flourish on Toronto's sidewalks and public squares. Instead, the many would-be vendors attracted by the newspaper's campaign became the victims of a long and tortuous politico-legal process. The upshot of this was the imposition of a welter of regulations that made the previous compulsory hot dog rules look reasonable.

For example, potential vendors had to promise to staff their food carts themselves 70 percent of the time, a highly impractical regulation, especially if vendors had any notion of being involved in shopping for ingredients and cooking the food. This regulation (which does not apply to existing hot dog carts) was not justified in any public venue. It may be that the idea was simply borrowed from rules applying to the newer category of taxi license, the "Ambassador" plate, which is given only on the condition that the licensee himself drive the cab, since the same bureaucrats who govern hot dog carts also govern taxi licenses. But be that as it may, the inappropriateness of the sole-proprietor rule was then compounded by the fact that since Public Health would not allow the public sale of any food cooked in one's home, however clean and sanitized, the potential vendors had to be either owners or employees of an already-approved restaurant or institutional kitchen—that is, precisely *not* the independent self-employed entrepreneurs imagined by the reformers.

While the licensing and permitting bureaucracy took the province's repeal of the hot dog rule as an opportunity to begin micromanaging the economic and legal conditions of the future providers of Toronto's "diversity menu," the city council, on its part, also undertook its own micromanaging campaign—aimed not at the licensees, however, but at the actual carts. During these council discussions, much time was spent debating whether the city should put in an order with a manufacturer, buy a number of carts, and lease them to vendors—or whether the city should instead require vendors to order and purchase carts on their own, but to the city's specifications. Vendors and potential vendors were not given a voice in these discussions (as far as the public record reveals, at any rate). Against the grain of current neoliberal governance trends, the council initially decided to "municipalize" the (as yet unbuilt) food carts; but in the end the decision was taken to provide the specifications but not the actual carts, which had to be ordered and bought by would-be vendors at a cost of between $15,000 and $28,000.[23]

As any experienced hot dog vendor could have predicted, city councillors' foray into industrial design combined with the bureaucrats' financially unrealistic rules to create a completely unworkable governance system. The "diversity menu" campaign drew large numbers of interested would-be entrepreneurs, probably because the *Toronto Star* had given the campaign much favorable publicity for a long period of time; but as we shall see momentarily, the unworkable system drove most of the few entrepreneurs who survived the long and expensive process into financial ruin.

In January 2009, the city announced that anyone wanting to apply for a license had to first attend one of two mandatory "information sessions" (a requirement not demanded of any other entrepreneur, to my knowledge). About two hundred people in total attended these sessions. However, most of these went away discouraged due to the high price of the carts and to the fact that the city informed them that it would additionally impose a "location cost" of between $5,000 and $15,000 (a figure comparable to the price of a permit for the hot dog carts located in the most lucrative locations). As if that were not enough, the license fee (which as explained earlier, is not the same as the permit for a particular space) would be $375.61 per year, higher than most business licenses, which typically run closer to $100 per year. In addition, all potential vendors had to cook up some food items, serve them to an official committee, wait to see if their food was approved, and then elaborate a very small menu with nothing but preapproved items. If something proved unpopular, the vendors would not be able to do what restaurants do, that is, change the menu.

When asked by the *Star* if the regulations were excessive and impractical, the head of the project, Yvonne de Wit, associate director of Toronto Public Health, said, "Regulations are in place in order to err on the side of caution. . . . We're being very cautious because we're dealing with health. We're dealing with food safety. . . . If things go well, those regulations may increase. Or they may decrease."

It was clear to everyone except the bureaucrats and the councillors that the risks that would make the program sink rather than swim were not pathogens but rather unrealistic financial and regulatory requirements. Very high license fees, very little freedom in choosing profitable locations, expensive carts, and the paternalistic demand about having all food items approved in advance by a committee added up to complete regulatory failure. Eight carts were eventually put on assigned bits of sidewalk, but few of them were able to make enough money to pay the licensing and other fees and the financing costs. And as one could have predicted, the carts did not work well, since, due to the absence of vendor input, they were not properly designed. The program, baptized "A la Cart," was abandoned officially in 2011. The handful of survivors (eight) were given financial breaks by the city and were allowed to keep their locations (perhaps out of pity, or perhaps for fear of a lawsuit), but they were told to remove the "A la Cart" name and logo. The city's experiment with municipal control over diverse food had come to an end.

The story of an "ethnic-food" entrepreneur couple, who survived to tell the tale, will here illustrate the predictable failure of the city's long-desired "Toronto a la Cart" program.

Blair and Kathy Bonavento sold Greek souvlaki in front of Nathan Phillips Square as part of Toronto a la Cart, a three-year pilot project that began in May. The couple kept the cart going for a little over a month. Eventually they shut down, saying their allotted location—at the west end of a long line of hot dog carts and chip trucks—wasn't viable and they weren't making enough money.

Since then, they've spent weeks wrangling with the city hoping for a new location, but in vain. . . . As one of eight vendors accepted into the project, the Bonaventos had to buy a cart built to the city's specifications, buy a cube truck to transport it and fork out $15,000 for the right to use the spot, among other expenses. All told, they say, they sank $80,000 into it. And their sales? Only $100 to $150 per day . . .

Heavy regulations were a major problem. Unlike nearby hot dog vendors, they were limited to just one drink cooler and couldn't use a generator to power the cart's fridge. The cart also lacked a covering to keep off sun and rain, causing an employee to quit. . . .

The project has long been criticized as over-regulated. The city tried to create a uniform brand by having custom carts built and submitting would-be vendors to a taste test by a panel of judges. Some argued the city should simply set parameters and let vendors set up the business for themselves.

"This is micromanagement and this is bad business," said Marianne Moroney, who heads an association representing 100 of the city's hot dog vendors. "Good business ideas never come from the city."[24]

That "good business ideas" were needed to have the diversity menu become reality, and that neither bureaucrats in the licensing department nor city councillors generated such ideas, is hardly a surprising finding. But the story of the city's failure to truly "put diversity on the menu" does not merely tell us what we already know from previous chapters about both bureaucrats and politicians. It also sheds new light on an old, indeed ancient, sociolegal question that rarely comes to the fore in policy debates but which undergirds the collection of stories told in this chapter: the way in which intrusive, antieconomic and paternalistic regulations are not only tolerated but also expected at the municipal scale of governance, even as they are disappearing from higher levels of government.

In the concluding section, therefore, we will turn away from the tragicomic story of Toronto's vendors and focus instead on broader questions that concern the legal "essence" of municipal governance, namely, the municipal corporation.

Licenses and Permits: The Legal Logic of the Municipal Corporation

Criminal jurisdiction is jealously guarded by "higher" levels of government; nevertheless, it is well known both to city officials and to legal scholars that municipalities can and do prohibit, and punish, a whole range of behaviors and activities. In general, prohibitions aimed at individuals— rather than at businesses or at buildings—are not absolute, since then they would be criminal or quasi-criminal laws. Instead, the rules are space-specific or time-specific, or both. Thus, municipalities in both Canada and the United States cannot, by law, prohibit all panhandling, since that would infringe on "real" criminal codes. They can only regulate panhandling by specifying the time, place, and manner. Of course, cities can limit the time and space of panhandling or sleeping outdoors so much as to almost ban it;[25] but it is nevertheless important to note that absolute bans are not within cities' legal powers. The same goes for food vending. A total ban on any and all food carts could be challenged in court as a breach of the right of people to make a livelihood, especially people who have had licenses in the past; but cities can and do impose complex and unworkable rules about time, space, and manner.

Since municipalities have been forced by higher courts to leave some public spaces public at least some of the time, politicians and city officials and lawyers who share the ancient middle-class fear of disorderly streets and informal-economy entrepreneurs are constantly coming up with regulatory inventions that not only spatially isolate but also stigmatize and punish "undesirables." The existence of this welter of rules, taken as a whole, conveys the message that spaces that are notionally public—in that the public paid for their creation and upkeep, as well as in the sense that they are open to the public, without admission—are actually the private property of municipal officials, who decide who can go where and when, doing what.

Municipal rules that greatly restrict the use of public spaces have received much critical attention from urban scholars, criminologists, and others. But by and large this critical literature ignores the specific legal forms that municipalities use. The phrase "criminalization of the poor," while politically useful, obscures the very important differences between criminalizing certain acts absolutely, on the one hand, and oppressing people by limiting the time, space, and manner of their conduct, on the other. The literature also tends to assume that residents of a city are divided into two groups—the marginal, who are hounded out of public spaces, and the respectable "public," on the other. But while municipal regulations bear down more coercively on some people at some times, the city is not divided into two opposing camps. The hot dog and souvlaki vendors featured in this chapter are not "outlaws." And there are countless small-business people who, while rarely encountering the extremes of micro-management documented here, are regularly treated as if we still lived in a feudal society, where carrying on a trade required the explicit permission of the local lord. Opening a restaurant, just to name one example, requires seven different and uncoordinated permission processes.

Hendrik Hartog's brilliant book on the legal history of the municipal corporation of New York City is a source that can help us understand municipalities' penchant for acting as if small-time capitalism is suspect and should only be carried on after obtaining a series of permits and licenses.

As Hartog highlights, the municipal corporation of the early modern period (an early experiment in legal forms of collective personhood that would much later give us the limited-liability company) was not an off-the-shelf legal entity. On the contrary, the essence of each corporation lay in the specific details set out in its charter—the "privileges," as the telling phrase went, of that particular corporate body. Thus, Albany was through its city charter given monopoly control over the fur trade, whereas New York's charter gave that city control over the harbor and ferries across the Hudson.

But in the eighteenth century (as is the case still today), the municipal corporation was not only a public authority with sovereign-granted power to make rules. It was also, and perhaps more importantly, an economic entity, a true corporation with properties and revenues. And each municipal corporation had its own portfolio of real estate and other sources of income. Over time, however, judges and state legislators became suspicious of the economic and regulatory power of municipal corporations. Speaking in the name of private citizens' property rights, courts succeeded in creating a more or less uniform body of law—the law of municipal corporations—that undercut the economic power of the wealthy municipal corporations that had developed in major commercial trading centers. This body of law, as Hartog points out, insists on treating New York City as if it were the same, for legal purposes, as the smallest rural municipality.[26]

In English Canada, some colonial cities were given charters with specific clauses, as was the case in the thirteen colonies; but Toronto, incorporated only in 1834, arrived too late on the historical stage to be eligible for a charter. To make a long story short, the law of municipal corporations described by Hartog was established more uniformly and quickly in Upper Canada (later Ontario) than in New York. And while some accoutrements of the medieval corporations of guild masters still exist (the mayor's golden chain of office, for example), nevertheless, city government in our era acts mainly as a conduit to deliver services dictated by higher levels of government—that is, as a subordinate public authority, rather than as a corporation with both public and private aspects.[27] And the city of Toronto's legal powers are virtually the same as those of the smallest of Northern Ontario towns.[28]

What does all of this have to do with the legal techniques used to manage public space, and specifically with the story of street-food vending? The answer has to remain somewhat speculative, given the absence of a literature on the legal history of licenses and permits. But existing work on the legal history of municipal corporations in England and the United

States suggests that there are deep historical roots that help to explain the origins of the city governments' apparent obsession with micromanaging who can sell food on the street, where exactly they should stand, with what accoutrements, for how long, and under what economic conditions.

Licensing is one of the oldest—and least researched—functions of local government. While recent legal developments in administrative law have changed how licensing is done—for example, the standard "good moral character" traditionally demanded of licensees would no longer be deemed constitutional in most jurisdictions—nevertheless, the way in which licenses govern people and spaces has not substantially changed over the centuries. Licensing used to apply to virtually everything. In medieval times a town council or other local authority (e.g., a feudal court) might decide to allow a market to be held outside the church on certain feast days, for instance, with all commerce that was not specifically licensed being prohibited. And peddlers who went from market to market and from farm to farm were required to have a license—just like every other kind of business (except for publishers, usually controlled and licensed by the monarch, given the sensitivity of political publishing). Commerce was not free; and municipal corporations and other local authorities were the essential commercial regulatory authorities, for many centuries.[29] Local bodies, whether judicial or legislative, even set the price of essential commodities such as bread. But at the same time that it acted as a key regulator of commerce (at a time when the default setting for commerce was regulation rather than freedom), the municipal corporation, particularly in large commercial cities, also acted as an economic actor in its own right, carrying on business and seeking to augment revenues by various means, including charging rents and levying fees and tolls.

The private aspect of the municipal corporation as described by Hartog is still visible in the way in which the city of Toronto handles the management of street life. A counterexample might help to illustrate the point. The city of Portland, Oregon, broke with the traditional approach to street-food vending when it decided to let vendors rent space from private owners (e.g., owners of parking lots), rather than insisting that food vending be allowed only on licensed and permitted municipal space (namely sidewalks). Giving up the city's monopoly on space devoted to outdoor food vending, thus leaving food carts to be regulated only by public health authorities and not by any licensing body, has reportedly created a real boom in interesting, "diverse" street food, with vendors and their customers using Twitter to report where the best tacos are being sold, in real time.[30]

But in the Toronto context no vendor seems to have thought about approaching a private owner with a parking lot or other underused property adjacent to the sidewalk. Economically marginal microbusinesses attempted to use public spaces *as* public spaces, and the activists that supported them thought of their project as reforming the rules for the use of public space; privatization was not in their vocabulary. But any business that is conducted on city-owned rather than private property can be saddled with the kinds of detailed rules and ordinances that characterized medieval markets. In the municipal regulation of street-based businesses, everything that is not compulsory is prohibited: a pre-liberal, premodern logic of governance that is more reminiscent of absolute monarchies than of modern democracy.

CHAPTER 7

Driving a Taxi

City Fathers' Myth of Immigrant Self-Employment

In many cities in North America, taxi driving is one of the few occupations open to certain groups of recently arrived male immigrants. In Toronto, the Bangladeshi or Somali doctor who drives a cab because his credentials have not been recognized is a local cliché; but as a matter of fact, I have often met taxi drivers who had indeed been professors or engineers back home.[1]

The economics of the industry, the regulatory structure, and the demographics of the taxi-driving population differ in their details from city to city: but there are many commonalities. The most important economic fact about the industry is that those who do the bulk of the driving rarely own the most valuable means of production in the taxi business, which is the municipal license to operate a taxi (called a "plate" in Toronto and a "medallion" in Chicago and New York). The second crucial fact is that, unlike in occupations such as construction, kitchen work, and cleaning (sectors employing large numbers of recent immigrants), taxi drivers are not paid an hourly wage. Instead, most drivers rent the plate for a fixed amount of money, by the day, the week, or the month. They first have to pay the plate rent, then they pay for gas and insurance, and keep the rest—an amount that varies a great deal but that compares unfavorably to minimum wage jobs. The financial structure means that drivers have a very strong incentive to break speed limits and other traffic rules, since the more fares they squeeze into a given day, the more money they can keep for themselves. Owner-drivers also have a strong incentive to work extra hours, given that vehicle and licensing costs are fixed; but drivers who have to first work several hours just to pay for the plate rental are more strongly driven to break traffic laws and to work past the point of fatigue.

Since taxi drivers are not considered employees, even when a corporation rather than an individual owns the plate and/or the vehicle, twelve-hour shifts, abolished in both blue-collar and white-collar formal employment for over a century now, are the industry standard, in Toronto as in other major cities. Provisions for sick leave and pensions are similarly unknown (although drivers of yellow "medallion" taxis in New York City do have a workers' compensation plan).

Drivers enter the low end of the industry hoping to eventually acquire a plate. The dream of acquiring capital in the form of a plate resonates very well with the more general immigrant dream of founding a business in a new country—and it also fits perfectly with city politicians and bureaucrats' self-flattering image of North American cities as open and free societies in which hard work pays off even if one is a newcomer with no contacts. Indeed, the taxi business is more than a business. In urban North America, the taxi business works also as a cultural arena in which immigrants' often unrealistic dreams about prosperity in North America converge, in a dysfunctional manner, with the equally mythical North American cities' own narrative of New World cities as sites in which immigrants can go from rags to riches in one generation.

The facts give the lie to the rags-to-riches immigration story. Researchers familiar with the political economy of immigrant-attracting cities in the age of global capital flows and finance-driven capitalism will not be surprised to hear that investors, only some of whom are former drivers, have found ways to buy significant numbers of plates, sometimes creating oligopolies. Since North American cities generally limit the total number of plates—unlike in London, where a license to drive one of the famous "black cabs" can be acquired by anyone who passes the difficult "knowledge" test, with numbers being regulated only by the marketplace—most drivers' dream of owning one or two plates and thus ensuring a decent retirement never comes true.

The most notorious example of taxi capitalism is Chicago's Symon Garber (a friend of Mayor Daley's son Patrick Daley). He owns over eight hundred medallions and, as if that capital were not sufficient, he has found a way to charge his drivers much higher rates for leasing his cars than those set by city taxi regulators.[2] But even without close links to individual politicians, taxi capitalism is alive and well, in Toronto as elsewhere, despite the city's official story of taxi driving as a stronghold of self-employed immigrant entrepreneurialism. This chapter will show that driving a taxi is not, for most people, the first chapter of a story of rags-to-riches upward mobility. On the contrary, the taxi business is a good example of what has happened as the blue-collar industrial cities of the mid-twentieth century fade into the historical mist and are replaced (sometimes in the same space, as in Toronto's case) by highly unequal urban workforces in which select groups of well-paid professionals and managers provide precarious, badly paid, un-unionized work for the tens of thousands of Filipino nannies, Somali taxi drivers, Chinese restaurant workers, and Latin American construction workers whose unsung work make successful financial centers like Toronto possible.[3]

This chapter is divided into two parts. First we will examine the dysfunctional two-tier taxi licensing system that Toronto has had since 1998 and that New York City has considered as a potential option for the taxi capital of North America, Manhattan. The system is analyzed not as an economist or a labor sociologist might do it, that is in terms of capital and labor, but rather by looking at the delicate interplay between legal structures and legal rules, on the one hand, and social and cultural processes and assumptions, on the other. The figure of the self-made immigrant entrepreneur (whose power, like the power of mythical figures generally, is by no means diminished by proof that it is statistically unusual) turns out to be the key to understanding why a contradictory and irrational taxi licensing system continues to creak along, with no hope of radical reform visible on the horizon despite the presence (in Toronto) of a major legal challenge.[4]

The second part will shift gears. Turning away from regulatory architecture, it will focus instead on face-to-face interactions at Toronto's licensing tribunal—the quasi-judicial body before which taxi drivers challenging their loss or denial of the municipal taxi license appear. This microlevel study of a quasi court reveals that ethnocentric (specifically, Christian-centric and common-law-centric) assumptions about what it is to make a successful appearance "before the law" pervade a municipal legal body set up by the city that touts itself as "the world's most diverse city." Confessing one's errors and legal misdeeds and showing remorse in classic Christian manner work very well for errant drivers seeking reinstatement, my observational study reveals; but this assumption is not part of the formal rules published in the *Statutory Powers Procedure Act* (the procedural bible for Ontario administrative tribunals) or any other text, and so it has not been challenged, whereas the racial stratification of the taxi labor force has been under scrutiny at the Ontario Human Rights Tribunal.

Observation and interview research at the tribunal shows that the profound cultural gap separating the Canadian tribunal members from the recent immigrants from countries with very different legal traditions who appear before the tribunal results in a dialogue-of-the-deaf situation. Drivers offer what they believe is evidence of worthiness, only to find that their legal-moral currency is not worth anything and can even count against them. That a city seeking to be a diversity-loving "hub of humanity" might need to think about the substance of law and regulation as well as about the cultural presuppositions of everyday bureaucratic and legal interactions is a conclusion that applies not only to Toronto but also to all of today's metropolitan, demographically diverse cities.[5]

The Self-Made Immigrant Entrepreneur Ideal as the City's "Social Shock Absorber"

Asafo Addai is a Toronto African immigrant who drives for himself. He owns one of the two thousand or so "Ambassador" license plates that the city began issuing in 1998. In January 2010, lawyer Peter Rosenthal, a retired University of Toronto math professor who became an activist lawyer late in life, launched a complaint at the Ontario Human Rights Tribunal on behalf of Addai and his fellow Ambassador cabbies. The basis of the complaint was that the two-tier system comprised of (a) "standard" plates that can be owned by corporations or absentee owners and leased, and (b) Ambassador plates, which cannot be leased or traded, has systemic racist effects. Rosenthal did not argue that there was deliberate discrimination (and indeed such a claim would not have been well founded). He made the more subtle argument that the system had differential effects that amounted to systemic discrimination: the vast majority of the Ambassador plate owners are relatively recent immigrant men from racialized minority groups, whereas the vast majority of standard plates belong to nonracialized people.[6] (It should be explained that under Canadian human rights law, it is possible, though not easy, to win cases purely through evidence—usually provided by social scientists—of systemic discriminatory effects on historically disadvantaged groups; one does not have to prove that the legislators or the bureaucrats implementing the law or policy intended to discriminate or even knew that discrimination was happening, structurally.)

The tribunal began to grapple with the evidentiary issues five months later, in late June. The city licensing department (Municipal Licensing and

Standards, MLS) was asked whether it could reproduce drivers' license photos from its computer system, which was the only available evidence of the racial composition of the different taxi license categories.

A whole year later, in early June 2011, the hearing continued. The city lawyer, forced by his position to defend the existing bylaw, had tried to argue that race cannot be determined merely by looking at license photos. The legal process was stuck because the city and the complainant had not been able to agree on what kind of expert should be given the job of determining race from the pictures. The adjudicator thus decided to sideline expertise altogether and take the matter into her own hands: "I did not have any difficulty in determining that there was a preponderance of racialized men in the Ambassador program," she stated at the resumed hearing.[7]

The preponderance of "racialized" people (the locally politically correct term for the groups that government discourse still calls "visible minorities") may not be sufficient to prove that there was illegal discrimination. As is the case elsewhere, in Toronto there are numerous occupations, including many licensed by the city, with very marked concentrations of a small number of ethnic groups. The result of the hearing is not a foregone conclusion, therefore. But the human rights complaint, whatever its ultimate fate, is important in that it involved several institutions in issues that were historically of interest only to the taxi industry itself and to perhaps one city councillor. In addition, the complaint was more than an individual person's quest for justice: the resumption of the hearing in June 2011 was accompanied by a street protest in which cabs blocked the road, and a delegation of Ambassador cabbies with heartrending stories appeared at a meeting of the licensing committee of the city council.

Why did city authorities design the two-tier system in the first place? What kind of image of the immigrant cabbies, and of themselves as leaders of a diversity-loving city, were they operating with?

The Ambassador plate was introduced with great fanfare in 1998 as a regulatory invention designed first and foremost to improve passenger experience. There had been numerous complaints about dirty and badly maintained cabs, about surly drivers who did not seem to know the city, and so forth. The Ambassador program was thus at one level a tourism-promotion initiative to improve both customer service and the image of the city. Ambassador drivers have to take extra training, and their cabs are subject to more strict mechanical and cleanliness standards than the "regular" ones. The second and equally important goal of the program, however, was said to be to enable drivers, who by the late 1990s were overwhelmingly new immigrants from Africa, the Middle East, or South Asia, to achieve the dream of plate ownership.

Initially, city leaders wanted to simply abolish the existing plates and start all over again, essentially expropriating the plate owners and forcing them to lease the plates back from the city. Councillor Howard Moscoe, a more or less left-wing councillor who was for a long time the city's licensing czar, explained: "At the time [1998], we wanted to return the industry to the people who drove the vehicles."[8] But municipal nationalization was nixed by the city's legal department, no doubt out of fear that the plate owners would sue the city and win. Councillor Moscoe thus resorted to a badly thought-out Plan B. This involved leaving the legally protected standard plates alone, but freezing their number indefinitely, and passing a new regulation that prevented existing plates from being bought up by anyone other than those with cab-driving experience.

The old plates, it was thought, would eventually pass into the hands of actual drivers as the old owners died. However, a loophole in the rules allows the sale and purchase of the *corporations* that own standard plates, often in some numbers. This loophole is likely responsible for the fact that in 2008 the number of standard plates was almost the same as it had been in 1998 (about 3,500).

Understanding how standard plates work requires some explanation about lease arrangements. A few older cabbies own a standard plate and drive themselves part of the time, but for the most part the standard plates are leased. Leasing a plate can be done directly, through a private transaction between plate owner and driver, but often it is done by means of an "agent" or broker who acts on behalf of plate owners, finds drivers, collects money from them, and looks after maintenance and licensing. Drivers who work for owners directly make a little more money than those who work for a middleman, not surprisingly. But all drivers who do not own plates work in astoundingly poor conditions: an independent study carried out in 2008 showed that they work around seventy-seven hours per week for around $3 an hour.[9] Drivers who do not own plates have to lease the plate (at an average cost, in 2008, of $1,150 per month) and have to pay for the gas, which means that they have to work several hours just to break even. During rain or snowstorms they can make a decent wage; but there are many "dead" times in most weeks of the year—hence the low income, and the built-in incentive to work inhumanly long hours.

While this exploitative system created by the standard plate and the associated lease arrangements was decried by every city politician back in 1998, when the reforms were made, the system has continued, largely unabated. The nondisappearance of the standard plates should not have come as a surprise to Councillor Moscoe and his colleagues: clearly, if one has capital worth around $250,000, a price often quoted in discussions of these plates, there's a strong incentive to set oneself up as a corporation and thus pass the capital on to one's children, who will then work through a broker to ensure a maximum profit from the inherited plate.

But in 1998 city leaders imagined that over time ownership would indeed pass into the hands of the workers, that is, the drivers. With the exception of special plates for vehicles adapted for wheelchairs, all new plates were to be awarded under the new "Ambassador" category, which forbids leasing or renting the plate to other drivers, and furthermore forbids the sale of the plate on the open market (even in the event of long-term disability or death). The new system thus instituted a very rigid system of self-employment—but one applying only to the newer, second-tier, largely racialized taxi drivers, who were told they could never aspire to owning the much more lucrative standard plate.

The inescapable conclusion is that about fifteen hundred "new Canadian" Torontonians (or more, if one assumes, as is only reasonable, that many of the Ambassador taxis are not in fact staying parked while their owners rest, whatever the law says) are stuck in a situation in which the regulations prevent them from hiring someone to work while they're resting, which, given current fares and gas prices, is the only way they could build up enough of a nest egg to retire.

But when confronted with these data, city officials always fall back on the good intentions of the 1998 reform, as if good intentions sufficed to justify policies. They also speak as if there is something intrinsically wrong with Ambassador cabbies' wish to become capitalists rather than self-employed struggling entrepreneurs. At a meeting of the licensing committee of the council in June 2011, Councillor Glenn De Baeremaeker (who often votes with the left wing of the council) stated that they (Ambassador cabbies) "have legitimate complaints, but if the only thing is these guys are angry because they can't rent out their licence and exploit other people, then our job is very simple: keep the system the way it is. They were never promised lottery winnings." In a city full of bank and other corporate head offices, it seems a little peculiar to hear a councillor speak about cabbies' desire to hire a single solitary second driver described as a plot to "exploit other people."

But the mythical figure of the self-employed immigrant who somehow prospers on the streets of New World cities, despite being surrounded by transnational corporate capital, lives on. At the same city council committee meeting, similar feelings were voiced by Councillor Denzil Minnan-Wong. Minnan-Wong is right wing, and so doesn't speak about banning exploitation or about workers owning the means of production as Councillor Moscoe used to do; but the result is the same: "What they want," he said, "what they want—it's like the city writing them a cheque for $300,000 overnight."[10] Three hundred thousand dollars is on the high end of current estimates of the cost of a standard plate, but whatever the actual figure— and of course the price would drop sharply if the Ambassador plates were all turned into regular plates—it is odd that a councillor should imagine that if the city removes an unfair regulatory barrier, that amounts to writing someone a check.

And it is not the case that taxi driving would be left unregulated if the Ambassador system were repealed. First of all, all would-be drivers and owners have to sign up for a three-week compulsory training course (costing $590), for which there is a monthlong waiting list. This course demands daily attendance and subjects drivers to two quizzes per week, plus a final exam, and only a 70 percent grade is acceptable. Just to make things more difficult, one has to go in person to a city office in a location not on a subway line to register for this course. One has to also pass a first aid and CPR course, and obtain a medical certificate to the effect that one is fit to drive a taxi, all at one's own expense. Then, if one owns the vehicle (rather than leasing it along with the plate), one has to pay about $3,800 per year to the city by way of a license fee. (New York City has similar testing requirements. However, in keeping with American custom, a drug test and fingerprinting are also demanded of would-be drivers.) There is a new requirement for standard plate owners to have three years' driving experience; but presumably this does not apply to the corporations that own the plates.

On top of the standard requirements imposed on all Toronto drivers and current owners, would-be future owners of Ambassador plates have to take an extra course. The idea is that these drivers will be particularly knowledgeable about city attractions, hotels, and so forth—that they will indeed act as "ambassadors," not as mere drivers. But given that the city has used only sticks, and not a single carrot, to produce this group of city ambassadors, skepticism is in order. Torontonians and tourists who complain about surly drivers probably do not realize that a driver who has already worked eleven hours or twelve hours straight may be calculating whether to call it quits or work another couple of hours, as he is being flagged down.

The city fathers who seem to be blind to the racially biased regulatory mess they have created include not only old-style blue-collar politicos like Howard Moscoe and right-wing councillors like Minnan-Wong, who is likely to defer to the established businessmen who benefit from the existing system, but even the policy-informed, notoriously clean, golden-haired Harvard-trained lawyer who was mayor from 2003 to 2010, David Miller. A few weeks after taking office, the social-democratic, pro-diversity Mayor Miller, who had earlier been a city councillor, made a surprise appearance at the graduation ceremony for immigrants who completed the special Ambassador course. He warmly thanked those taxi drivers who supported him during the election and proclaimed that the Ambassador program gives drivers "the opportunity to own their own business."[11]

By 2003 it should have been crystal clear to all city councillors including Miller that Ambassador plate owners would be bound to complain about the unfairness of not being allowed to hire a second driver and about the difficulties caused when ill health or other problems forced the Ambassador drivers to stop driving . But the numerous problems documented in the industry newsletter *Taxinews* did not reach the broader public sphere. It was only in 2010–11 that a combination of a Human Rights Tribunal hearing and some savvy organizing by the cabbies drew attention to the flaws of the system.

Given the absence of reflection and the consequent collective failure to learn from regulatory mistakes, it is not surprising that the injustices inherent in the Ambassador plate system designed in 1998 came to haunt the hapless operators of the "Toronto a la Cart" food-vending operations whose story was told in the previous chapter. Like the "A la Cart" operators, who are prevented from hiring assistants, the Ambassador plate owners are forced by the city council to live out the mythical dream of the precapitalist entrepreneur who survives and even thrives without ever becoming either a wage laborer or a capitalist.

What policy lessons can be learned from the Ambassador plate fiasco? A concern to prevent monopolies and exploitation might seem to be a positive feature of local government, even if sometimes it leads to counterproductive regulations. But a closer look at both the Ambassador system and the "A la Cart" program shows that councillors are not in fact slowing the march of monopoly capitalism. Instead, they are imposing unrealistic rules that do not apply to big corporations but only to the tiniest of capitalists, such as hot dog vendors and taxi-plate owners. Large capital's effects on the city are almost completely beyond the jurisdiction of the city council, of course. But that is no excuse for turning all the energy that might have gone into regulating large-scale capital onto the hapless entrepreneurs of the street. Given the largely laissez-faire attitude toward development generally that characterized Toronto even during the tenure of a progressive mayor supported by a majority of the council (2003–10), the insistence on not allowing marginal mini-capitalists to hire a helper seems bizarre.

But even bizarre rules have their logic and their reasons. A knowledge-able observer opines that "the Ambassador plate is not a response to a legitimate need for taxi service but is primarily a device by which the city gets as many new immigrants as possible working," and adds that "the political-bureaucratic system of the City of Toronto is using the taxi indus-try to solve its own problems, not taxi industry problems. . . . The Ambas-sador plate program is only the latest means of using the taxi industry as a social shock absorber."[12]

The "social shock absorber" theory of taxi regulation would certainly account for the otherwise unexplainable rules we have documented here. Councillors do not worry about how many immigrants get to be on the boards of the five major banks whose buildings dominate the Toronto skyline, since big corporate capital is not charged with the task of social shock absorption. But they seem obsessed with preventing one group of small-scale capitalists from "exploiting" their fellow immigrants, perhaps because of the (probably unconscious) weight of the cultural stereotype of the taxi business being somehow destined to be one in which individ-ual immigrants make their way upward by sheer hard work, but without becoming real capitalists. The realities of car loans, high gas prices, and leasing arrangements will only be seen for what they are once the myth of the happy hardworking, self-employed immigrant cabbie is shown for what it is.

The Myth of the "Big Yellow Taxi"

A similar blindness to the realities of the capitalist economy mars New York City's taxi regulation system. Before going on to the detailed study of the tribulations of taxi drivers hauled up for infractions before the To-ronto Licensing Tribunal, a brief consideration of New York City's taxi regulation system will be helpful to put the Toronto taxi regulation system in a broader context.

In New York City too, myth seems to drive regulation more than fact—myths about cities and myths about immigrants' place in cities. And in New York City too there is a two-tier system, but one in which the tiers are separate universes, since the reasonably well-regulated yellow taxis found in Manhattan turn out to be a small part of the overall New York City taxi business, with the much larger universe consisting of appropriately named "black cabs," which operate in near–Third World conditions.

The classic yellow cabs of Hollywood film fame romanticized in Joni Mitchell's 1980 hit song "Big Yellow Taxi" are regulated in such a way as to ensure that some drivers can (eventually) own a plate, even though they will be in debt for hundreds of thousands of dollars when they do so. A 2007 study found that 25 percent of the medallion (yellow) cabs were owned by the person who drove them; 25 percent were owned by multitaxi fleets; and 50 percent were owned by former drivers or other individuals. Despite the continuing presence of the corporate fleets that city regulators have always wanted to eliminate, it is thus true that some New York immigrants have indeed come to own medallions and thus participate in the petty-capitalist dream, mainly because "since 1990 the Taxi Licensing Commission has required purchasers of individual medallions to drive at least 210 shifts per year, gradually restoring the balance of owner-drivers."[13]

The phrase "gradually restoring" is telling: the authors of the *Taxi 07* New York report clearly shared Toronto's official view that driving a taxi is no mere job—it is a romantic opportunity provided by the generous city to the successful self-employed immigrant, who will eventually be rewarded for his hard work as he purchases a medallion and thus comes to own a piece of the American dream. But rather tellingly, the lengthy, multidisciplinary, impressive-looking official report from which the phrase "gradually restoring the balance of owner-drivers" is taken did not gather information about the working conditions of nonowner drivers. In 2009, another, more objective study found that the tens of thousands of New Yorkers who do not own medallions drive an average of eleven hours per day for $65–$85 clear pay—with no vacation pay, no pension, and nothing like the universal health insurance that all Torontonians, like all Canadians, have.[14] Their pay is higher than that of the average Toronto nonowner cabbie, but it's still in the realm of Dickensian working conditions, and health care insurance or actual health care costs could mean that for many drivers the take-home pay is lower.

Despite these rather bleak facts, the myth of the self-made immigrant continues to be touted. In keeping with this, the 2007 report recommended that New York City consider adopting Toronto's Ambassador plate system. "TLC [the commission] could consider restricting new medallions to a single shift. The best way to enforce this restriction would be to permit only the owner to drive these medallions."[15] This move is justified by an argument about overall, aggregate efficiency that is quite irrelevant to individual drivers, namely that if double shifts of twelve hours each are the norm, many vehicles will be driving around at times in which there is little business. The single-shift system would presumably encourage individuals to drive only at peak times—though, given that there's much taxi business from late evening partiers as well as from early morning commuters running late, the economically ideal driver shift would be a split shift never allowing eight hours' straight sleep.

Whatever happens with the New York City medallion system for yellow cabs, the real regulatory issues lie in the vast quasi-informal sector made up of "for-hire vehicles" (FHVs) and "community cars." These are dispatched in response to phone calls and are thus far less visible than the yellow cabs. Contrary to what a tourist or a Manhattanite might imagine, for most New Yorkers these non-yellow cabs are the main form of taxi transportation.

The non-yellow taxis have set fares to airports, but otherwise they seem to be able to negotiate individually with passengers, Third World style. Clearly, they are a major industry—there are about twenty-five thousand of these vehicles, compared to about thirteen thousand yellow cabs—but all that the *Taxi 07* official investigation says about them is that the fares are "lightly regulated," which seems to be a euphemism for "unregulated." The fact that the vast amount of time and energy spent by city officials, taxi owners, and other stakeholders in devising regulatory conditions and setting up enforcement and inspection systems for yellow cabs only affects less than a third of the real taxi economy—which includes the twenty-five thousand "community cars" and "for-hire vehicles" plying their trade north of 125th street and in outer boroughs, as well as the several thousand "black cars" that have ongoing contracts with corporations for executive transportation—is not of much interest either to city officials or to the media.

Despite resorting to neoliberal economic reasoning to sing the praises of the Toronto Ambassador system, New York's *Taxi 07* report is mainly a cultural manifesto. Produced beautifully, with artsy black-and-white photos that make real cabs look like film props, the report is full of romantic prose eulogizing the mythical image of the yellow cab. The introduction states:

> Hailing a cab, with its promise of freedom, power, and anonymity, is the quintessential New York City act. Stick an arm in the air, and a taxi will take you where you want to go at any time of day or night. With each journey, driver and passenger enter a brief, strangely intimate, and occasionally profound relationship in which New York's diverse communities—economic, social, racial—collide. It's no surprise that the yellow cab has become a globally recognized symbol of the city. That symbol also represents both sweat and dreams: countless immigrants have gotten behind the wheel of a yellow cab in search of a better life. (10)

This passage can serve as a fitting concluding quote for the analysis of municipal regulatory attitudes. It encapsulates most of the key problems identified thus far in our analysis, as well as being an example of the kind of rosy-colored poetic prose whose romance takes attention away from the practical problems experienced by drivers. In the quote, the point of view that counts is clearly that of the passenger, not the driver: "hailing a cab" is the archetypal urban act being eulogized in evocative, even lyrical prose—not driving it. Second, insofar as the driver is mentioned, he is portrayed not as a citizen and a worker with rights but as an ant-like member of the huddled masses of New York City lore. The economic fact that, in today's global-capital world, precarious self-employment is hardly a good recipe for success is swept under the rug—not surprisingly, since as cultural studies scholars have long shown, mythical or iconic images are characterized precisely by their uncanny ability to use sentiment to steamroll inconvenient facts. Third, the regulatory fact that only the thirteen thousand yellow cabs that ply their trade in Manhattan south of 125th street can legally stop if someone sticks his or her arm out in the air is suppressed here. Tourists and bankers in Manhattan do experience the freedom of hailing a cab, but not inhabitants of Harlem or the Bronx, who must call ahead of time and then wait. And fourth, the class and race divide that separates the majority of drivers from the majority of the customers is also swept under a rhetorical rug as the authors talk about "diverse communities" "colliding."

That the cabbies might not be free individuals colliding in exciting cosmopolitan urban encounters but rather victims of both economic structures and municipal regulatory systems is the only conclusion that can be drawn from the available evidence. But the myth of the self-made, immigrant small entrepreneur is unlikely to be abandoned by mainly white city leaders who love to romanticize certain aspects of urban life while remaining blind to the stark realities of what William Sites, writing about New York's economy and riffing on Karl Marx's analysis of "primitive" capital accumulation, has called "primitive globalization."[16]

The Toronto Licensing Tribunal: "Looking at the Whole Man" in a Multicultural Setting

We now move from the legal machinery that produces legal taxis and legal drivers and puts them on the road to another piece of legal machinery, one designed to deal with "deviant" taxis and drivers: the licensing tribunal. All businesses that are required to obtain a municipal business license, from hair salons to massage parlors, can potentially end up at this tribunal. Some businesses thought to be inherently risky are governed more closely, with owners having to justify, in person, even a routine transfer of ownership (sexually oriented "adult entertainment parlors" are among these). Others, such as taxi drivers, only end up at the tribunal if something goes wrong. However, in a process that is similar to the plea bargaining that goes on in the shadow of criminal courts, negotiations between city officials and the errant drivers or license holders often result in deals that make hearings unnecessary (or reduce the hearing time to the two minutes required to rubber-stamp the deal). While the tribunal deals with a large variety of businesses, the majority of the tribunal's hearing time is devoted to appeals of taxi drivers' license denials and suspensions.[17] Taxi drivers have the automatic right to appeal to the tribunal, and about half of them do so. Plate owners could potentially be brought before the tribunal for infractions committed by their agents or drivers, but this does not seem to happen, perhaps because—as taxi drivers claim—owners are rarely charged, or perhaps because they obtain lawyers who work on a deal behind the scenes.[18]

The arm's-length administrative tribunal, operating independently from the licensing bureaucracy, was created in 1998, as the adjudicative function was removed from the city department in charge of licensing, Municipal Licensing and Standards.[19] This is unusual. In New York City as in other places, complaints about unfair or incorrect taxi license denials or suspensions continue to be heard by the same organization that issues licenses. The licensing tribunal could thus be seen as an example of what the law-and-society literature would call "juridification"—although until 2006, the tribunal membership was drawn from the same motley crew of former city councillors and assorted civic figures who sit on bodies such as the Parking Authority or the Committee of Adjustment (zoning appeals board), so it was hardly a model of legalism.

The tribunal has seven members, who usually sit in panels of three. In 2003–4 all the tribunal members were white and English-speaking, and most had little or no legal training. After a major reform in 2006, motivated by persistent concerns that the tribunal constantly undermined the city's policies by "pardoning" errant drivers, even those with serious criminal convictions, the tribunal personnel changed drastically, in the direction of professionalization. Three out of the new seven members are lawyers; one is a paralegal; another is an engineer; and yet another represents small businesses. Three out of the seven also appear to be members of racialized minorities (in keeping with the city's overall diversity policies, not because of any specific concerns about the demographics of the former tribunal).

While the tribunal personnel changed over the study period, the errant taxi-driver population did not. Virtually all the taxi drivers appearing before the tribunal, in 2007 as in 2003–4, were African, Middle Eastern, or South Asian men, with the vast majority of these being relatively new immigrants (judging from English fluency, accent, and the biographical facts recounted in legal proceedings). Thus, the licensing tribunal provides a good opportunity to examine how a run-of-the-mill municipal legal venue deals with "diversity," and especially with racialized immigrants.

The data collected did not lend itself to answering the usual sociolegal questions about fairness and racial discrimination that gave rise to the Human Rights Tribunal complaint described in the earlier section of this chapter, since there were no white English-speaking taxi drivers in our sample to provide comparisons. The data shed new light not so much on the content of legal decisions (i.e., whether racialized license holders receive harsher punishments than whites) but rather on the process, especially the underlying assumptions about what legal venues such as the tribunals are all about (which are rarely studied in policy-driven analyses of judicial and quasi-judicial proceedings). The outcome of the hearings was of course the only thing that really mattered to the individual participants. But from the point of view of the complex relations between cultural background assumptions and legal processes that is the theme of this chapter, observing face-to-face interactions exposed some unspoken assumptions about what it is to appear "before the law," what makes a good witness, what makes a good, redeemable, sympathetic offender. The assumptions that undergirded many of the interactions observed imported into law culturally specific notions of truth, authenticity, and personhood, notions with deep roots in Christian thinking about the soul.

A tribunal member who consistently opposed the bureaucracy's persistent attempts to implement rules, and who was also clearly hostile to the city solicitors' rather aggressive prosecutorial tactics, was asked (in an interview) whether ordinary experience sufficed to do the adjudication work, given the obvious cultural gap between the new-immigrant, largely Muslim taxi drivers and the (at that time) all-white, all English-speaking tribunal. Misunderstanding the question, she responded that the possible cultural bias of rules does not matter, since the tribunal is committed to "looking at the whole man." This phrase may seem like a throwaway comment, a gesture demonstrating one tribunal member's lack of interest in legal details; but the phrase stayed with me, because it resonated with many of my research findings. It is well known that judicial perceptions of character are crucial in criminal court contexts; but I had not expected official perceptions of honesty and morality to play such a major role in venues dealing with often trivial municipal rules. The criminal law has always been centrally concerned with both public morals and individual character; but regulating the taxi business seems like an odd arena in which to scrutinize people's souls. That is, however, what I witnessed. It is important to note that the cases that got a full hearing and thus became venues for moral scrutiny were by definition unusual, statistically, since the majority of conflicts are resolved in a quasi–plea bargain process that is not available for inspection to researchers such as myself; but a process that is quantitatively rare (i.e., the full hearing) can still be qualitatively significant, if it sheds light on an unexpected and thus unknown feature of the governance process.

To see how citizen adjudicators actually examine "the whole man" in that particular transcultural context, it is necessary to slow down the pace and tell a few stories in some detail.

The first story is highly unusual in that the errant driver in question was white and English-speaking.[20] Not coincidentally, he was a tow truck driver, not a cabbie; tow truck driving is still to a large extent the preserve of working-class Anglo males, in Toronto at any rate. Mr. C, as we shall call him, seemed Irish-Canadian and was definitely working-class. He appeared in blue jeans—in contrast to the efforts made by virtually all immigrants to dress up for their hearing—and he was quite at ease in the room, again in contrast to the marked nervousness shown by the vast majority of racialized license holders. While the jeans and the down-home, blue-collar masculine manner (complete with the "f" word) would have come across as disrespectful in a real court of law, in this low-level tribunal, whose members often wore informal office attire, not suits, much less robes, Mr. C's presentation of self came across as authentic—and therefore truthful. Similarly, while in a higher court he would have suffered by virtue of being unrepresented, in this context, having no lawyer or even agent was somewhat beneficial. A lawyer might have prevented some of the faux pas he made or prevented some self-incriminating moments; but, on the other hand, tribunal members are consistently willing to bend the rules of procedure in favor of unrepresented people, and often give useful help along the way. But whether having a lawyer would have helped or hindered from the point of view of the outcome, in regard to his ability to present a picture of truthfulness and authenticity, being unrepresented was most definitely an advantage. He spoke perfect Canadian English and possessed the personal savvy and the cultural background knowledge needed to read facial expressions and tones of voice and adjust his performance to what the tribunal members seemed to want.

The city solicitor began her attempt to take away Mr. C's tow truck license by calling a municipal inspector, who testified that Mr. C had shown up at the scene of an accident and had proceeded to engage in a physical fight with a competing tow truck driver who also wanted the business. The inspector had not seen the assault himself, but he testified that Mr. C had been criminally charged by the police officer who had been called to the scene of the accident. Under cross-examination, Mr. C admitted that he spit on the competing driver but claimed that the other driver had punched him first. Much to the dismay of the tribunal, the police officer in question had not shown up at the hearing, and so no authoritative version of the facts could be established. Nevertheless, after hearing both the inspector and Mr. C, I concluded that a physical fight had indeed taken place, not just spitting.

At that point, Mr. C decided to invoke not his knowledge but his ignorance of law and his lack of representation as a resource: "Why are you asking me all these questions? . . . I don't have a lawyer with me and you're asking me all these questions and I think I might be incriminating myself since I haven't even had my trial yet." Of course, his point about self-incrimination in light of his future criminal trial demonstrated a good knowledge of the criminal law, but the tribunal members did not seem to realize this. (In an interview, a licensing manager asked to comment on this case explained that a licensing hearing does not in any way either affect or depend on criminal proceedings: "We're not concerned with the outcome of the criminal case. He didn't dispute the fact that he punched the other guy and that was our point. We can't have guys out there licensed by the city beating other people up.")

The tribunal panel, however, which at that time (pre-2006) tended to side with the errant drivers and against the city, even in cases where convictions, not just charges, existed,[21] took a different view. They briefly retired and came back to essentially forgive Mr. C. Surprisingly, admitting to punching the other guy had actually worked in Mr. C's favor. The perceived honesty trumped the obvious legal wrongdoing. In keeping with the Christian idea of looking at the soul, not the act, and showing more concern for the tow truck driver's cleansed soul than for the safety of the public (which is supposed to be the tribunal's key concern), the tow truck driver received not a suspension but a kind of Catholic absolution. "Your license will be reinstated immediately, Mr. C. That means you can go back to work on Monday. Tomorrow, even, if you're ready." But "from now on, if something on the street upsets you, don't react." "As you've found out, it isn't worth it. Don't let your anger get the better of you. If trouble comes calling, just walk away. . . . Try to exercise some self-control." No doubt habituated from his schoolboy days to the boys-will-be-boys-but-try-to-control-your-temper talk, Mr. C knew exactly how to respond. He stood up, looked directly into the eyes of the fatherly tribunal member who was forgiving him, and said, "I will. Thank you."

This exchange may seem to be culture-neutral; but in fact it is based on and presupposes certain culturally specific, Eurocentric assumptions. Philosopher Charles Taylor's detailed history of the culturally specific "self" valued by European cultures shows that what began with early Christianity's techniques for scrutinizing and cleansing the soul, and later became the formal examination of conscience, confession, and forgiveness rituals of Roman Catholicism, has provided much of the content for the modern, secular, autonomous self of contemporary psychology, the self that prizes authenticity at all costs.[22] Remorse and repentance are of course integral to criminal justice and correctional practices; but one would have thought that a very low-level administrative tribunal would be more concerned with bureaucratic rules, rather than being swayed by a presentation of an authentic self that can admit to manly mistakes such as losing one's temper but can then obtain forgiveness by promising not to follow the rules, but simply to "try" to "exercise some self-control."

Mr. C's success in getting his license reinstated was partly rooted in the fact that, at the time of his hearing (2004), the tribunal members collectively deplored "lawyerization." Many tribunal members took pleasure in overturning bureaucratic decisions and distancing themselves from the city's prosecutorial efforts (in the same way that city councillors often enjoy taking up the anti–city hall, people's friend role). But despite the general antilawyer and antibureaucrat attitude of most tribunal members, other drivers appearing before the tribunal in the same time period were not able to benefit from the hostilities between adjudication and administration in the same way as Mr. C. One important fact distinguishing Mr. C from the vast majority of his counterparts was that he knew not only the language but also the prevailing cultural assumptions. As we shall now see, language difficulties are provided for at this tribunal by means of interpreters. However, the new immigrants who end up at the tribunal due to infractions get no help in managing their encounter with the tribunal's culturally rooted assumptions about what it is to appear before "the law." A few vignettes drawn from tribunal observations will show how Christian and European cultural assumptions embedded in the tribunal's process disadvantage the vast majority of the taxi drivers who appear there.

A tall, elegant would-be taxi driver, dressed in a suit and tie and accompanied by a well-dressed wife and an adorable toddler, appeared before the tribunal one day in early 2004 to persuade the tribunal to overturn the bureaucracy's decision to not give him a taxi driver's license. He was represented by an "agent," which was somewhat unusual, since the vast majority of taxi drivers appeared before the tribunal completely unrepresented.[23] The presence of an agent, combined with the strikingly elegant attire of the family, suggested that the gentleman was one of those numerous new immigrants who were doctors or professors in their own country but are reduced to taxi driving in Toronto.

The city solicitor—a young white woman of southern European descent but with a perfect Canadian accent—began by arguing that every single word of the proceedings had to be translated into Somali. The tribunal chair pragmatically suggested that in the interests of time, the interpreter could limit herself to helping out where needed. But the solicitor, who (as had become apparent to me after seeing her in earlier cases) conducted herself as if every case were a murder trial, dismissed the concern with efficiency by dangling the specter of "big law" and judicial review in front of the tribunal: "We won't know what he understands until the judicial review comes in." The threat worked. Without anyone asking the applicant how well he understood English, everything was translated.

Interpretation is provided free of charge in all judicial and quasi-judicial municipal venues including the tribunal, a very expensive concession to official diversity politics. (By contrast, the provincial government provides court services in French for Ontario's francophone minority, in keeping with official Canadian bilingualism, but does not pay for interpreters for the more numerous speakers of other languages.) The tribunal members no doubt know that one of the conditions of taxi drivers' licenses (posted on the back of the driver's seat in every cab) is good knowledge of English; but the contradiction between that condition and the provision of interpreters at the tribunal goes unaddressed (in interviews as well as in hearings).

The city solicitor calls her first witness, a manager from Municipal Licensing and Standards (MLS), a young woman with a slight eastern European accent whom we shall call Ms. O. The manager explains that Mr. S had his application for a new license turned down three months earlier because he had a "serious record of conviction." In New York City, or in Toronto today, people with serious criminal convictions cannot get a municipal license, but as we saw in the case of the tow truck driver the Toronto tribunal was at that time (2004) prone to forgiving criminals. Therefore, the manager had to build a case in a quasi-criminal manner, instead of simply having to show proof of conviction. Thus, she began by relating that upon receiving the conviction information when doing the routine check that applicants must undergo, Mr. S was called for an interview. In the interview the applicant explained the conviction away as the result of a misunderstanding.

The tribunal, and everyone else in the room (including people waiting for their own case and a reporter), then heard the story of the conviction secondhand, from Ms. O. Apparently, Mr. S was working as a store manager in a cigar shop. A woman walked in with an employment application, and Mr. S decided to interview her for a clerk position on the spot, in the stockroom. As reported by Ms. O, Mr. S said that the woman being interviewed found an "adult" magazine in the stockroom, proceeded to look through it, and gazed at Mr. S "suggestively." This led to a "liaison" (in Ms. O's words). A couple of days afterward, Mr. S was arrested pursuant to a complaint made to police by the woman. The police charged him with several offences, with some being later dropped as Mr. S was persuaded to plead guilty to one of the lesser charges. (This overcharging story is very plausible, incidentally, at least to anyone with knowledge of criminal justice in Toronto.) Mr. S's bargained guilty plea resulted in a noncustodial

sentence, which apparently included having his penis tested for suscepti-
bility to pornographic imagery.

During this testimony, the three tribunal members surreptitiously
glanced at Mr. S's wife and child, probably wondering if the wife understood English well enough to follow the drift. There was awkwardness in
the air, but nobody said or did anything until an event disrupted the legal
discourse: the adorable toddler burst into tears. The crying was ignored
at first, but after some time, one of the tribunal members asked the elderly gentleman (a former city employee) who volunteers at the tribunal
to please have the wife and the "unhappy little fellow" escorted out of the
room. This was promptly done. The crying was still audible, however, and
so the tribunal chair asked the volunteer clerk to accompany the wife and
child further away, "preferably to the lower level of the building."

The removal of the child and the hard-line instructions to the volunteer
clerk seemed more of a punishment for Mr. S's apparent disregard for
Canadian norms regarding the telling of personal sexual stories than a
precaution about order, since the tribunal proceedings at that time were
not nearly as formal and orderly as court proceedings. Mr. S then made
things worse for himself by refusing to take advantage of the child's well-
timed misbehavior to save his wife from embarrassment. Instead of encouraging his wife to leave, which the tribunal chair was clearly hoping
would happen, he did the opposite, asking, through the Somali interpreter,
to be allowed to go out of the room to console the child who was "crying
because he is away from me." The tribunal chair positively bristled at this
request: "You cannot leave in the middle of testimony."

At this point in the proceedings, the looks on the tribunal members'
faces reminded me of another hearing. There, a Pakistani driver received
the same looks when, in an effort to change an unfavorable legal tide, he
burst into tears and sobbed, saying something (largely inaudible) concerning his father's death. Toddler's tears constitute a breach of decorum, and
parents are clearly expected to remove the child immediately or suffer a
loss of legal capital; but if the tears are those of an adult male, they can
have additional negative effects. Neither babies nor tears nor any other
sign of vulnerability counts as legal capital—and can indeed count against
one. Remorse is fine if performed with manliness, as Mr. C did; but tribunal members resent what one of them, in an interview, called "manipulation." The tears of the Pakistani driver were interpreted as manipulation,
clearly.

But returning to Mr. S's hearing: when Mr. S and his agent were finally given a chance to tell the story of the cigar-store "liaison" in their own words, the agent tried to argue that the plea bargain was not a real admission of guilt but rather a pragmatic choice made by a vulnerable new immigrant under pressure. The agent then began to introduce evidence of Mr. S's upstanding moral character (though "good moral character" is no longer required of license applicants,[24] only the absence of serious criminal convictions). The city solicitor immediately objected to the extraneous papers. These were not visible to the audience, but the agent explained that one of them was a testimonial by a "British lady," a doctor with UNICEF, who worked in a school for refugees attended by Mr. S in Africa. At this point the city lawyer became truly incensed, pointing out that she had not seen the documents, and that they were in any case "irrelevant." The agent, however, countered that the documents were a kind of character reference, and that "at the end of the day this is a case about character. My client's character. And I want to present his character." The tribunal chair appeared annoyed. He stated that "matters pertaining to character are important but not critical in this case," with the city lawyer piping in that "it is not my awareness that character is the issue in this proceeding." The city lawyer then contradicted herself, however, by adding "with the very obvious exception of the sexual assault."

When the hearing ended, soon after this exchange, the tribunal briefly retired and returned with a decision. Against the strong recommendation of city staff, the tribunal decided to grant Mr. S his taxi driver's license, with the condition (a standard one) that a copy of his criminal record be provided to the city every year for three years. How did this happen, given that the driver had alienated the tribunal by his conduct around the baby crying as well as by the attempt to introduce somewhat irrelevant evidence of character? As far as one can tell from the orally given reasons, the driver got his license because even if his own character was by no means vindicated, the tribunal members (two men and one woman) decided that the (absent) woman who had been interviewed for the cigar-store clerk position had a worse character. The tribunal chair concluded: "Without in any way diminishing the seriousness of a sexual assault charge, based on the evidence you gave us, we accept that there may have been some leading on that you misinterpreted by the young woman." The Somali driver was thus saved by the fact that the combination of his criminal offence and his cultural faux pas were found not to weigh as much as the assumed bad character of the (absent) young woman.

In interviews, one senior tribunal member, who not coincidentally denounced the then-proposed "lawyerization" of the tribunal in strong terms, told me that even a murder conviction should not be an absolute bar to a city municipal license. Another member commented (a year or so before a major police investigation of Hells Angels' control over Toronto's tow truck business) that "because a guy is in the Hells Angels, he shouldn't be absolutely barred from getting a tow truck license to earn a living," adding that "if you don't give them a chance to earn a living, they'll earn a dishonest living." Presumably this adjudicator would have been happy to give a murderer a tow truck license as long as the driver promised to "try" to "exercise self-control."

Another case, one involving a Punjabi-speaking driver, sheds further light on the perils of making licenses depend on the "whole man" test. Mr. M was caught driving a taxi without a valid license, and only after this did he apply for one. If bureaucratic rules had prevailed, this would have been a straightforward case and Mr. M would have been denied his application. But given the tribunal's preference for inquiries into the soul, the hearing ended up focusing on his commitment to truth-telling.

The city lawyer (the same as in Mr. S's case) focused her quasi prosecu-tion on the claim that the form certifying Mr. M's fitness to drive a cab, which Mr. M had submitted to the bureaucracy, had a forged signature. A great deal of time was spent trying to elicit the details of this forgery, and it was unclear whether the interpreter was helping or hindering. But the facts, as I understood them, were that Mr. M had indeed visited a doctor to get the certificate but had obtained a handwritten note on letterhead rather than a signature on the official form. Instead of returning to request that the doctor sign the correct bureaucratic form (a request which would likely have cost him around $50, given that Ontario health insurance does not cover such form-filling), Mr. M simply copied the signature from the note onto the form.

Mr. M did not know that if he had admitted copying the signature, explained his wrongdoing by informing the tribunal that the doctor was charging extra, and then shown appropriate remorse, the "sin" would prob-ably have been forgiven. After all, his sin was much more venial than that of the tow truck driver mentioned above. His agent should have known that confession and remorse would have been more effective than stone-walling, but the agent—the same one appearing for Mr. S—did not give his client the correct cultural information. Uninformed about the value of admitting one's sins and repenting, Mr. M tried to persist in saying that the signature was authentic—even though, quite unusually,[25] the physician's secretary had appeared to testify against him. After her damning testi-mony, the driver realized the game was up. He then shifted gears. Instead of continuing to deny wrongdoing, he sought to appeal to the mercy of the tribunal: "I only had two choices: suicide myself or drive a cab without a license. . . . I could not find any other work and I was desperate." But the tribunal members' expressions hardened rather than softened at the mention of suicide.

On their part, the bureaucracy disregarded the plea for mercy, and instead began to make an additional claim of dishonesty, namely that the driving school in which Mr. M claims to have received his compulsory "refresher course" did not exist, because the bureaucrats could not find it in their database. "This school is not licensed. It does not exist," exclaimed Ms. O. The tribunal chair, ever keen to shatter the bureaucracy's faith in its own information, argued back, saying that the school might well exist: "Why didn't you make a phone call to the number on the letterhead?" This evoked further hostility; the bureaucrat refused to make the phone call.

The spat between adjudicator and bureaucrat did not help the driver, since the specter of forgery was not dispelled by the fight about the lack of fit between law and reality. In her concluding remarks, the city lawyer stated that "the fact that Mr. M has difficulty stating the truth is central to this"; "Mr. M has not been truthful with the tribunal. He therefore cannot be considered trustworthy." He cannot be trusted to follow bylaws because he "did something extremely dishonest" with the medical certificate. "He has breached the law and has a problem with his integrity and will continue to do so," she reiterated.

Mr. M's agent tried to counter the city lawyer's argument on its own terms: "If you look at the overall picture and his demeanor, you'll see that he has shown remorse. . . . He will not do this again. . . . He should be given a license with severe restrictions. . . . He has learnt his lesson and will pull his bootstraps up."

Remorse, of course, was exactly what Mr. M had failed to convincingly produce. Nobody had told him that the Christian spectacle of confession and repentance was crucial to the tribunal's sense of itself.[26] It was not Mr. M's copying of a doctor's signature onto a form that sealed his fate, much less his rather appalling record of driving infractions, which was barely mentioned. The tribunal's oral comments focused instead on the issues of truthfulness and remorse already highlighted by both city lawyer and agent: "In general, his explanation appears to be lacking in conviction and his answers are misleading." Mr. M tried instead to invoke pity by mentioning his suicidal thoughts; but in the Christian tradition, pity is seen as best bestowed on repentant sinners, not on people who are merely poor and exploited.

Several other drivers, all from African or South Asian countries, had also tried to evoke pity by various tactics, all unsuccessfully. Some mentioned the number of children they had to support, not knowing that in Canada having many children can be seen as a sign of bad planning or even recklessness. One Nigerian driver talked about being sick, and lifted up his shirt to reveal some kind of medical equipment, only to meet with a stony silence, as a tribunal member cleared his throat and changed the subject, noting, "You currently have seven demerit points on your driver's license."

Visible signs of suffering might work in another context to trigger the traditional judicial and sovereign gifts of mercy and compassion. But in the absence of appropriate remorse for one's sins, signs of suffering were not sufficient to evoke mercy—perhaps because it was not judicial mercy that was at play, but rather Christian-style forgiveness, which is dependent on honest repentance but is unconditioned by material circumstances.

This does not mean the tribunal members were racist. While blind to the cultural assumptions reproduced in the minute-by-minute judgments about credibility and worthiness that make up the tribunal's adjudication work, they were on the whole very sympathetic to the conditions that force the racialized and poverty-stricken immigrant taxi drivers to constantly risk illegality, which was why the tribunal was not overly concerned with poor driving records. But putting to one side the attitudes of individual adjudicators, one can use the methods of legal anthropology to explore the hidden cultural assumptions not of adjudicators as individuals, but of taken-for-granted legal procedures—with "procedure" here referring not to the technicalities of evidence law but rather to the everyday words, gestures, and largely intuitive decisions about truthfulness and moral worth that go almost completely unrecorded in law's official record.

At the policy level, this chapter has shown that the well-meaning and rather expensive decision taken by city leaders to provide interpreters, free of charge, to the myriad immigrant groups who encounter problems with the city's committees and tribunals does not affect some of the hidden Eurocentric cultural dynamics that help to shape the everyday functioning of low-level legal processes. Appointing racially diverse citizens to boards and tribunals, as has been happening in recent years, may help somewhat, but since a major part of the 2006 reforms revolved around what the older members had called "lawyerization," it may be that those citizens who are appointed, however racially diverse, are immersed in the underlying Eurocentrism of everyday legal processes. This of course does not mean cities ought to stop taking pro-diversity measures such as providing free interpreter services; it just means that becoming truly diverse is not a matter of good intentions or even of funding innovations.

The next chapter will tackle the same question of cultural and racial diversity but at another scale altogether: we will examine legal proceedings concerning not people and licenses but rather the local law of religious buildings.

CHAPTER 8

From Local to Global and Back Again

Mosques and the Politics of Local Planning

In the fall of 2010, as plans to build a large mosque two blocks from the former site of the World Trade Center were publicized, first throughout the United States and then around the world, the politics of local land-use control received unprecedented attention. That locating a building on one street rather than on another can provoke all manner of emotional reactions is not news to the city councillors, neighborhood leaders, and officials whose daily rounds have been documented throughout this book, and hence not news to any reader who has come this far; but seldom do these emotional outbursts shift from the local to the global scale, and back again to the local, in such a dramatic manner.

Anyone familiar with the semantic niceties of Middle East politics could have predicted that as the mosque plans were debated, different participants would choose completely different names to refer to the (future) building. Imam Feisal Abdul Rauf's chosen name for his proposed lower Manhattan religious center is "Cordoba House," after the medieval Muslim caliphate in southern Spain that famously fostered learning and culture and tolerated large communities of Jews and Christians within its boundaries. In his public comments, Rauf tried to evoke the enlightened atmosphere of Muslim Cordoba by explaining that a multifaith memorial to the victims of the 9/11 attack would be included in the proposed cultural center. But in the voluminous news coverage, and the even more voluminous and often irate commentary on the blogosphere, the most commonly used term for the proposed building was not Cordoba House, but rather "ground zero mosque." This provocative term uses the ultimate spatialized symbol of American victims of terrorism—"ground zero"—as the filter through which to look at an issue that, from the strictly legal point of view, is a mere matter of checking whether the property in question is appropriately zoned for places of worship.

Given the political and media visibility of the former World Trade Center site, it was perhaps inevitable that this mosque project would transcend the municipal sphere. Even President Obama chimed in, in support of Muslims freely worshipping anywhere (a move that did nothing to boost his domestic popularity). But local governments all around the world deal with delicate matters such as this one on a daily basis, with both civic debate and legal process remaining, for the most part, at the local level, and indeed often being confined to the strictly micro-local sphere.

As seen throughout this book, highly local matters often move people more powerfully than questions that appear as distant, such as the economy, the national debt, or climate change. In cosmopolitan cities that have experienced major demographic changes as a result of changing patterns of global migration, certain issues that are the subject of negotiations between developers and planners—or developers, neighborhood groups, and city councils—frequently become lightning rods for fears and anxieties about cultural differences that often remain otherwise unspoken, especially in cities like Toronto, where locals consider it very impolite to say anything about other cultures that is not nice.

This chapter begins by examining some recent disputes about the municipal governance of Islamic religious spaces in the Toronto region in order to shed light on the underlying governance process. Governance being broader and less tied to formal law than government, the mini-study will cover both the formal, legal rules for such land uses as "places of worship" and the nonlegal but still powerful norms and habits that result, for example, in public meetings being called even when planning law does not require such a meeting. These institutional habits create expectations and feelings of entitlement—or as the case may be, of disentitlement—as much as formal law does.[1]

Material presented in earlier chapters showed that all manner of disputes about who and what belongs in the city, or who the city belongs to, are regularly funneled through low-level legal mechanisms, such as municipal business licensing or zoning law, that were not designed for such tasks. Unfortunately, in increasingly cosmopolitan cities, these outdated and cumbersome legal machineries are often the only ones available for citizens to engage in public discussions about such issues as the relationship between global terrorism of the 9/11 type and their local mosque.

When Switzerland instituted a ban on minarets, after 57 percent of the population voted in a referendum to ban this type of construction, in November 2009, it was taken for granted by all concerned that the new rule was more about a certain religion and/or culture than about building design; but it was not at all coincidental that the legal target was the physical structure of the minaret, rather than Muslims as persons. In liberal legal systems, it is far easier to try to expel minarets from a city or a country than to expel or discriminate against populations. Buildings have no human rights. And municipal codes are not usually subject to constitutional equality provisions, since, as the North American planning mantra goes, local rules govern "time, space, and manner," not persons.

But while buildings catering to a particular minority can be regulated much more coercively than any identifiable group, nevertheless, the "ground zero mosque" dispute is also telling in that as is usual in planning law, the opinions of local residents about the mosque counted for a great deal. By contrast, the same local residents had not been consulted in regard to the prior immigration processes that had brought the Muslim immigrants to Manhattan, as if community opinion mattered only when a state-scale or global process (migration of Muslim people) suddenly becomes visible locally.

While urban studies scholars (and sometimes city mayors) routinely deplore the lack of municipal involvement in matters that very much affect cities, such as immigration policies, not all "local" matters, however, are subject to public consultation and debate. The focus of this chapter is disputes that take place in planning-law venues and community meetings. But it is important to note, before we present the research on mosques and other religious buildings, that the kind of popular involvement in arguments about mosques, public housing, shelters for homeless people, and so on that has been documented in this book does not extend to all spheres of municipal government activity. In particular, the economic flows that are as necessary as bricks to bring new buildings into existence, whether they are private or public, are not rendered visible, much less debatable, in the public venues that are part of the governance process. That is why capital, local or global, has remained largely in the background thus far. If I had asked planners to reveal the financial details of the projects they were handling (details that in any case may not have been known even to the planners), they would have declined. Fleur Johns, a legal scholar who has studied global finance, has pointed out that the "deal" that is constantly mythologized in management literature is regarded as naturally deserving protection and secrecy, even when tax revenue and public authority are involved. Major infrastructure projects depend on such "deals." Residents often know very little about how the future revenues will be divided and what will happen if revenue (say, from a toll highway or a toll tunnel) is lower than projected. Global capital plays little or no role in the mosque-building business, at least in the Toronto area; but the governance process that determines whether mosques or minarets are allowed to proceed is the same one that also gives us the bridges and tunnels and signature waterfront spaces whose design process is open to public input but whose financing is shrouded in secrecy.[2]

Islamic Parking? The Zoning Category "Place of Worship"

In the greater Toronto area, the Muslim population has grown by leaps and bounds over the past twenty or thirty years, due to shifts in patterns of immigration. Christian denominations have been selling or renting out buildings and have amalgamated congregations, especially in the older parts of the city. In the meantime, Muslim communities throughout the Greater Toronto Area have been forced to hone their legal and political skills, as well as their fund-raising capacity, in order to expand and/or to institutionalize adequate spaces for worship and related activities.

Most of the decisions that either facilitate or block such community-building efforts involve only local planning staff, councillors, and "Committees of Adjustment" (boards of zoning appeals), and are thus below the formal legal radar; but several of them have reached the Ontario Municipal Board, a quasi-judicial provincial planning tribunal with great powers to undo municipal decisions.

A study of OMB decisions involving mosques (six, almost all from the greater Toronto area), supplemented by a search of relevant articles from the *Toronto Star* (which covers local politics not only in Toronto proper but in the larger metropolitan area), reveals some outbursts whose volume seems out of keeping with the importance of the issue at hand. While the vehement opposition to mosque expansions from some residents and some local politicians suggests a whiff, or more, of Islamophobia, nevertheless, if one places the mosque disputes in Toronto in comparative perspective, it becomes clear that the "Diversity is our strength" city motto is not wholly empty, since, at least in publicly available sources, there were no attacks on Islam as such in and around Toronto—in contrast to much of the discourse prompted by the "ground zero mosque."[3]

But this difference does not mean that the disputes analyzed here are of no relevance to the United States or to Europe. If one wanted to quantify racism and Islamophobia and compare Toronto to other cities with a view to giving out grades, one would look for social factors that make public debates about cultural difference less vitriolic than in other places. This has been done in a variety of reports containing "tolerance" rankings and other multiple-regression measurements of collective urban virtue. But the aim here is not to hand out prizes based on more or less arbitrarily chosen indicators. It is rather to document and analyze, qualitatively and dynamically, the workings of governance processes that are commonly found in municipalities. The creaky mechanisms of urban governance lead to distinct, often unpredictable, outcomes, depending on a host of local factors; but the mechanisms can be analyzed not to provide ratings but rather with a view to seeing how they tend to empower certain groups and disempower others, and how they funnel disputes so as to authorize certain questions and foreclose others. Thus, the fact that prejudices against Muslims or other groups may be more virulent in other places does not make this study irrelevant elsewhere.

The first controversy examined here took place in the city of Mississauga, which is located just west of Toronto and contains Toronto's international airport. From the point of view of planning law, what is most unusual about this case is that Mayor Hazel McCallion, the octogenarian battle-axe who has ruled the city of Mississauga for longer than most of its citizens can remember, chose to make an appearance, in person, before the OMB, during an appeal of a planning application from an Islamic foundation. This might create the impression that Mississauga is a village lacking in lawyers, but that would be incorrect. Mississauga (named after the dispossessed Indian nation that is still to this day attempting to sue governments over land claims) is a city of over six hundred thousand. It mushroomed in the 1950s as a largely white middle-class bedroom community, but in the past couple of decades it has become highly cosmopolitan. Its demographic distinctness in the Toronto area lies in its large South Asian population. In 1996, 11.3 percent of the population claimed to be "South Asian," but by 2006 this proportion had doubled, to 21.6 percent, as the city made the symbolically important transition to being majority nonwhite (Chinese and Filipino origin are the next largest categories).

In terms of religion, Muslims make up the largest non-Christian group in Mississauga—though this is still a small minority, at 6.83 percent in the 2006 census—with Hindus and Sikhs being recorded as 4.73 percent and 3.82 percent of the 2006 population respectively.[4] (These numbers may be an underestimate, since recent immigrants may be reluctant to report their religion to a "government" authority, and the totals of the main three South Asian religions do not add up to anywhere near the 21.6 percent of the population that identifies as South Asian.) But be that as it may, the anxieties that affect the well-being of minority religions/cultures are likely to be rooted not so much in brute demographic facts as in subterranean and often unconscious processes. The speed of change is as important as the snapshot, onetime breakdown of populations. And Mississauga has experienced particularly rapid demographic change: according to the 2001 census, 40 percent of all its immigrants had arrived in Canada within the past ten years. Rapid demographic change can make "old timers" feel threatened or overrun by newcomers, even if no particular group of newcomers has formed anything approaching a majority.[5]

But not all newcomers draw the same attention or produce the same anxieties. The eleven top linguistic minorities in Mississauga each have more than ten thousand members; but some of these groups have features that made them less "alien." For example, the Tagalog speakers (who are from the Philippines) are overwhelmingly Catholic, which is the most popular religion in the city (with people of Polish, Italian, and Portuguese descent being also present in large numbers). Although in popular discourse Mississauga is regarded as a South Asian enclave, the fact is that among the "recent immigrants" (that is, those arriving between 1991 and 2001), only 20.6 percent were from India, 14.3 percent from Pakistan, 4.6 percent from China, and 2 percent from Iran. Thus, only half of Mississauga's immigrants have come from Asia and the Middle East. But there are cultural and geopolitical reasons why certain groups become visible in the local media or in planning disputes, while other groups, recently arrived or not, do not draw any public comment.

This is the demographic and social background of the story that follows. In 1995, the Canadian Islamic Trust Foundation bought a large property just off the Queen Elizabeth Way, the major highway that borders Lake Ontario and links Toronto to Buffalo. The existing zoning designation allowed for a place of worship "as of right"—or so the trust was told by their agents. But the property was larger than what was required for a mosque, and the trust decided to try to add several related operations that, unfortunately for them, are treated in planning law as distinct land uses: a social hall that would generate revenue from weddings and similar events, a travel agency (specializing in trips to Mecca), and a private Muslim school. The trustees were told that a private school was not a permitted use, or at least not "as of right," but that since another semipublic school (belonging to the Catholic board) had recently obtained permission to locate a large high school nearby, it was very likely that planning permission for the private Islamic school would also be granted. That the mosque itself would require a zoning variance was not known to the promoters for a long time.

The public debate started when in early 1996 a local newspaper advertisement soliciting contributions to build a large mosque on that site drew the attention of the (non-Muslim) mayor's office. As the planning board decision puts it, "Members of the project committee were requested to attend a meeting with the mayor of Mississauga. There were obviously very different perceptions of the tone and underlying motivation of the meeting. In fact, there were suggestions throughout the hearing that the opposition that was mobilized by this proposal was based on considerations other than planning law."[6] The meeting hosted by the mayor and attended by the local councillor and a planner must have been very hostile indeed, because the trustees were told to go find another location, even though the closing date of the real estate transaction was only days away. This was not a legally motivated request, since the mayor's people seemed as ignorant of local zoning rules as the Muslim leaders and did not point out to the trustees that the mosque itself, never mind any other business, would need a zoning variance.

In the absence of correct legal knowledge, the trustees, believing the law was on their side, and perhaps provoked by the fact that the opposition, as the board euphemistically put it, "was based on considerations other than planning," chose to go ahead with the purchase. Subsequently, both Mayor Hazel McCallion and the city council continued to oppose the mosque and related facilities. The city called not one but two public meetings at which some residents expressed very "strenuous objections"—but still without deploying relevant legal arguments. In the end, the Mississauga city council refused to approve the project. They were able to deny permission because the property needed rezoning—a fact discovered by a city planner at some unspecified time subsequent to the land purchase. Feeling that they had been misled about the zoning rules as well as mistreated, the Islamic Trust then appealed the decision to the Ontario Municipal Board.

Faced with the prospect of the board's near-almighty power (board decisions are almost never subject to judicial review), the trust proceeded proactively to make the kinds of concessions that developers and homeowners facing community opposition to their projects usually make to facilitate board approval. The proposed building was downsized from almost 10,000 square feet to 6,620 square feet; and the proposed school was now described as small, with a single initial grade 9 class.

In this as in other cases, those who opposed the mosque quickly realized that their objections had to somehow fit into the formats and logics of planning law. Thus, they objected to the size of the building—an objection already anticipated by the revised plans—and also to the risk that there would be traffic jams and insufficient parking. (Scarce parking is, not coincidentally, the most common objection voiced by people who object to affordable-housing or supportive-housing developments.) The trust had made provision for no less than 361 parking spaces, but this was said to be insufficient by the opponents—even though no residences abutted the property in question, which meant that even if parking was scarce, few residents would be significantly affected.

The city's lawyer attempted to give the standard arguments about parking a new, culturally specific twist. He stated that while the city's official plan encourages the sharing of parking facilities between schools and places of worship, sharing could not take place in this instance because the neighboring Catholic school would be operating at the same time as the Friday prayers at the mosque. Other legally creative arguments were put forward, many lacking any serious connection to planning rationales.

The city then made what might have been its worst legal mistake, which was to bring—or perhaps to allow—Mayor McCallion herself to testify at the board hearing. In other similar disputes in neighboring municipalities, mayors have acted to appeal to reason, calm fears, and prevent cultural anxieties from getting out of hand—as President Obama tried to do in the context of the "ground zero mosque" controversy. But McCallion chose to stoke the fire. She talked at length about the problems caused by worshippers parking on residential streets—which was irrelevant, since the property was in a former industrial park now used for a variety of mainly commercial uses.

The final decision of the board—whose lengthiest sections, predictably, were "parking" and "traffic"—was, in terms of the outcome, very much in keeping with board decisions involving contentious developments. For instance, tall condo buildings that are opposed by neighbors are often approved by the OMB but only if several stories are shaved from the plans and/or some minimal amenities are added to the area. In the Islamic Trust case, there were no immediate neighbors with an interest in aesthetic or other amenities. But in keeping with the board's habit of mollifying opponents, on principle, and generating decisions that make the board look like the reasonable arbiter who calms the civic waters and arrives at a compromise, the mosque promoters were told to eliminate the "social hall" and to put in additional parking spots, as well as to add a fence. The school, however, was approved.

One feature of the board decision was highly unusual: a several-paragraph-long description of Muslim religious practices. Since decisions on other buildings rarely take much time to describe what goes on in that type of building, one can only assume that the long explanation was provided specifically for the purpose of educating the decision's readers—including Mississauga city lawyers, councillors, and officials (and the mayor herself, no doubt). I cite only a portion of this long passage:

> With respect to the mosque, it was explained to the Board that the Islamic religion requires that its members integrate their religion into their daily life. Members are required to pray five times a day. The times of the prayer are exact, but will vary over the year depending on the time of sunrise and sunset. . . .
>
> While it is obviously ideal that prayers take place in a mosque, in acknowledgement of the exigencies of modern life, members are permitted to pray wherever there is a quiet place that can be set aside for the purpose, both at work and at home. However, there is one prayer a week that is a more significant prayer: the Friday noon prayer, or Juma prayer. Members of the religion are encouraged to attend a mosque for this prayer. Many members seek to find a mosque which is close to their home and place of work, and make efforts to attend the Friday prayer. However, because the number of mosques, until recently, have been disparate [*sic*] and few, the Board heard testimony of travels of twenty minutes or more [by car] . . . (par. 25, 26)
>
> Activities in the mosque require worshippers to face east toward Mecca . . . (par. 28)
>
> In respect to schooling, the evidence was that study was an integral part of the Islamic faith. Apparently, there are only two Islamic private schools in the entire Greater Toronto area. The principal/Imam of [one] school indicated that there was an extensive waiting list for children . . . (par. 29)
>
> Smoking, drinking, and drugs are strictly prohibited. Attendees of any events taking place at the social hall (eg. weddings, social dinners, teas, or other events) will either have come from worship at the mosque or will at some point attend the mosque for prayer. (par. 30)

The legally irrelevant sentence about smoking and drinking being banned was clearly meant as a rebuke to those who associated mosques with danger and disorder. Overall, the decision, straying quite far from the usual planning jargon, forcefully conveyed a didactic message about the need to understand rather than condemn minority religions and cultures. Here the OMB, which is known for its highly technical and often unreadable decisions, took the time to not only preach but also perform Canadian multiculturalism.

Nevertheless, despite the board's sincere effort to understand and then explain why Islamic community institutions might require buildings of a certain size and shape and containing particular functions (e.g., they realized a travel agency was needed because pilgrimages to Mecca are best provided by an Islamic agency), in the end, they still forced the Islamic Trust to downsize its plans as a concession to the city's (and residents') objections. The fact that the case would very likely never have reached the board (with the concomitant expense of hiring specialized lawyers and expert witnesses) and would thus not have been modified if the proposal had been for a church rather than a mosque was never mentioned either in the decision itself or in the media coverage.

The second case, also from 1995, illustrates the fact that in a city such as Toronto, intercultural conflicts do not always pit Anglo-Saxons or Christians against "others." Sometimes two different "ethnic" groups openly debate or dispute. When this happens, Anglo-Canadian born politicians and civic leaders often feel called upon to preach multiculturalism, tolerance, and diversity to the less enlightened "ethnics," as happened in the "East York mosque" case.

In what was then (prior to 1998) the small, largely working-class autonomous borough of East York, which has had a significant Greek-speaking minority for many decades, Sunni Muslims attempting to turn a disused industrial lot surrounded by unattractive high-rises into a mosque ran up against a series of objections that, like Mayor McCallion's plea about parking, were not what they appeared to be. The first argument against the mosque was that the city would lose $91,000 in taxes (since places of worship do not pay municipal taxes)—which was not a strong argument, since industries had been for years leaving that area of the city, and it was not likely that the space vacated by an industry would be occupied by another industry in the foreseeable future.[7]

The second issue was, as one would expect, parking. The scarce-parking argument was invoked by some councillors who introduced a motion to reverse the municipality's earlier approval and deny the mosque the necessary planning permission. The newspaper reported: "The crucial swing votes in the 6–3 decision were those of councillors George Vasilopoulos and John Antonopoulos, who decided the parking proposal put forward by the Muslims and the borough's planning commissioner wasn't good enough."[8] The councillors with the Greek names, it turned out, had been pressured by the Cypriot-Greek association, which, unfortunately for the Sunnis, had its citywide headquarters next to the property wanted for the mosque.

The mosque leaders were aware of the importance of ample parking in securing planning permission, and they had already approached the Greek-Cypriot group in the hopes of drawing up a plan for sharing parking that would satisfy the council of the borough. The Muslim leaders pointed out that the Cypriots did not use the parking lot on Fridays, which was the busiest day at the mosque. This argument seemed to fall on deaf ears, however.

No doubt many Greek-Canadians are not especially concerned about mosques; but the East York situation was not an isolated instance of Greek-Muslim tensions being voiced via discussions of buildings. In the mid- and late 1980s, a proposed mosque in Scarborough (an east-end municipality absorbed into the megacity in 1998) had faced repeated opposition from a local Greek restaurant owner, who reportedly managed to delay the mosque's opening by several years, by appealing first to the Ontario Municipal Board and then to divisional court. Interviewed by the local press in the wake of the 1995 East York dispute, the restaurant owner responsible for the earlier legal battle, Peter Kalyvitis, was adamant: "Sure, you can scream and shout discrimination, but maybe the problem is really parking. . . . It was a mistake [to allow the mosque]. . . . If you come here on a Friday afternoon, the area is paralyzed. There is still nowhere near enough parking."[9]

The *Toronto Star*, always a promoter of diversity, weighed in with a paternalistic editorial criticizing East York's reversal of the mosque approval—but it did so in language that revives old northern European stereotypes about Mediterranean cultures:

> When East York councillors approved the parking arrangements for a planned mosque in their borough last month most residents applauded the compromise that would bring the Islamic Society of Toronto a most cherished wish—their own place of worship in their Thorncliffe Park community.
>
> Sadly, stubborn councillors—some motivated by age-old conflicts born on foreign soil—are prepared to sully the reputation of Canada's only borough by

insisting on fighting off the mosque. . . . The mosque is to be erected in a neighbourhood that already has a Greek Orthodox and a Macedonian church, neither of which pays taxes nor has insufficient parking. Some of their parishioners
have brazenly resurrected old country hatreds—Greece vs Turkey, especially
over Cyprus—to thwart fellow Canadians who are Muslims.[10]

For the *Star*, which had covered the story in great detail for months, the
hero of the story was East York mayor Mike Prue, presented as a true
and enlightened Canadian upholding constitutional rights and diversity
and defending the rights of the Muslim minority. Prue was certainly acting as the voice of reason, as other mayors (other than McCallion) have
done in similar circumstances.[11] But the fact that like other white English-
speaking Torontonians he was presented throughout as a man with no
particular cultural or religious preferences made it easy for the editorial
writer to contrast his reasonableness to the "old country hatreds" and
"age-old conflicts born on foreign soil" attributed to the disputants. Needless to say, the *Star*'s own choice of words invoked the myth of hotheaded
Mediterranean races with inexplicable, ancient ethnic rivalries—but the
message of the editorial, at face value, was one of diversity.

The image of the reasonable, nonracialized mayor upholding the Canadian values of tolerance and multiculturalism (values said to be lacking
in other cultures) was also disseminated in a different situation, namely
the news coverage of neighbor opposition to the use of a private multimil-
lion dollar mansion, in the suburban city of Brampton, for Sikh religious
gatherings. Initial complaints by neighbors had resulted in the city putting
a parking prohibition on the street in question, in line with Mississauga
mayor McCallion's approach. But since the Sikh leader had two brothers
living on the same wealthy street, on lots that were sufficiently large to
accommodate all cars, the city had no further legal tools to use. This did
not stop the neighbors, however, who attempted to introduce a new bylaw
banning gatherings of more than twenty people.

The mayor of Brampton (presumably conscious of the high property
taxes being paid by the three mansion-owning Sikh brothers in question,
but perhaps also sincerely committed to multiculturalism) made it clear
that she would not countenance any such legal change: "The reality is if
you invite a bunch of people over to watch the Super Bowl, that's your
business. If you invite a bunch of people over to pray, that's your business.
That's your home. The city dealt with the parking. It's not within the parameters of land use planning as to how many people gather."[12]

This mayor's response shows an awareness of the way in which public participation in land-use planning often becomes a vehicle for resentments and anxieties that lurk under the surface in the most apparently harmonious multicultural communities but which have few formal outlets. And yet, complaining about how planning meetings are misused to express cultural and aesthetic prejudices does nothing to shed light on the structure of local planning law. In fact, planning law does make a distinction between Super Bowl–watching and praying: the latter, if conducted by some kind of minister in a group setting, is supposed to be confined to officially approved "places of worship," whereas the former is not considered a distinct land use.

But one can forgive the mayor for not knowing that planning law makes a distinction between watching the Super Bowl and praying as a group. Planning law, especially at the local level, is a regulatory maze whose complexities have increased from decade to decade, as new categories and new rules are added. The province of Ontario has engaged in some larger-scale rationalization, creating a large "Greenbelt" and imposing some overall policies. But locally, municipalities continue to operate with little if any overall principles, and as a result, the rules set out in official plans and zoning bylaws are broken or suspended with great ease. When official plans and comprehensive zoning bylaws were first implemented in Ontario— which was not until the 1950s—zoning bylaws distinguished light industrial from heavy industrial, low-rise residential from high-rise residential, and so forth. But as time went on, legal exceptions accumulated—and these were then used as precedents by nearby property owners seeking exceptional status for their properties. In addition, new rules have been introduced over time to deal with new and seemingly risky activities and endeavors. These rules have been generated in an ad hoc fashion, however, not as part of a systematic codification effort.

Thus, that the mayor of Brampton did not know that praying in public is a distinct land use is understandable. Similarly, that legal staff at Mississauga city hall did not know, for a considerable period of time, that the Islamic Trust property that caused so much controversy could not be turned into a mosque without a zoning bylaw exception is not a sign of their incompetence, but rather a symptom of a Kafkaesque system of rules whose complexity and irrationality make individuals and groups feel powerless and even deceived by bureaucrats and politicians alike. And as seen in situations involving subsidized housing as well as in the mosque incidents, because there are few other opportunities for neighbors to talk in public about what they want and don't want for their communities, planning and zoning processes easily turn into arenas in which all manner of concerns and fears and anxieties are aired, often in a dysfunctional manner.

The NIMBY Syndrome?

The use of planning law and related consultation mechanisms to air views about who or what belongs or does not belong in a city or a neighborhood has often been criticized by progressive urban studies scholars as "NIMBYism" (from "Not In My Back Yard").[13] Anyone familiar with local politics will recognize the "NIMBY syndrome"—that is, the way in which any number of proposed developments, from wind turbines to public housing, can easily draw a huge amount of negative attention from neighbors, sometimes for reasons that do not appear to be rational. Professional planning journals often devote much space to sharing strategies and ideas about how planners can counteract or fight against "NIMBYism."

While doing research for this book I certainly had plenty of opportunities to silently fume about "NIMBYism" as I sat at community meetings or planning hearings listening to people articulate objections that were often ill-founded and legally irrelevant, and which sometimes (though by no means always) showed prejudice against marginalized groups. However, when reflecting on the processes described as NIMBYism with the benefit of hindsight, it seems to me that calling a group or an individual a "NIMBY" does not help us to understand how and why certain venues and certain processes seem to be designed in such a way as to fuel social and political fires rather than to provide opportunities for constructive engagement and mutual education. It is all too easy to criticize the ill-informed or prejudiced comments of this or that person or neighborhood group; but what is more important is to think about what we could call the governance architecture, that is, the way in which the process is designed.

The inhabitants of Mississauga—and of other cities undergoing rapid demographic change—would very much benefit from participating in well-organized, informed, calm discussions about the city's changing demographics. Such discussions do take place; but they are usually organized not by city leaders but by social agencies serving immigrants, or by interfaith initiatives, and so they have a limited audience and often preach only to the converted. It is remarkable that national and municipal governments that welcome thousands of new immigrants from far-off countries every year do not feel obliged to provide regular opportunities to discuss immigration policies and to acquire the information that is needed to engage in practices of citizenship at all scales.[14]

In the absence of public education and public discussion about the processes of "diversity," residents, who often feel very strongly about their street, their neighborhood, and their city, but lack information about migration patterns, immigration policies, and the cultural practices of certain co-citizens, are liable to becoming suddenly mobilized in a reactive and uninformed manner whenever a specific change—say, a mosque needing planning permission for a new minaret—appears on the immediate horizon. Once motivated to get out of the house to attend such a site-specific meeting, they will then discover that those who called the meeting, worried that "considerations other than planning" might derail the process and generate too much heat, usually insist on restricting the discussion.

It makes sense that a mosque or a planner or a planning tribunal would chastise or simply ignore comments and submissions that raise issues outside the scope of planning law. But if a zoning hearing is not the right place to talk about how people feel about changing patterns of migration and settlement, where can one talk about these things? The mismatch between what people want to talk about and what the legal framework allows and requires has predictable results. Residents feel dissatisfied and claim that "city hall is not listening," while planners and other experts fume about the public's emotionalism. Municipal politicians, on their part, end up feeling torn. On the one hand, they do want to engage with their constituents (unlike the lawyers and planners) and, depending on their politics, they want to either validate or critique prejudices against newcomers. But on the other hand, they know that a planning process is supposed to stick to buildings, parking, and parks, and they know that populist mutterings about the social housing or the mosque being planned for their neighborhood can easily be seen as a symptom that "city hall" is nefariously plotting against the locals. Councillors who do not want to be swept out of power by populist resentment politics often make a point of distancing themselves from "city hall" and even from government in general—as was seen in the Toronto municipal election campaign of the fall of 2010, which resulted in the surprise election of Mayor Rob Ford, a councillor long famous for vociferously criticizing his own bureaucracy as wasteful and incompetent.

Left-wing academics (and community activists working on housing and similar issues) love to gather in small groups to deplore right-wing populism. But residents are not wholly to blame if they do not know much or anything about other cultures and religions. They are also not to blame for not understanding the limits of planning law or the workings of local government.

The structural governance issues that this book has described result in a situation in which the anxieties associated with rapid social and economic change end up being funneled through the very inadequate legal mechanisms of land-use planning. Those who dominate the arenas provided for land-use consultations are not necessarily narrow-mindedly defending property values, and they are not necessarily bigots and racists. My own research corroborates Mark Purcell's careful study of neighborhood activism in suburban middle-class municipalities in California, which shows that neither race issues nor real estate values, contrary to what many left-wing urbanists think, are always the key forces in neighborhood politics. He concludes that homeowners' activism can certainly provide a venue for race and class fears, but it is rooted less in direct economic or social self-interest and more in an emotional attachment to place. The kind of local political activity that admittedly often leads to out-and-out NIMBY-ism is not just a knee-jerk reaction to protect class and race interests. Such activity also has a more proactive and less negative dimension, since it "is designed to defend and proactively realize [homeowners'] spatial vision in the material space of their neighbourhoods."[15]

The dozens of Committee of Adjustment hearings that my research assistants and I witnessed showed that in a surprisingly large number of cases—perhaps the majority, though quantification is not possible—neighbors showed up to oppose development applications that would actually increase property values, often defending the postwar bungalow form against more contemporary and more valuable renovations. Purcell perhaps overestimates the "proactive" dimension of homeowner politics: my research leads inescapably to the conclusion that sentimental nostalgia for "community," rather than a rationally articulated vision of what the future should look like, is by far the dominant mode of citizen engagement in local debates regarding everything from park design to mosque-building. And yet, his work and that of other scholars engaged in similar studies helpfully take critical urbanism beyond the ritual denunciation of class and race interests, and invite us to take seriously the emotional charge as well as the content of what neighbors say when they go to public meetings.[16] When faced with a passionate group of neighbors that expresses vehement opposition to a highway or a solar-power development, or a public-housing development, denouncing NIMBYism is unhelpful. It is definitely true that, as an overview of urban-governance issues put it, in a cautionary note about the dangers of simply calling public meetings, "in many cases participation requires public education and building leadership capacity in the community."[17] Existing structures tend to favor self-appointed leaders, organized mainly around home owning, and they systematically exclude renters, young people, and, to some extent, racialized groups, especially those who are poor and/or live in rental housing. Serious public participation, not only in decisions that are part of planning law but also more generally in community building, requires at least some prior organizing work to ensure that the marginal groups are not further marginalized by the consultation process, and may require educating people about social inequality, the legal powers of municipalities, and so forth.

Diverse cities that aim to facilitate both democratic engagement and justice toward newcomers will have to think creatively about how to design opportunities for exchanges and interactions that equip local leaders to discuss the challenges of diversity in an informed manner—not simply stating their views. For that reason, planning-law hearings and meetings about particular proposals regarding individual properties, which are often the only place where citizens engage politically at the local level, are not helpful in relation to the governance needs of diverse cities in a time of economic uncertainty. Planning law and planning-related civic activity have in recent years become less rather than more suited to furthering inclusion and diversity. It is clear from the whole of the book thus far, not just from the stories in this chapter, that the kind of reactive, ad hoc, one-property-at-a-time logic that dominates both city governance and neighbor participation tends to encourage a myopic politics of resentment—"save our park" or "save our community" is often code for "not in my backyard." And rather than argue whether a mosque or a group home should be in this backyard or that one, it would be more helpful to look up past one's own home and try to see the city as a whole.

To reform governance processes so as to improve urban life on a citywide scale for all residents (and not just for homeowners with a sense of entitlement), one first has to take a close and critical look at those often invisible legal and administrative mechanisms that govern, at least in theory, the city as a whole. The tale of the rise and fall of the Toronto harmonized zoning bylaw told in the concluding chapter suggests that even if overall plans (such as the harmonized bylaw) are imperfect, abandoning the citywide perspective altogether in favor of village-elder micro-local compromises is likely to further inequality and exclusion. City planning, as Toronto's urban guru Jane Jacobs eloquently showed, can sometimes ride roughshod over democracy (though it did so much more in her day than in ours); but now that city planning has largely been abandoned in favor of single-building solutions and, at best, "precinct plans," it's time to reconsider whether the Jacobs front-stoop perspective can cope with today's problems.

CHAPTER 9

The Death of Planning and the Challenges of Diversity

Concluding Reflections

In many large cities that attract global migrants, the majority view is that urban diversity is a good thing. In the global context this is no small achievement. Given the backlash against ethnic, cultural, and religious diversity occurring in many places (including previously tolerant countries in northern Europe), it makes sense that bureaucrats, politicians, and activists who are depressed about today's urban economic and governance crises should cheer themselves up by gazing at international reports showing their city as a world leader in diversity and tolerance, as is the case in Toronto. And yet, the research presented in this book shows that underneath the pride in urban diversity that—with some hiccups—constitutes the Toronto local ethic, a pride also visible in other cities and neighborhoods in North America, serious conflicts and inequalities exist. As discussed in the introductory chapter, many urban gurus now see diversity mainly from the point of view of global markets in capital and labor, and thus think of cities not as democratic political entities but rather as economic actors needing to exhibit the type of urban diversity that represents a competitive advantage.[1] Neoliberal urban diversity includes more than ethnic restaurants and a lively night life; corporate leaders do recognize the importance of properly utilizing an ethnically diverse skilled labor force. And many neoliberal urbanists (e.g., Toronto's Richard Florida, internationally renowned for his "creative cities" idea) do favor some government intervention, such as public investment in education and infrastructure, two areas in which capitalism is happy to rely largely on the state.

But pursuing market-friendly forms of diversity does nothing to address the plight of those whose particular diversity cannot be linked to cities' global competitive advantage. Older blue-collar workers, young high school dropouts, recent immigrants, those who for health reasons need supportive housing, rooming house tenants—these and other marginalized groups, who form part of all cities' diversity mix, are ignored by those promoting a neoliberal vision of gentrified urban diversity.

That today's cosmopolitan cities are more diverse but also much more unequal than they were forty years ago is well known to urban scholars. What is new here, what this book has contributed, is a detailed study of the role that cities' regulatory arsenal plays, or might play, in supporting the kinds of diversity that are not necessarily valued by the new global (and local) economy. The study has shown that cities rarely use their legal and regulatory tools to promote inclusion. To compound the problem, cities seem to have no mechanism for gathering collective experiences and using them to generate new legal and regulatory policies, in part because nearly all civic energy is spent either on micro-local issues (improving or preserving this or that amenity or streetscape) or in single-issue campaigns, say to create bike lanes or set up farmers' markets.[2]

Why does this happen? Sometimes social inclusion is defeated by concerted political attacks from the right. But in traditionally liberal cities, such as Toronto, social inclusion is often left out of the agenda due to inertia and/or lack of vision. Legal rules based on archaic assumptions (such as the idea that nonfamily households constitute "locally undesirable land uses" that need to be governed through separation distances) persist despite their clash with today's diversity and inclusion ideals. Archaic laws persist because while there's lots of room in local law to get exceptions, and occasionally even to change this or that single-issue rule, there's no venue for reflecting collectively on the rules themselves, as a whole. In the absence of a mechanism to constantly reflect on and evaluate collective experience, the regulatory habits laid out in long-outdated municipal codes live on, as do the political habits developed long ago, in far less diverse times. A good example of such an anachronistic governance tradition—one that is found in formal law but also in nonlegal political and civic mechanisms—is the assumption that whoever shows up to complain about a local matter should be heard and mollified, whereas the needs of those who do not live nearby, or are unlikely to show up for structural reasons, can simply be ignored. How municipal law is interpreted and applied in practice, and how the formal rules of urban municipalities interact with nonlegal governance traditions, had not been hitherto documented in any systematic way. And as we have seen in chapter after chapter, and in issue after issue, local regulation is characterized by a lack of systematic policy: it is a nonsystem in which ad hoc decision-making enshrines the wishes of civic society's squeaky wheels in law, while neglecting the needs of the city as a whole.

So what could be done to stimulate collective reflection, to promote collective "learnings" and, on the basis of that, revise and edit cities' regulatory toolboxes to better support the kinds of diversity that the marketplace ignores or excludes?

Typically, critical urbanists getting to the end of a book make ringing calls for popular action against capitalism, against racism, and so forth. But I prefer to avoid political speeches, at least when writing books based on empirical research. Reflecting on the research, and thinking about what lessons might be of use, well beyond Toronto and well beyond this year or next, I believe the key moral of this book's story is that most important civic issues, including diversity, need to be addressed on a citywide basis, using city (and/or regional) perspectives, rather than at the scale of the neighborhood. Taking a city or region-wide perspective means breaking with the fashion of micro-local planning, a fashion sparked by Jane Jacobs, among others. It is high time to recognize that the populist attack on city, regional, and national planning waged from the 1960s onward by a wide range of folks, from populist advocates of neighborhood involvement to right-wing Tea Party critics of government as such, has been very successful, indeed too successful. The baby was thrown out with the bathwater. Politicians look only after the needs of those constituents who speak up; bureaucrats enforce outdated and irrational rules because neither politicians nor the public trusts them to use their brains and suggest new, better rules; and civic activism focuses almost completely on single issues at the local level (often under the banner of "neighborhood diversity") while the citywide gap between rich and poor, and between old-timers and immigrants, yawns ever wider.

That the populist antiplanning ethos of Jacobs and her admirers has been all too successful is illustrated by a story that received scant attention but that can here serve as a concluding reflection. This Toronto story, whose significance is far more than local, involves the failure of the planning department's major project of 2009–10, namely the harmonized, comprehensive zoning bylaw that would have finally unified, for zoning purposes, the "megacity" created out of six municipalities in 1998.[3]

The harmonized zoning bylaw painstakingly elaborated over many years by the planning department was finally approved by the council, with no enthusiasm, in 2010, during the last council meeting of Mayor David Miller's term. This was a very rare instance of a planned change in the legal rules affecting the whole city (indeed, the only such citywide change in legal rules I witnessed during six years of research).[4] The process as well as the content of the law stood in sharp contrast to the urban governance norm of seat-of-the-pants, reactive, highly local decision-making. The change was much needed. From 1998 on, the zoning law for the city consisted of forty-three separate bylaws, totaling over a million words in length. A ridiculous nonsystem of rooming house licensing, through which the city spends regulatory resources on the shrinking downtown single-room housing stock while ignoring the proliferation of similar housing in areas beyond the old city, is only one of numerous irrationalities that a harmonized citywide law might have mitigated.

The proposed harmonized law was no Robert Moses–style grandiose plan; it was very much in keeping with the current ethos of modest government. At one public meeting, the planning department offered, as its chosen "sample" of the new bylaw, a demonstration of how a new, harmonized way of measuring roof heights would make construction and renovation work much more straightforward. It was also explained that a new rule would prevent homeowners whose plots ended in ravines from erecting any new structures close to the edge, for environmental reasons. Also for environmental reasons, a new rule would ensure that at least 50 percent of backyards remained as either lawn or garden (rather than being paved for parking or being turned into a large swimming pool). Similarly, while drive-throughs at fast-food restaurants were still allowed, the distance between a drive-through and the nearest residence was slightly increased.

Although the new law encompassed the whole city, it was essentially a consolidation exercise, not a reform, much less a revolution. Harmonization was highly limited; for example, suburban areas that had had mandatory large side-yards got to keep them in the new law. And planners ensured that policy questions, especially regarding social issues, were consistently ruled out of order. At one public meeting, a question about possibly adding rules facilitating or requiring a certain number of units of affordable housing in new condominium developments was dismissed, as the chief planner told the speaker (incorrectly) that such a change was not within the city's powers and would have to come from the provincial government.[5] The voluminous documentation produced for this legal exercise as well as the statements made by planners during public meetings and council meetings made it clear that the new bylaw was a technical exercise, and a very limited one at that; there was no diversity-oriented social policy, and only the faintest of environmental rationales.

Despite the fact that the planners made sure they did not wander into issues perceived as political, there was nevertheless only weak support for the new bylaw at the city council. At the February 2010 meeting of the planning and growth committee, one councillor attempted to direct the planning department to come up with different rules for each ward. Planners tried to explain that the "zones" of a zoning bylaw do not refer to geographic wards but to categories such as "industrial" or "single-family residential." Other councillors were aware that the ward-specific zoning idea was bizarre, but their priority was to press planners to confirm that all variances that were already approved, whether or not they had been acted upon, would be preserved. The councillor chairing the committee, on his part, reassured the public present that the planning department had no intention of changing its traditional practice of making changes to rules and granting exceptions more or less on demand.

Why were councillors so loath to straighten out any of the zoning mess? The answer is that byzantine and highly localized rules with uneven enforcement mean that a market is created for fixers and brokers who will facilitate one-off compromises. Since councillors usually act as fixers, they have no incentive to make the legal system clearer, simpler, and more accessible, either in regard to zoning or any other issue. They instead have strong incentives to be seen as powerful village elders able to get better rules or exceptions for local businesses and local residents. That the city's rules are supposed to be public law designed in the public interest, rather than opportunities for mediation to make private parties happy, is not something that councillors appear to understand.

A telling detail was that councillors complained that they could not read the immensely long and complicated new bylaw, and demanded an easy-to-read map instead. The planning department attempted to comply. Given the existence of hundreds of special-rules areas and exceptional spaces, however, no map large enough to show the zoning categories legibly could be drawn. The planners ended up drawing 921 separate maps instead. They were too polite to point out that it was precisely the historical demands made by councillors for mountains of special districts, special rules, and exceptions that had created the Borges-like situation of a city whose legal complexity could not be reduced to legibility either through texts or through any manageable number of maps.[6]

Continuing with the same village-elder behavior that had produced the legal monster of the forty-three added-together bylaws, councillors showed little or no interest in having the larger purposes of the bylaw explained by the planners but were instead highly deferential toward a series of deputations. In keeping with the fragmented and single-issue character of city politics, each group focused exclusively on one of hundreds of changes and opposed the law on that basis. A fancy lawyer representing fast-food restaurants threatened to appeal the whole bylaw to the Ontario Municipal Board because of the drive-through separation distance. A federation of North Toronto (that is, upper-class) residents' association objected vigorously to the loss of property rights inherent in the new rule about building on erosion-prone ravine edges. And a representative from the chemical industry objected to proposed new separation distances for chemical storage facilities, put in the new bylaw in response to a fatal accident at an oil storage depot. (Later on, the planning department changed the rule so it would affect only oil tanks, not other chemical storage facilities.) In addition, it was reported that the pool and hot tub manufacturers' objection to the 50 percent backyard planting rule had been successful, and that planning staff had made changes that satisfied the industry. That the amendments to the backyard rule were treated as a private, mediated solution, rather than as a public legal change of public interest, was apparent from the fact that neither the planners nor the committee chair explained the change or sought the committee's approval for it.

The planners had undermined their own project so much that a property lawyer described the law as a "Swiss cheese bylaw," in reference to the planners' inventive solution to the burgeoning demand for exemptions, which was to classify numerous areas of the city as "holes in the bylaw."[7] But even a Swiss cheese bylaw was too much of a threat to the village-elder system. In May 2011, the council (now led by a pro-business, anti-public-servant mayor) repealed the brand-new harmonized zoning plan, with virtually no publicity.

This story does not quite show that planning as such is dead. The planners had failed to persuade the councillors, despite having bent over backward to reassure people that the three thousand variances that had been granted in just the previous year would still be legal. But the planning department did not vanish in a puff of smoke. The death-of-planning thesis announced at the beginning of the chapter means not that the profession is dead, but rather that the Toronto story is an example of today's trend away from citywide, evidence-based plans, and toward one-project-at-a-time, reactive planning—"let's make a deal planning," as professional publications put it.

While the bulk of city planning work is concerned with single parcels of land, the signature projects (the work that planners like to do) take place at a scale that is not quite the same as that of individual ownership. The scale of today's "let's make a deal" plans, however, is certainly not the scale of the whole, complex, diverse city. And when considering scale (a crucial dimension in urban governance), it needs to be noted that the scale of a project includes more than the amount of territory covered. Each project has a temporal as well as a spatial scale; and spatial scales are connected to temporal scales. A single building can be renovated with no reference to city- or nationwide economic and social trends, for example; but working on the city as a whole requires taking socioeconomic trends into account. City planning is necessarily future-oriented and needs to take large-scale trends into account.[8]

Citywide diversity may in some instances be supported and promoted by microscale projects. Citywide diversity on the basis of mental health, for example, was certainly promoted by those developing the tiny supportive-housing development in East Chinatown described in chapter 5. But that only happens occasionally. Most of the time, both official action (especially by councillors) and civic action are reactive in nature, and address the needs or desires of those who already live there and who feel a sense of entitlement. Supporting citywide, inclusive diversity of all kinds—and not just the kinds of diversity that today's economy favors—requires citywide planning; and citywide planning requires examining aggregate data and anticipating future needs.

If urban diversity in all its forms—including tenants as well as home-owners, young people as well as the middle-aged, recent immigrants as well as old-timers, people who need supportive or institutional housing as well as families—is to be properly supported, a citywide perspective is necessary. A group of neighbors who all live in single-family homes, even if they are ethnically diverse, are unlikely to take the needs of homeless citizens and rooming house tenants into account in their deliberations. And if local politicians talk to nobody but home-owning families and business people in their area, they too are highly unlikely to take the needs of more marginalized groups into account.

Diversity is often invoked by both citizens and planners involved in current projects. But pursuing certain kinds of diversity in highly localized projects may mask cities' failure to practice socially inclusive diversity at the scale of the whole city. To explain this contradiction between different scales of planning (and of activism), we need to briefly return to the introductory chapter's main protagonist, Jane Jacobs.

In the 1960s, Jane Jacobs—the greatest urban guru Toronto has ever had and the twentieth century's most influential urban thinker—dreamt of a diverse and welcoming city governed largely by spontaneous cooperative action, like a village. The image of a city that would work like a village, or like a group of villages, has since then held great sway over ordinary citizens as well as among architects and planners. Toronto is not the only city that prides itself on being first and foremost a city of neighborhoods.

It seems rather churlish to say anything critical about the trend to see and experience the city at the level of the small district. Don't people identify with their local area, much more than with large sprawling urban agglomerations? Aren't local streets much nicer than arterial roads? Isn't it true that people buy homes in particular areas, rather than shopping around the whole city? Undeniably, much of what makes urban life pleasant and satisfying takes place at the scale of the neighborhood, or even the microneighborhood. Like others, I enjoy walking down to the local cheese shop and running into the same people I see at my kids' school. But these pleasures, today, do not have the same meaning and the same social function as they did in Jane Jacobs's day. At that time, being recognized by name by local shopkeepers was a welcome respite from both the gray anonymity of "Organization Man" (the fifties' paradigm of corporate lifetime employment), and from the bureaucratic excesses of large-scale, citywide and nationwide planning practices. When Jacobs joined with her neighbors to fight against a proposed expressway that would have cut the neighborhood in half, that was clearly a progressive, democratic political act.

But urban life today is hardly suffering from an excess of centralized planning and big, public, citywide projects. Few cities (outside of China, perhaps) are currently carrying out large-scale reforms that affect all of their urban space. Cities are certainly pursuing improvement projects; but these are now usually oriented to tourism rather than to the needs of inhabitants, on the lines of the Baltimore Harbor or Faneuil Hall in Boston, and they are limited by profitability considerations, since they are almost always public-private partnerships. These projects do bring some jobs (though usually service jobs) to decaying urban centers, and they do help to stop the kind of decay that has corroded both business districts and older residential areas in postindustrial cities, in Europe as well as in North America. But these "revitalization" or "regeneration" projects do not seek to transform the city as a whole. All citizens might be indeed free to enjoy the new boardwalks; but the commercial as well as the noncommercial opportunities provided in these "showcase" developments are heavily geared to a certain demographic. There are bike paths, but not skateboard parks; there are organic bakeries, but no outlets for discount groceries.[9]

Some aspects of the postwar grandiose approach to urban design were certainly problematic. However, the main conclusion that emerges from this book is that the pendulum has swung too far the other way. Nowadays, the needs of the city *as a whole* are routinely neglected. In particular, diversity in language, ethnic origin, and to some extent religion is acceptable and even celebrated in progressive cosmopolitan urban centers, at least within certain limits. And municipal regulatory tools, such as zoning, do not systematically target ethnic or racial groups today, as they did in the past. However, diversity in household composition and housing tenure, and along socioeconomic lines, is invisible at the level of official policy and is positively discouraged by the mechanisms of planning law and planning custom, as we have seen in this book.

All planning, even if focused on the details of sewers or roof heights or actuarial tables, is social planning. Planning is the organization of activities and spaces to maximize aggregate well-being (what municipal codes have long called "public welfare," *salus populi*). Planning is governing people and things collectively; planning is taking collective measures to pool risks on a society-wide basis. Many benevolent and not so benevolent dictators, at the local as well as at the national level, seized the idea and the techniques of planning to carry out schemes said to be designed to improve the human condition, which in some cases had very negative results. This, however, is by now more than well known. We cannot simply continue repeating Jane Jacobs's mantras. While postwar public-housing projects were fraught with practical and social problems, turning to public-private partnerships (the trend today) will mean that only those communities that happen to live on or near valuable real estate will get "revitalized." Letting private developers choose which public housing or public amenity to renovate or rebuild is likely to increase inequalities, among the poor as well as between rich and poor.

The question I want to leave readers with is this: given the speed at which the remaining fragments of the postwar welfare state are fraying, in Europe as well as in North America, is it not time to ask whether the pendulum has swung too far? Does the old idea that cities should be planned, as such, still deserve to be condemned? Communal spontaneity can work for micro-local projects, but it cannot be a citywide multi-issue alternative to using public law to regulate urban life. The only practical alternative to planning cities on public-interest grounds—the one being pursued now across the globe—is letting the private sector decide. And in regard to diversity and social inclusion, the private sector will support only certain kinds of diversity. When Jane Jacobs promoted, with good reason, widespread skepticism about "bureaucrats" and about citywide rules and projects, she did not know that she would eventually win the battle against the planners—but lose the war of social inclusion.

Notes

Chapter 1

1. Michael Keith, *After the cosmopolitan? Multicultural cities and the future of racism* (London, Routledge, 2005), 1.

2. The best readily accessible overview of these worrying trends is found in the detailed maps of change over the last thirty years produced by J. David Hulchanski and his team at the University of Toronto, "The three cities within Toronto: Income polarization among Toronto's neighbourhoods 1970–2005." The report is available on the website of the University of Toronto's Cities Centre. See also the 2010 report "Vertical poverty: Poverty by Postal Code 2," available on the website of the United Way of Greater Toronto.

3. In an old but still relevant article, Peter Bachrach and Morton S. Baratz pointed out that sociologists tend to think that power is unified because they privilege the scale of invisible social structures, while pluralist political scientists think power is dispersed because they work at the scale of observable interactions. "Two faces of power," *American Political Science Review*, vol. 56 (1962), 947–952. The present book mainly documents frontline interactions, but it subscribes neither to the pluralist theory nor to theories of a unified elite, since for me the interesting questions are about how various, uncoordinated forms of power are exercised, not in asking who has how much power. My primary data consists mainly of microlevel interactions, but to interpret their significance I rely largely on the background knowledge I have, as a scholar and as a citizen, of the basic social and political architecture of Toronto today.

4. A literature largely neglected by sociologists and political scientists that sheds a great deal of light on the day-to-day dilemmas of governance is loosely called "regulation studies." One of the most important empirical studies of regulatory work is Keith Hawkins's massive study of health and safety inspection work in the UK, *Law as last resort: Prosecution decision-making in a regulatory agency* (Oxford, Oxford University Press, 2002). Municipal inspectors also tend to use law

as a "last resort" (with some notable exceptions), as do many of the regulatory officials whose work has been studied by others.

5. This argument is developed in the context of the history of urban planning in Mariana Valverde, "Seeing like a city: The dialectic of premodern and modern ways of seeing in urban governance," *Law and Society Review*, vol. 45, no. 2 (2011), 277–312.

6. See Michael J. Doucet, "The anatomy of an urban legend," 2004 paper available on the website of the Metropolis project (ceris.metropolis.net). Interestingly, Wikipedia includes the "most diverse city in the world" claim as a notable example of a "factoid" (see entry for "factoid," accessed June 1, 2011).

7. On a small scale, I collaborated with urban studies colleagues to produce a jointly authored report on governance for use by the local media during the 2010 municipal elections. "Governance in Toronto: Issues and questions," available through citiescentre.utoronto.ca.

8. See, for example, Patricia Ewick and Susan Silbey, *The common place of law: Stories from everyday life* (Chicago, University of Chicago Press, 1998); Sally Merry, *Getting justice and getting even: The legal consciousness of working-class Americans* (Chicago, University of Chicago Press, 1990); and Austin Sarat and Thomas Kearns, eds., *Law in everyday life* (Ann Arbor, University of Michigan Press, 1993).

9. Ron Levi and Mariana Valverde, "Freedom of the city? Canadian cities and the quest for governmental status," *Osgoode Hall Law Journal*, vol. 44, no. 3 (2006), 409–460.

10. Much information on municipal law enforcement is found in studies that do not explicitly focus on local law. A study that sheds much light on how building codes, municipal licenses, and zoning rules are or are not enforced is Robert P. Fairbanks, *How it works: Recovering citizens in post-welfare Philadelphia* (Chicago, University of Chicago Press, 2009). See also Mitchell Duneier's detailed study of municipal law and governance affecting street vendors in Greenwich Village, *Sidewalk* (New York, Farrar, Straus and Giroux, 1999).

11. I owe the phrase "ant-like" to Bruno Latour, whose ethnographies of legal and governance processes have influenced my method greatly. "Ant" is a pun on "ANT," the acronym for an approach to research developed by Latour among others, "Actor Network Theory." For more on how Latour's work can be used by sociolegal scholars see Ron Levi and Mariana Valverde, "Making law by association: Latour's ethnography of the Conseil d'Etat," *Law and Social Inquiry*, vol. 33, no. 3 (2008), 805–826.

12. John and Jean Comaroff, *Ethnicity, Inc.* (Chicago, University of Chicago Press, 2008).

13. Edesio Fernandes and Ann Varley, *Illegal cities: Law and urban change in developing countries* (London, Zed Books, 1998), 6.

14. A notable exception is the Canadian magazine *Spacing*, devoted to issues of public space, which carries its share of megaproject boosterism but consistently

attempts to also document and even celebrate ordinary neighborhoods. See www
.spacing.ca.

15. A rare, and very valuable, close-up study of "ordinary" municipal law in
action was carried out by an anthropologist, Constance Perin, who departed from
the American urban sociology tradition by concentrating on suburban rather than
downtown life. *Everything in its place: Social order and land use in America* (Princeton, N.J., Princeton University Press, 1977). I am not aware of any subsequent studies that use the same approach to shed light on how local law shapes everyday
middle-class experience.

16. Neil Smith's influential work on "the revanchist city," for example, only dis-
cusses social exclusionary ordinances and city policies. Neil Smith, *The new urban
frontier: Gentrification and the revanchist city* (London, Routledge, 1996).

17. Using Michel Foucault's influential language, we could say that urban studies
scholars usually see law only when some exceptional exercise of sovereign power
takes place, which distorts the picture by ignoring the quieter and less overtly coercive workings of "governmentalized" law. For Foucauldian approaches to sociolegal studies, see Mariana Valverde, "Spectres of Foucault in sociolegal scholarship,"
Annual Review of Law and Social Science, vol. 6 (2010), 45–60.

18. Jane Jacobs, *The death and life of great American cities* (New York, Vintage, 1961). Curiously given Jacobs's keenness to document microlevel interactions, her later books did not include any detailed study of Toronto urban life,
perhaps because she realized that would have resulted in a dismissal of those works
as "provincial," whereas her famous descriptions of Greenwich Village were read
as universally applicable.

19. Duneier, *Sidewalk*.

20. For the broader context of the expressway fight, see John Sewell, *The shape
of the suburbs* (Toronto, University of Toronto Press, 2009).

21. David Ley's *The new middle class and the remaking of the central city* (Oxford, Oxford University Press, 1996), a hugely influential empirical study of gentrification, contains a case study of Cabbagetown, a Toronto neighborhood that
underwent a similar but more drastic gentrification process starting in the 1970s.

22. See Christopher Klemek, "From political outsider to power broker in two
'Great American Cities,' " *Journal of Urban History*, vol. 34, no. 2 (2008), 309–332.
While bizarrely turning Toronto into an American city, Klemek's article usefully
puts Toronto's urban design trends in the context of North America. He notes that
Jacobs was revered by at least two Toronto mayors, David Crombie (1972–78) and
John Sewell (1978–80).

23. See especially William H. Whyte, *City: Rediscovering the center* (New York,
Doubleday, 1988), a fascinating study of sidewalk behavior, complete with reams of
photographs and diagrams showing how people walk, stop, and talk.

24. Important scholarly organizations promoting this type of analysis include:
the Law and Society Association (of the United States, though a large part of its
membership is international), the Japanese Law and Society Association, the

British Socio-Legal Studies Association, the Canadian Law and Society Association, and the International Institute for the Sociology of Law in Onati. All of these have websites that give current information about research activities and meetings.

25. Gerald Frug and David Barron, "International Local Government Law," *Urban Lawyer*, vol. 38 (2006), 1–62. See also Yishai Blank, "The city and the world," *Columbia Journal of Transnational Law*, vol. 44 (2006), 866–931.

26. See papers by Steve Shrybman posted on the website of the national office of the Canadian Union of Public Employees, especially "Municipal obligations under NAFTA and the WTO," October 2001, www.cupe.ca/ShrybamReport. Accessed October 1, 2010.

27. See Fleur Johns, "Performing power: The deal, corporate rule and the constitution of global legal order," *Journal of Law and Society*, vol. 34, no. 1 (2007), 116–138; and "Financing as governance," *Oxford Journal of Legal Studies*, vol. 31, no. 2 (2011), 391–415.

28. An influential study by noted sociologist and "global cities" scholar Saskia Sassen, *Territory, Authority, Rights: From medieval to global assemblages* (Princeton, N.J., Princeton University Press, 2006), shows that it is very misleading to talk as if globalization meant a disempowering of national and subnational levels of government, since national and subnational governments are busy transforming and even empowering themselves by actively pursuing global agendas.

29. Raymond Williams, *Keywords: A vocabulary of culture and society* (Harmondsworth, UK, Penguin, 1976). Reflecting the then-great influence of Marxist language, Williams has an entry for "dialectic" but not for "diversity." And again reflecting the trends of the time, the lengthy entry for "culture" includes several subterms, including "culture-vulture," but not "multiculturalism."

30. Ellen Berrey, "Divided over diversity: Political discourse in a Chicago neighborhood," *City and Community*, vol. 4, no. 2 (2005), 144.

31. Lauren Edelman, Sally Riggs Fuller, and Iona Mara-Ditta, "Diversity rhetoric and the managerialization of law," *American Journal of Sociology*, vol. 106, no. 6 (2001), 1590.

32. For a powerful critique of the idea of "tolerance," see Wendy Brown, *Regulating aversion: Tolerance in the age of identity and empire* (Princeton, N.J., Princeton University Press, 2006).

33. In his Toronto appearances Florida always pays homage to Jane Jacobs. However, the differences between Jane Jacobs's lifestyle and Richard Florida's are informative. In a lifestyle piece in *Toronto Life* ("Richard Florida: Ten things I can't live without," April 26, 2010), Florida's ten essential things are said to include "indie beer," "modern design," and "custom wheels" (a custom-made racing bike "designed for my exact measurements"). Jane Jacobs's trademark old shawl was arguably as much a product of her time and place as Florida's custom-made bicycle.

34. Richard Florida, *The rise of the creative class* (New York, Basic Books, 2002), 226. In this book Florida praises Jacobs as an early prophet of creativity and diver-

sity (42) and, referring to "organization man" writer William F. Whyte, goes on to claim that "ironically, but not surprisingly, Jacobs and Whyte were the closest of friends. . . . For much of the past half century, intelligent observers of modern life believed it was Whyte's world that had triumphed. But now it appears that Jacobs' world may well carry the day" (42–43).

35. Ibid., 79.

36. Quoted in Jamie Peck, "Struggling with the creative class," *International Journal of Urban and Regional Research*, vol. 29, no. 4 (2005), 762.

37. Christopher Mele and Sharon Zukin are two New York–based scholars whose work generally shows that "diversity" merges with gentrification and increased social inequality. See Christopher Mele, *Selling the Lower East Side: Culture, real estate, and resistance in New York City* (Minneapolis, University of Minnesota Press, 2000); and Sharon Zukin, *Loft living* (Baltimore, Johns Hopkins University Press, 1982) and *The cultures of cities* (Oxford, UK, Blackwell, 1995).

38. See Richard Florida, *Who's your city? How the creative economy is making where to live the most important decision of your life* (New York, Random House, 2008).

Chapter 2

1. Mariana Valverde, "Jurisdiction and scale: Using legal "technicalities" as resources for theory," *Social and Legal Studies*, vol. 18 (2009), 139–158; and Mariana Valverde, "Seeing like a city: The dialectic of premodern and modern ways of seeing in urban governance," *Law and Society Review*, vol. 45, no. 2 (2011), 277–312.

2. The best overview of the North American city as a legal entity is Gerald Frug, *City making: Building cities without building walls* (Princeton, N.J., Princeton University Press, 1999). See also Engin Isin, *Cities without citizens: Modernity of the city as a corporation* (Montreal, Black Rose, 1992). On how nineteenth-century US courts interpreted the expansive "police" powers of municipalities under the *salus populi* / public welfare rubric, see William Novak, *The people's welfare: The police power* (Chapel Hill, University of North Carolina Press, 1996).

3. Michel Foucault, *Security, territory, population: Lectures at the College de France, 1977–78* (New York, Picador, 2004).

4. See the US Supreme Court's 2005 decision in *Kelo v. City of New London*. In its wake, many states passed property-rights statutes limiting municipal eminent-domain powers, but in many states expropriating homes to sell to a more desirable private owner remains legal. The *Kelo* decision is arguably a symptom not only of the hidden coercive powers of municipalities but also, paradoxically, of privatization trends; few if any courts would now demand that if cities expropriate they do so only to build fully public housing and public roads. The extraordinary powers of

expropriation and eminent domain that cities have are increasingly utilized on behalf of corporate owners, even if some public amenities are included in the deal.

5. The United Kingdom, by contrast, has very different systems of municipal governance. It is impossible to make general comparisons, in part because in the UK there is not one but many systems—London, most famously, continues to have a greatly fragmented system, with the old corporation of the City of London still enjoying some of its unique medieval powers. The persistence of county-level governance in England as well as the ancient tradition of using justices of the peace (who are not accountable to municipalities) to resolve many of the disputes that in North America would go before city officials or local councils are some of the factors that show that while at other scales of law Canada has been greatly influenced by English law, municipal governance in Canada has been primarily influenced by American developments. For an excellent account of the slow erosion of local legal powers in twentieth-century England, see Martin Loughlin, *Legality and locality: The role of law in central-local government relations* (Oxford, UK, Clarendon, 1996).

6. On legal complexes as assemblages of objects, papers, and humans, see Bruno Latour, *The making of law: An ethnography of the Conseil d'Etat* (Cambridge, UK, Polity Press, 2010).

7. My attention was drawn to these quasi-legal lines that are literally drawn on the sidewalk by Irus Braverman. See " 'Everybody loves trees': Policing American cities through street trees," *Duke Environmental Law and Policy Forum*, vol. 19, no. 1 (2008), 81–102. The proliferation of fiber-optic cables owned by private companies may well be in the process of "privatizing" underground city spaces, more profoundly than the proliferation of corporate advertising on bus shelters and garbage receptacles.

8. Jamie Benidickson, *The culture of flushing: A legal and social history of sewage* (Vancouver, University of British Columbia Press, 2009).

9. See Eran Ben-Joseph, *The code of the city: Standards and the hidden language of place making* (Cambridge, Mass., MIT Press, 2005). Ben-Joseph's study only covers street standards, however, leaving to the side both the subterranean level and the level of overhead utility lines.

10. Some Committees of Adjustment (what in the United States are known as boards of zoning appeals) make regular use of the online survey (shown on a screen with the help of a technician) to help them adjudicate disputes, whereas others operate in a pre-computer environment. In the latter case, disputing neighbors have to congregate around the committee's table to peer over each other's shoulders trying to decipher hard-copy documents, a physical stance that tends to encourage very informal, nonjudicial modes of interaction.

11. The motto of the redneck mayor elected in Toronto in October 2010, Rob Ford, is "Respect for taxpayers." In the municipal context, and not just in Toronto, "taxpayer" is code for "homeowner" and "business owner." The 50 percent of the Toronto population that rents, however, pays more than its share of local taxes,

since property taxes are higher for rental buildings than for owner-occupied premises, as is the case generally throughout North America.

12. See David Bell and Mark Jayne, *City of quarters: Urban villages in the contemporary city* (Aldershot, UK, Ashgate, 2004).

13. Jane Jacobs initially distinguished between the microneighborhood that is used every day by most residents—which can be as small as a street block—and what she calls "the district," a larger area that can coincide with the boundaries of named neighborhoods. Jacobs, *The death and life of great American cities* (New York, Random House, 1961), 114–115. In Toronto, districts in this sense have become very popular and have in some cases displaced traditional neighborhoods that had more diffuse and usually larger boundaries.

14. See Bernard Frieden and Lynne Sagalyn, *Downtown, Inc.: How America rebuilds cities* (Cambridge, Mass., MIT Press, 1989); and Libby Porter and Kate Shawn, eds., *Whose urban renaissance? An international comparison of urban regeneration strategies* (London, Routledge, 2009).

15. An excellent study of the economics and politics of regeneration in East London that has much relevance for all cities relying on public-private partnerships is Nicholas Deakin and John Edwards, *The enterprise culture and the inner city* (London, Routledge, 1993).

16. Nicholas Blomley, *Rights of passage: Sidewalks and the regulation of public flow* (Abingdon, UK, Routledge, 2011).

17. A study of the governance issues involved in the city of Toronto's remaking of the central Yonge-Dundas intersection shows the key role played by international planners and architects, and draws conclusions that are applicable elsewhere. See Evelyn Ruppert, *The moral economy of cities: Shaping good citizens* (Toronto, University of Toronto Press, 2006).

18. Braverman, " 'Everybody loves trees,' " 81–102.

19. In the late 1990s some homeless people regularly camped/slept under the bleachers of Varsity Stadium, on Bloor one block east of St. George, and often left wet sleeping bags or shopping carts there during the day, much to the dismay of some of my students. The new stadium, opened in 2009, is a much smaller and lighter structure, and it has become nearly impossible to gain shelter there.

20. Alan Hunt, "Police and the regulation of traffic: Policing as a civilizing process?," in Markus Dubber and Mariana Valverde, eds., *The new police science: The police power in domestic and international governance* (Stanford, Calif., Stanford University Press, 2006), 168–184.

21. This finding is based on systematic observation, over two summers, of all four Toronto Committees of Adjustment. Incidentally, there is no legal definition of a "minor" variance; on occasion, a proposed building with almost 100 percent more floor area (habitable space) than the bylaw allows will get approval as a minor variance.

22. S. J. Makielski, *The politics of zoning: The New York experience* (New York,

Columbia University Press, 1966); and Keith Revell, *Building Gotham: Civic culture and public policy in New York City 1898–1938* (Baltimore, Johns Hopkins University Press, 2003).

23. Robert Caro, *The power broker: Robert Moses and the fall of New York* (New York, Knopf, 1974).

24. Mitchell Duneier, *Sidewalk* (New York, Farrar, Straus and Giroux, 1999).

Chapter 3

1. Blomley's fascinating study of how people think about property and quasi-property issues in relation to neighbors' front yards shows that in Vancouver, Chinese people's preference (actual or perceived) for vegetables rather than flowers plays an important role in street interactions. Nicholas Blomley, "The borrowed view: Privacy, propriety, and the entanglements of property," *Law and Social Inquiry*, vol. 30, no. 4 (2006), 617–661.

2. Markus Dubber has argued that paternalism shapes liberal Anglo-American law generally. See Markus Dubber, *The police power: Patriarchy and the foundations of American government* (New York, Columbia University Press, 2005). I do not necessarily disagree, but here I want to emphasize that local law is more paternalistic than national-level law.

3. Constance Perin, *Everything in its place: Social order and land use in America* (Princeton, N.J., Princeton University Press, 1977).

4. The term "blight" has done a lot of urban-clearance work in the United States. "Blight" is a fascinatingly hybrid, moral-physical, cultural-economic term. See Wendell Pritchett, "The "public menace" of blight: Urban renewal and the private uses of eminent domain," *Yale Law and Policy Review*, vol. 21 (2003), 1–52.

5. Daniel Linz et al., "An examination of the assumption that adult businesses are associated with crime," *Law & Society Review*, vol. 38, no. 1 (2004), 60–104.

6. "Debate follows bill to remove clothesline bans," *New York Times*, October 10, 2009 (online).

7. Jamie Benidickson, *The culture of flushing: A social and legal history of sewage* (Vancouver, University of British Columbia Press, 2007); Joel F. Brenner, "Nuisance law and the industrial revolution," *Journal of Legal Studies*, vol. 3, no. 2 (1974), 403–433.

8. Louise Elliott, "Neighbours raise stink about kitchen-smell lawsuit," *Globe and Mail*, July 28, 1999, B6.

9. Maureen Murray, "Stir-fry set to sizzle as suit gets settled," *Toronto Star*, August 14, 1999, A7.

10. Both quotes in Elliott, "Neighbours raise stink."

11. Open letter to "community" from CCNC, February 8, 2002; attached open letter by Tung Chu and Tze Chun Huang, dated January 19, 2002.

12. It is risky to make broad historical generalizations, but it may be useful here to venture the claim that safe drinking water and trash and human-waste disposal figured as the key issues facing cities in the period from the Renaissance to the mid-nineteenth century. Since the establishment of municipal water supplies, sewers, and regular trash collection, noise, which by nature is resistant to being channeled, buried, or cleaned, may be the most contentious issue in everyday urban life. Municipal inspectors interviewed highlighted noise and illegal trash disposal as the two key sources of property-related complaints.

13. Davina Cooper, " 'Far beyond the crowing of a farmyard cock': Revisiting the place of nuisance within legal and political discourse," *Social and Legal Studies*, vol. 11 (2002), 5–35.

14. Melissa Leong, "Docks loses liquor licence over noise," *National Post*, July 25, 2006, A10.

15. In addition to the "generalist" officers (about 140–150 strong), small groups of officers are entrusted with special enforcement campaigns, such as policing illegal trash dumping (with Toronto's various Chinatowns receiving particular attention in this regard) or (more rarely) issuing tickets to dog owners who breach leash and "stoop and scoop" bylaws in particular parks.

16. Vito's obvious bias in favor of respectable people was not shared by all officers, it has to be said. It should also be said that the choice of an Italian pseudonym is not random: a large proportion of the "generalist" MLS inspectors were Italian-Canadian, at least in the 2004–5 period.

17. Sally Merry, *Getting justice and getting even: The legal consciousness of working-class Americans* (Chicago, University of Chicago Press, 1990), 44.

18. *Ottawa (City) v. Freidman*, Ontario Provincial Court (1998) Carswell Ont 5974.

19. *Montreal (City) v. 2952–1366 Quebec Inc* (2005) 3 S.C.R. 141.

20. It was unclear whether the phrase "homeowner pride" was the councillor's or the officer's.

21. A national news program devoted a segment to this dispute: CTV television, W5, April 9, 1996. Ms. Fox then complained to the Canadian Broadcasting Standards Council that she was misrepresented in the program. The council's decision, available online, recounts some of the dispute. See www.cbsc.ca/English/decisions/1996/96102. Accessed May 20, 2006.

22. An excellent overview of US case law in this (very old) area of municipal aesthetic regulation is found in David Burnett, "Note: Judging the aesthetics of billboards," *Journal of Law and Politics*, vol. 2 (2007), 171–233. Canadian law on billboards (and postering) is very similar.

23. The Civil Code of the Province of Quebec states—rather in conflict with the Montreal noise bylaw—that "neighbours shall suffer the normal neighbourhood annoyances that are not beyond the limit of tolerance they owe each other, according to the nature or the location of their land or local custom" (S.976).

Chapter 4

1. Emily Mathieu, "Mayor urges flexibility in seniors park spat," *Toronto Star*, October 14, 2009, GT1.

2. Open letter to residents dated October 14, posted on Mark Grimes's website, markgrimes.ca. Accessed October 30, 2009. The television news item was accessed on October 29 on the Global TV website but is no longer available.

3. Insidetoronto.com/news/local/article/157005 (October 22, 2009).

4. An excellent account of the 1950s formation of the "Metro" level of government and the eventual demise of this entity in the 1998 amalgamation is found in Frances Frisken, *The public metropolis: The political dynamics of urban expansion in the Toronto region 1924–2003* (Toronto, Canadian Scholars' Press, 2007). Frisken points out that while the neoconservative regime of Ontario premier Mike Harris (1995–2002) is locally blamed for downloading, the process by which the province began to disavow responsibility for urban services began as early as the 1970s. For a broader perspective, see Katherine Graham and Susan Phillips, *Urban governance in Canada: Representation, resources, and restructuring* (Toronto, Thomas Nelson, 1998). While comparisons are difficult given the dearth of empirical studies of urban governance, Toronto may be an extreme example of the abandonment of cities by higher levels of government that afflicts cities in many jurisdictions.

5. See Julie-Anne Boudreau, Roger Keil, and Douglas Young, *Changing Toronto: Governing urban neoliberalism* (Toronto, University of Toronto Press, 2009), 69–92.

6. This process was vividly explained to me by a former senior bureaucrat, who was eventually forced to resign.

7. Max Weber, *Weber: Selections in translation*, ed. W. G. Runciman, trans. Eric Matthews (Cambridge, Cambridge University Press, 1978), 348.

8. Scholars working in the sociology of knowledge have produced numerous studies of the governance effects of particular "practices of inscription" (e.g., the categories preprinted on standardized, fill-in-the-blanks documents such as census forms or government funding forms). But such studies usually focus only on preformatted varieties of official paper. Older state knowledge formats, such as direct visual inspection, that still exist today and play an important role in local governance have received very little attention from scholars.

9. Brenna Keatinge, "Sex battles: Civic politics and the regulation of adult entertainment urban space in a Toronto inner suburb," MA thesis, Sociology, University of Toronto, 2009.

10. Ibid., 38

11. Helping neighbors fight an uphill battle to close a seedy club was also credited with boosting the political career of Councillor (and later mayor) David Miller, but in that case the "big bad city" was represented by inept or corrupt police managers, not city staff. Linda Diebel, "How they shut Meow," *Toronto Star*, June 7,

2004, E1. Diebel mentions that a financial mogul and local resident who spent his own money on legal battles against the club "was so impressed with Miller that he helped put together his winning mayoral election team in 2003."

12. The planning department's five-year report on the experimental permissive zoning policy spends much time giving itself environmental pats on the back: over a third of district residents polled in 2002 did not own a car, and just as many walked to work, either locally or downtown (the financial district is within walking distance.) Instead, the fact that over one thousand industrial jobs had been lost is mentioned but with no comment at all. City of Toronto, Urban Development Services, *Regeneration in the Kings*, 2002.

13. Several feature articles in the *Toronto Star*, most written by reporter Raju Mudhar, documented this process. The most useful is "Night and Day collide: Urban revitalization done too well," May 28, 2007, L1.

14. Raju Mudhar, "Night and Day," *Toronto Star*, May 28, 2007, L7.

15. Councillor Chevy's conduct is a good example of what Max Weber famously called "kadi justice" (after the Arabic word for a local elder who settles disputes in a one-off manner, using his knowledge of the parties and the situation, not a law code).

16. Bruce DeMara, "Politics bedevil plan for pub patio," *Toronto Star*, July 19, 2004, B4.

17. Ibid.

18. Observation of Committee of Adjustment meetings shows that councillors often show up or send their assistant to oppose a minor variance or rezoning at Committee of Adjustment; but, more worryingly, an experienced city employee revealed that councillors also often make phone calls to the adjudicators beforehand.

19. A study of the same area at a slightly earlier period that pays close attention to municipal governance is Tom Slater, "Municipally managed gentrification in South Parkdale, Toronto," *Canadian Geographer*, vol. 48, no. 3 (2004), 303–325.

20. David Hayes, "Renter-activist has eyes on Queen Street West," *Toronto Star*, June 14, 2008, CL8

21. Raju Mudhar, "Bar wars," *Toronto Star*, February 18, 2006, J1.

22. Ibid.

23. Hasson and Ley's comparative study of neighborhood politics in Canada and in Israel shows that in most cases local civic groups had little binding them together except a common dislike, often bordering on hatred, for "city hall." Shlomo Hasson and David Ley, *Neighbourhood organizations and the welfare state* (Toronto, University of Toronto Press, 1994).

24. Observing several meetings of the planning committee of the council, I often saw councillors (of all political stripes) get up to shake hands with or hug constituents and neighborhood leaders, sometimes leaving the meeting room with them. City staff, by contrast, almost never left their seats.

Chapter 5

1. Castells shows that while class and race often fracture urban politics, urban grassroots movements often focus on governance issues and on housing issues that have a broad appeal. Manuel Castells, *The city and the grassroots* (Berkeley, University of California Press, 1983).

2. See Susan Fainstein, *The city builders: Property, politics and planning in London and New York* (London, Routledge, 2001).

3. Statistics Canada data collected and analyzed by Lysandra Marshall for the M4M postal code, which includes the port and related industrial areas as well as residential Leslieville. If it were possible to separate out data for Leslieville proper (as indicated by street signs) and to update the data to the present, the changes would be even more striking.

4. Robert Fairbanks, *How it works: Recovering citizens in post-welfare Philadelphia* (Chicago, University of Chicago Press, 2009).

5. Theodore Porter's influential study of French and American engineers in the nineteenth century shows that producing and using numbers can add to a profession's prestige, but not always. Theodore Porter, *Trust in numbers* (Princeton, N.J., Princeton University Press, 1995). Lawyers and judges seem to have a love-hate relationship with numbers, and not just in the context of planning; but I am not aware of any studies of the role of numeric knowledge formats in law.

6. For an analysis of the wasted energy spent by Toronto City Council over a five-year period to reform the zoning rules governing municipal shelters for homeless persons, see Prashan Ranansinghe and Mariana Valverde, "Governing homelessness through zoning," *Canadian Journal of Sociology*, vol. 45, 325–349 (2006).

7. Variances are required not only for "nonconforming" separation distances but also for many minor changes in the shape, size, and use of a building. I am focusing on separation distances for heuristic reasons, since they starkly reveal the moralistic, nuclear family bias of urban law, but affordable-housing providers, especially those who build or operate nonfamily housing, face a large number of regulatory barriers.

8. *Village of Euclid v. Ambler Realty* 272 US 365 (1926). On this case and its implications, see Charles Haar and Jerold Kayden, eds., *Zoning and the American Dream: Promises still to keep* (Chicago, American Planning Association, 1989).

9. Lisa Freeman is writing a dissertation on the legal geography of rooming houses and rooming house–type housing in Toronto in the geography department at the University of Toronto; I thank her for sharing information and ideas.

10. Maps of the existing neighborhood and plans of the proposed development are held in the city archives, Metro Toronto Housing Authority holdings. The specific map described here is entitled "Clearance and rehabilitation areas; Don Mount Village: Riverdale area, sub-area A."

11. Bicycles would of course have allowed police good access to every nook and

cranny of Don Mount and other public-housing complexes built in the same style, but Toronto police did not have bicycles until well into the 1990s.

12. See "City called shortsighted and unfair over Napier Place expropriations," *Globe and Mail*, March 7, 1966, 5. Four more articles on the issue were published in the same week. The maps mentioned are found in "Don Mount Village Urban Renewal Scheme," in *Urban renewal project statistics*, Urban Affairs Library series T59.

13. The RARA group had brought a PowerPoint presentation to the OMB hearing, consisting mainly of photographs of trees. Lacking professional legal advice, they did not realize that these images, however useful they might have been in garnering support from local neighbors, had no legal weight whatsoever. The question of how ordinary citizens attempt to use "professional" knowledge formats, from PowerPoint slides to statistics to Geographic Information System data, has received very little attention, but it is an important aspect of citizen engagement with law. See Sarah Elwood, "Beyond cooptation or resistance: Urban spatial politics, community organizations, and GIS-based spatial narratives," *Annals of the Association of American Geographers*, vol. 96, no. 2 (2006), 323–341.

14. The full judgment, with reasons, was delayed for months; see "Memorandum of oral decision . . . with subsequent written reasons," OMB decision 2673, October 7, 2005.

15. Nonprofit housing providers explained (in a group interview) that the cost of neighbors' appealing their developments to the Ontario Municipal Board was usually built into the proposal, but the costs of holding the land pending an appeal—which include the inflation in building costs—are not included (October 14, 2005).

16. Over the past twenty years, blacks living in areas of Toronto with a relatively high proportion of blacks have become poorer, by comparison with the average; by contrast, several parts of the city and many areas in suburban municipalities have witnessed "highly concentrated but wealthy Chinese neighbourhoods." Alan Walks and Larry Bourne, "Ghettoes in Canada's cities? Racial segregation, ethnic enclaves and poverty concentration in Canadian urban areas," *Canadian Geographer*, vol. 50, no. 3 (2006), 279.

17. Quantitative data are not readily available, since the census records household income but not the economic status of local shops.

18. Lucia Lo, "Changing geography of Toronto's Chinese ethnic economy," in David H Kaplan and Wei Li, eds., *Landscapes of the ethnic economy* (New York, Rowman and Littlefield, 2006). Lo's article does not even mention East Chinatown, only the older and larger historic Chinatown on Spadina Avenue.

19. I thank Hongmei Cai for locating and translating most of the relevant articles.

20. Greg Harrison, "Angry residents storm meeting for local housing project," *Etc news*, September 22, 2005, 1 and 10.

21. See, for example, Castells, *City and the grassroots*; Deborah G. Martin, "Reconstructing urban politics: Neighborhood activism in land-use change," *Urban Affairs Review*, vol. 39, no. 5 (May 2004), 589–612; K. R. Cox, "Spaces of dependence, spaces of engagement and the politics of scale," *Political Geography*, vol. 17, no. 1 (1998), 1–23.

22. An influential and nontechnical discussion of the kind of dynamics visible in the story just told can be found in a symposium entitled "Rethinking NIMBY," in the *Journal of the American Planning Association* (Winter 1993), 59. The planning literature, however, tends to treat "the community" as a single entity that is either prejudiced or wise about local needs, without paying much attention to the fractures within "the community" that are not only revealed but sometimes created by badly managed public-consultation processes.

23. The first influential work along these lines was Henri Lefebvre's *Le droit a la ville* (Paris, Economica,1968).

24. Ontario Municipal Board decision PL05611, January 14, 2010.

Chapter 6

1. The UK did not have prohibition, and therefore liquor and beer licensing remained a local jurisdiction (though administered, until recently, by justices of the peace rather than by municipalities). See Mariana Valverde, "Police science, British style: Pub licensing and knowledges of urban disorder," *Economy and Society*, vol. 32, no. 2 (2003), 234–252.

2. Nicholas Blomley, *Rights of passage: Sidewalks and the regulation of public flow* (London, Routledge, 2011).

3. The city's war on vendors began in the early 1990s, under Mayor David Dinkins, and continued under Mayor Rudy Giuliani. See Anastasia Loukaitou-Sideris and Renia Ehrenfeucht, *Sidewalks: Conflict and negotiation over public space* (Cambridge, Mass., MIT Press, 2009); and Mitchell Duneier, *Sidewalk* (New York, Farrar, Straus and Giroux, 1999).

4. The supposed park on Cumberland Avenue is in fact a landscaped strip between the Cumberland Avenue sidewalk and the back doors of Bloor St. stores Williams-Sonoma and Pottery Barn.

5. Kerry Gillespie, "Hot-dog cart can't pass muster here," *Toronto Star*, September 19, 2003, GT1. See also John Barber, "Brilliant development proposal overshadowed by . . . food fight!," *Globe and Mail*, December 1, 2007, M3, recounting a similar story of council interference with one particular vendor's license. However, the *Star* story cited here served to gather support, and after collecting five hundred signatures on a petition, the two vendors were able to get a "reprieve," not without having considerable councillor time spent on this one hot dog cart. "Hot dog vendors win reprieve: Legal glitch saves food cart," *Toronto Star*, Sept. 23, 2003, C5.

6. Yonge-Bloor-Bay Business Association, "Seven critical issues for 2004."

7. See Loukaitou-Sideris and Ehrenfeucht, *Sidewalks*, 138–155.

8. An excellent case study of sidewalk vending ordinances and their effects is Peter Baldwin, *Domesticating the street: The reform of public space in Hartford, 1850–1930* (Springfield, University of Ohio Press, 1999).

9. Henry Mayhew, *London Labour and the London Poor*, 4 vols. (London, Guffin, Bohn, 1861).

10. Nineteenth-century municipal markets, whose architecture is now greatly valued, not only in London but in other cities (e.g., Barcelona), were created partly for public health reasons but also in a regulatory effort to concentrate retail food sales in a few, supervisable locations. On how markets, slaughterhouses, and other municipal projects helped to build a bourgeois urban space, see Patrick Joyce, *Rule of freedom: Liberalism and the modern city* (London, Verso, 2004).

11. As readers of Dickens's *Our Mutual Friend* will know, a "mudlark" was a London-specific type of worker: someone who searched through the Thames's tidal mud flats to find items of value.

12. William H. Whyte, *City: Rediscovering the center* (New York, Anchor, 1990); and William H. Whyte, *The social life of small urban spaces* (Washington, DC, Conservation Foundation, 1980).

13. Whyte, *City*, 27.

14. For a sampling of the large literature on the creation of "distinctive" trendy downtown districts, see Anne M. Cronin and Kevin Hetherington, eds., *Consuming the entrepreneurial city* (New York, Routledge, 2008); and Rowland Atkinson and Gary Bridge, eds., *Gentrification in a global context: The new urban colonialism* (New York, Routledge, 2005).

15. Unpublished research report by Tim Groves, done in 2007 for the "multistory" group's campaign to reform food-vending rules in Toronto, used by kind permission.

16. See Markus Dubber and Mariana Valverde, eds., *The new police science: The police power in domestic and international governance* (Stanford, Calif., Stanford University Press, 2006).

17. Melissa Leong, "Slaves to the hot dog," *Toronto Star*, July 25, 2004, B1. This article marks the beginning of this newspaper's long campaign to "put diversity on the menu," as a later article would put it.

18. Undated document in possession of author. The group had a website, multistorycomplex.org. The website no longer exists but its work has left many traces on the Internet. The New York City "Street Vendors Project," probably the most significant force in both advocating for vending and providing useful information and support, was a significant influence on the Toronto group.

19. Matthew Chung, "Putting diversity on the menu," *Toronto Star*, March 30, 2007 (Article 197641, online).

20. This quote is from a document distributed at the May meetings. A very

comprehensive and legally erudite document was later generated, in November 2007, by Katie Rabinowicz and Andrea Winkler, the leaders of the "multistory-complex" organization, under the title "Street food vending." (I thank Katie Rabinowicz in particular for sharing the research conducted by her group.)

21. Matthew Chung, "Which one do you think is hazardous?," *Toronto Star*, May 17, 2007, R1.

22. In addition to the wholly positive press coverage devoted to this campaign, there were also a number of public events promoting the diverse street-food campaign. No voices other than Public Health's were raised in opposition to the plan.

23. Dave McGinn, "So you want to cook bhajias or fajitas? Do we have a slate of rules for you," *Globe and Mail*, January 10, 2009, M3.

24. Adrian Morrow, "Red tape helps push food cart off the street," *Toronto Star* August 28, 2009, GT2; see also Adrian Morrow, "Tough ride for food carts," *Toronto Star*, July 20, 2009, GT1.

25. There is a vast literature on anti-"homeless" and similar measures. For an overview that is particularly sensitive to the way in which criminal law tools and enforcement mechanisms are now intertwined with, rather than separate from, municipal measures to govern through space and time, see Katherine Beckett and Steve Herbert, "Dealing with disorder: Social control in the post-industrial city," *Theoretical Criminology*, vol. 12, no. 1 (2008), 5–30.

26. Hendrik Hartog, *Public property and private power: The corporation of the city of New York in American law, 1730–1870* (Ithaca, N.Y., Cornell University Press, 1989). See also Gerald Frug, *City making: Building communities without building walls* (Princeton, N.J., Princeton University Press,1999).

27. See Engin Isin, *Cities without citizens: Modernity of the city as a corporation* (Montreal, Black Rose Books, 1992).

28. In 2006 a much-trumpeted "City of Toronto Act" came into force, but immediately, the Municipal Act that governs other Ontario municipalities was amended to give other municipalities the same scant additional powers Toronto had been given.

29. Sidney and Beatrice Webb's detailed, never-surpassed history of local authority in England points out that most local governance was not actually conducted by municipal corporations for most of England's history: bridge tolls, for instance, were often constituted as special purpose authorities. But for present purposes the distinction between formally incorporated municipalities and other more unique local authorities can be set aside. *English Local Government* (London, Cass, 1911).

30. See www.foodcartsportland.com.

Chapter 7

1. During the 1980s there was a large influx of mainly urban and educated Somalis into Toronto, many locating in a neighborhood of bleak apartment blocks,

near the airport, called "Little Mogadishu." Twenty to thirty thousand people of Somali origin live in the Toronto Census metropolitan area, and about three-quarters of children in Somali families live in poverty. See Michael Ornstein, "Ethno-racial inequality in Toronto: Analysis of the 1996 census," York University Institute for Social Research, 2000, report updated in 2006 and available through the City of Toronto website.

2. See "Russian emigre Garber now king of Chicago taxi empire," *Chicago Sun Times*, February 1, 2010, and "Chicago carriage cab drivers protest hikes in lease rates," *Chicago Sun Times*, July 13, 2010, republished in the *Huffington Post*, August 10, 2010.

3. While Toronto is not on a par with New York or London in terms of size, and while there are structural differences because a very large proportion of Canadian firms (with the important exception of the banks) are American owned, nevertheless, the analyses of urban economies and urban labor markets found in the "global cities" literature is largely relevant, mainly because Toronto has replaced Montreal as the Canadian center for banking, insurance, and related sectors, and is thus similar to London and New York despite its smaller size. Key works in this literature are Janet Abu-Lughod, *New York, Chicago, LA: America's global cities* (Minneapolis, University of Minnesota Press, 1993); and Saskia Sassen, *The global city* (Princeton, N.J., Princeton University Press 2001).

4. For a broader picture of the socioeconomic realities facing recent immigrants to global financial centers, see Abu-Lughod, *New York, Chicago, LA*; and Sassen, *Global city*. For a good case study of how global movements of capital and labor affect local communities, see Christopher Mele, *Selling the Lower East Side: Culture, real estate and resistance in New York City* (Minneapolis, University of Minnesota Press, 2000). For Toronto, there is no single book offering a similar political-economy analysis, but see David Hulchanski et al., "Three cities," 2010 report and maps available on the website of the Faculty of Social Work, University of Toronto.

5. "Hub of humanity" is a phrase used in the British Council report on selected global cities' multicultural practices, *Understanding Open Cities*, opencities .britishcouncil.org. The cities in question are Auckland, Dublin, Amsterdam, and Toronto.

6. "Not all cab licences equal, driver says," *Toronto Star*, January 25, 2010. See also *Taxinews*, August 2010.

7. Chloé Fedio, "Cabbie IDs reveal visible minorities own less lucrative licence plates," *Toronto Star*, June 7, 2011. (As if to confirm this perception, the human rights hearing was given publicity in India, in a story claiming that most Toronto cabbies are either Pakistani or Indian. See "A double standard for Toronto cabbies," *Times of India*, June 16, 2011.)

8. Moscoe quoted in "iTaxiworkers" big plans," *Taxinews*, August 2010.

9. Sara Abraham, Aparna Sundar, Dale Whitmore, "Toronto taxi drivers: Ambassadors of the city: A report on working conditions," January 2008, available at www.taxi-cab-dispatch-software.com. See also February 19, 2010, report from the

"Taxi working group" of the Toronto Police Services Board, available online from the board's website.

10. De Baeremaeker quote is from Patrick White, "City to study woes of taxi-licensing industry," *Globe and Mail*, May 31, 2011; Minnan-Wong quote from CBC news online, cbc.ca, "Taxi drivers chide councillor over licences," May 31, 2011.

11. "New Mayor David Miller high on Ambassadors," *Taxinews*, January 2004, 5.

12. Peter McSherry, "Who are the real beneficiaries of cab reform?," *Taxinews* January 2004, 10.

13. Taxi Licensing Commission of New York, *Taxi 07*, 41.

14. "Driver competition hot as NYC medallions hit $766,000," *USA Today*, August 7, 2009. See also "Villain or bogeyman? New York's taxi medallion system," report available at www.schallerconsult.com/taxi.

15. *Taxi 07*, 130.

16. William Sites, *Remaking New York: Primitive globalization and the politics of urban community* (Minneapolis, University of Minnesota Press, 2003).

17. Systematic observation of licensing tribunal hearings, by me and a research assistant, took place in 2003–4 (during about sixty hours); I also interviewed four of the six then sitting members and two licensing officials. In 2007 a research assistant did follow-up observations, for about fifteen hours, and I did three follow-up interviews with licensing officials.

18. *Taxinews*, the local newsletter, regularly complains about the fact that drivers, not owners and brokers, bear the brunt of taxi law enforcement, which is definitely the case in regard to street enforcement, by licensing inspectors and by police. But plate owners do face the risk of having their license suspended (something usually done without a hearing).

19. See the regular (biannual) reports from the licensing tribunal to the Planning and Transportation Committee of City Council, available through the city clerk.

20. Only three or four of the more than thirty "deviant" licensees and business owners appearing before the tribunal during our observations were white.

21. That magnanimous forgiveness was not confined to the three members who sat on that hearing is shown by the fact that the panel did not include the tribunal member who had told me in an interview that he would not "absolutely" bar a murderer from getting a municipal license to drive a cab or tow truck (an attitude that the 2006 tribunal reforms sought to stop).

22. Charles Taylor, *Sources of the modern self* (Cambridge, Mass., Harvard University Press,1989).

23. In the few cases when taxi drivers paid for a lawyer (the same one for all the represented drivers observed), he did not appear to help his clients get a better deal, in part because he seemed oblivious to the cultural mistranslation issues described here.

24. "Good moral character" was and to some extent still is a traditional requirement of municipal licensees and liquor license holders, one that shows that a license is not a right but a special permission to do something that would otherwise be forbidden. Many jurisdictions have abolished the good-character requirement, but licensing, as a legal tool, has never totally shed its legacy of state moral regulation, even where courts have said that citizens are entitled to apply for licenses and the state needs to have a good reason to deny them. See Mariana Valverde, "Police science, British style: Pub licensing and knowledges of urban disorder," *Economy and Society*, vol. 43, no. 2, 234–252 (May 2003).

25. In hearings and during interviews it became clear that the city often fails to enforce its rules as it wishes because neither citizens nor city officials outside of the licensing unit feel it is important to testify. Police officers in particular often fail to show up at tribunal hearings, which makes prosecuting errant licensees very difficult. This is one of the many frustrations facing the bureaucracy and contributes to its "misunderstood public servant" narrative.

26. On the rise of Christian confession as a mechanism constituting the responsible individual of European modernity, see Michel Foucault, *The history of sexuality*, vol. 1, trans. Robert Hurley (New York, Vintage, 1980).

Chapter 8

1. For an excellent analysis of a wholly nonlegal but nevertheless effective process of municipal governance to allocate and guarantee squatters' property, see Boaventura de Sousa Santos's groundbreaking study of a Brazil slum, "The law of the oppressed: The construction and reproduction of legality in Pasargada," *Law and Society Review*, vol. 12, no. 1 (1977), 5–126.

2. Fleur Johns, "Performing power: The deal, corporate rule, and the constitution of global legal order," *Journal of Law and Society*, vol. 34 (2007), 116–138.

3. The small number of OMB decisions on mosques does not mean that there was a small number of conflicts; the majority of local planning conflicts are settled without being appealed to the OMB, which is a cumbersome and expensive process. In addition, it has to be said that many mosques have expanded or moved to a new location with little or no public commentary. In my own neighborhood, a drab building on Danforth Avenue, long used as a mosque, underwent an expensive and showy renovation in 2009–10 and now features a large, very beautiful minaret that can be seen for a good kilometer. Neither the much improved, highly visible mosque nor the proliferation of halal pizza and similar shops in the area has caused any public debate, as far as I am aware.

4. The "first language" data from the 2006 census is not directly relevant to the mosque-building story but is useful to understand the broader "diversity" context. About half of Mississauga residents report English as the first language; after that,

the next largest category is "Chinese languages" (5.5 percent), followed by Urdu, Polish, Punjabi, Portuguese, Tagalog, Arabic, Italian, Spanish, Vietnamese, Tamil, Hindi, Gujarati, and a dozen other groups with statistically significant numbers. (Figures compiled from various sources.)

5. For a useful general discussion of religious and racial prejudice and law, see Eve Darian-Smith, *Religion, race and rights* (Oxford, UK, Hart, 2010).

6. *Canadian Islamic Trust Foundation v. Mississauga (City)* (1998), Ontario Municipal Board decision no. 299, paragraphs 11 and 12.

7. In other nearby parts of Toronto, vacant industrial space has been turned into lofts, condos, and knowledge-economy white-collar businesses, but gentrification was invisible in this particular area as late as 2010.

8. Phinjo Gombu, "Why a proposed mosque stirred up a hornet's nest," *Toronto Star*, October 8, 1995, F4. This and two similar cases are discussed in an article by Engin Isin and Myer Siematycki, "Fate and faith: Claiming urban citizenship in immigrant Toronto," CERIS Working Papers, June 1999 (Toronto, Joint Center of Excellence for Research on Immigration and Settlement).

9. Maureen Murray, "Religious wars," *Toronto Star*, October 8, 1995, F1.

10. Editorial, *Toronto Star*, March 3, 1996, F2.

11. Leslie Ferenc, "York mosque wins approval: Residents angered about imam's political views," *Toronto Star*, February 6, 2007, E1. In this dispute the mayor of Newmarket, a suburban middle-class bedroom community, refused to hold a public meeting (in addition to the legally mandated meeting of the council) on the mosque, despite requests by residents. The zoning here was "rural," and places of worship are allowed as of right in such zones; hence, no public consultations were required by law—but as we saw in the case of supportive-housing and public-housing developments in Toronto, councillors often call public meetings and other consultations if they face pressure from residents.

12. Mike Funston, "Religious gatherings trigger neighbourhood feud," *Toronto Star* April 27, 2009, GT1.

13. Some critical urban studies scholars in the United States, most influentially Neil Smith, have claimed that measures taken by municipalities to disperse or eliminate disorderly people as well as unsightly objects indicate a hardening, post–welfare state attitude that Smith calls "the revanchist city." However, British scholar Tom Slater (who is highly critical of economic inequality and gentrification) has concluded that "revanchism" is not an appropriate term to use in the Canadian context. Tom Slater, "Gentrification in Canadian cities," in Roland Atkinson and Gary Bridges, eds., *Gentrification in a global context* (London, Routledge, 2005).

14. Engin Isin's theorization of various historically significant practices of citizenship can help urban studies researchers go beyond the rather simplistic attacks on NIMBYism that one sees in planning and housing literatures by drawing attention to structural factors that underlie how citizenship is practiced, on an everyday basis. *Being political* (Minneapolis, University of Minnesota Press, 2003).

15. Mark Purcell, "Neighborhood activism among homeowners as a politics of space," *Professional Geographer*, vol. 53 no. 2 (2001), 178.

16. Deborah G. Martin, "Enacting neighborhood," *Urban Geography*, vol. 24 (2003), 361–385; Ellen Berrey, "Divided over diversity: Political discourses in a Chicago neighborhood," *City and Community*, vol. 4, no. 2 (June 2005), 143–170.

17. Katherine Graham and Susan Phillips, *Urban governance in Canada: Representation, resources, and restructuring* (Toronto, Thomson Nelson, 1998), 139.

Chapter 9

1. A report written by the Richard Florida group notes that Toronto has done well in the global economy but that "to move up the global ladder, however, Toronto must continue to develop and harness its primary competitive advantage: diversity." Karen King et al., "The importance of diversity to the economic and social prosperity of Toronto," August 2010 report available on the website of the Martin Prosperity Institute. Typically, the report does not mention any of the forms of diversity that are not easily turned into a city's "competitive advantage" (dependent old age, for example, or middle-aged unemployed blue collar workers).

2. Some of the people who have promoted farmers' markets, especially in poorer areas, do have a broader vision, and are involved in "food security" campaigns that include global climate change and local economic inequalities as well as practical food issues. In Toronto, the most important such organization is The Stop, www.thestop.org. But most civic groups are either homeowners' associations or temporary groups acting at the local scale, usually reactively, to stop something from happening.

3. I followed this story by reading voluminous planning department reports and attending five public meetings, two meetings of the planning committee of the council, and one meeting of the whole council.

4. A possible contender was the change to the regulatory system for billboards; billboard locations had hitherto been approved by local committees of councillors, but as part of a campaign to preserve public space as public, a new system was implemented in 2009–10 that required permission from a representative citywide committee and that taxed billboards more heavily (with the funds collected supposedly going to the arts). While citywide in scope, this change was clearly extremely limited, since it did not deal with corporate sponsorships of city spaces and vehicles or any other public-space issue other than billboards.

5. It may not have been legal for the city to demand affordable-housing units in all new condominium developments, as such; but since almost all such developments require zoning variances to grant them permission to build much higher than the legal maximum, affordable housing could have become the standard public benefit demanded from developers in exchange for the height, as is the case for many new urban parks and amenities.

6. Jorge Louis Borges's "Exactitude in science" is a short story about a king who was so concerned about accuracy that he ended up ordering cartographers to make a map the same size as his kingdom.

7. The "holes in the bylaw" phrase was used repeatedly at meetings and, as I understand it, it meant that many areas would not require property owners to even ask for exceptions and variances, since the new bylaw would simply not apply there. It is difficult to imagine that in any other area of law such black holes would be allowed to officially exist.

8. See, for example, Juliet Gainsborough, "A tale of two cities: Civic culture and public policy in Miami," *Journal of Urban Affairs*, vol. 30, no. 2 (2008), 419–435.

9. "Created either through the enhancement of historically distinctive areas, or by developing and generating signatures for previously . . . ambiguous areas, urban villages or quarters seek to appeal to the consumption practices of the emerging nouveau riche. . . . Working class traditions, ethnicity, sex and sexuality are also increasingly commodified in narratives of place." David Bell and Mark Jayne, *City of quarters: Urban villages in the contemporary city* (Aldershot, UK, Ashgate, 2004), 1.

Index